Date Loaned

EXPERIENCE WITH THE SUPERNATURAL
IN EARLY CHRISTIAN TIMES

EXPERIENCE
WITH THE
SUPERNATURAL
IN EARLY CHRISTIAN
TIMES

By

SHIRLEY JACKSON CASE

*Professor of the History of Early Christianity
and Chairman of the Department of Church
History in the University of Chicago*

THE CENTURY CO.

NEW YORK · LONDON

PRINTED IN U. S. A.

PREFACE

The Christians' Bible is rich in miracles. Supernaturalism runs like a scarlet thread through the whole book from Genesis to Revelation. For centuries this phenomenon was contemplated with entire satisfaction by both laity and clergy. But in modern times a different way of thinking has been gaining favor. Many a Christian to-day passes hastily over the miracle stories in the Scriptures and dwells with greater satisfaction on the less spectacular portrayal of men's moral ideals and spiritual struggles abundantly recorded in his sacred book. One whose inclinations move in this direction may sometimes feel at a loss to account for the prominence of the miraculous in Hebrew religion, and more particularly in early Christianity. Why did the advocates of the new religion concern themselves so extensively with the imagery of supernaturalism? To answer this question is the purpose of the present volume.

SHIRLEY JACKSON CASE

University of Chicago,
August 1, 1929

v

CONTENTS

EXPERIENCE WITH THE SUPERNATURAL
IN EARLY CHRISTIAN TIMES

CHAPTER I

AN AGE OF SUPERNATURALISM

THE sky hung low in the ancient world. Supernatural beings thronged the earth, crowding themselves uncomfortably into the society of mortals. In his description of Trimalchio's banquet Petronius made a Cumæan lady testify to such an abundance of divinities in the region where she resided that it was easier for her to meet a god than a man. As is usual with satirists, Petronius exaggerated, but only in the direction of the truth. Without seriously straining the hyperbole he might have said that the same conditions obtained generally throughout the Roman Empire.

If belief in a multiplicity of deities actively participating in an arbitrarily controlled world of human experience is taken to mean that men are "very religious," then Paul was certainly correct in his appraisal of the Athenians (Acts 17:22). With equal propriety he might have applied the epithet to the peoples of Corinth, Ephesus, Antioch, or the Mediterranean lands at large in the age of Nero. Divinities were abundant and supernaturalism was rampant over the whole territory where Paul and his fellow-missionaries to the Gentiles sought to make the new Christian religion at home.

I

Gods were everywhere. Even among Jews, despite their strong monotheistic leanings, a wide variety of supernatural powers conditioned the experiences of men.

3

In Palestine, as elsewhere, the sky was so near to the earth that angels traversed the intervening space with the utmost ease and in a brief period of time. The Palestinian heavens had not yet been scrutinized by the hundred-inch eye that to-day necessitates the measurement of sidereal distances with the staggering yardstick of light-years. The ancient man had at hand no *Outline of Science* where he might learn that an angel, even though he were to travel at the undiminished speed of a shell projected from the most powerful cannon, would consume five hundred years in traversing the diameter of Neptune's orbit, not to speak of the vast stretches of space lying beyond our relatively small solar system. Had the angel moved at the inconceivably greater speed of light — 186,000 miles per second — he would have required at least 50,000 years to fly from earth to that point in the heavens where God and his attendant spirits could dwell secure from the prying gaze of the twentieth-century telescope.

Just as the floor of heaven seemed scarcely higher than the tallest cedars on Lebanon, so also a lower world existed under ground not far below the surface of the earth. Intercourse with these nether regions was no less real than with heaven. The road to Hades was much traveled. Here all the spirits of deceased men took up their temporary abode. The people of that age were untroubled by any science of geology or geography. No Palestinian explorer had journeyed around the globe to discover that heaven and hell, as definite localities, must lie at a great variety of widely separated spots in the universe, as a spherical earth revolves on its axis in the course of a single day. The pious Jew in the time of Jesus had never been called upon to face the task of adjusting himself to a solar universe. For him both hell and heaven were as definitely local as the earth, and neither the question of distances nor the problem of time offered any difficulties for his way of thinking.

In this three-story world of popular Jewish imagery naturalism found no room to breathe. The most spacious quarters in this cosmic mansion were on the third floor where God and the angels resided. Also the appointments in the basement must have been conceived on a large scale. Provision had to be made in the lower regions for all dead men, whose numbers were rapidly multiplying with the passing of the centuries. In the intervening compartment, where mankind resided for a few brief years, not only was the space between ceiling and floor very shallow, but supernatural powers both from above and from beneath continually intruded upon this middle area. Man had no real privacy; angels and demons kept an ever watchful eye upon him. In fact, the forces of good and evil were thought to be so thoroughly at home on earth that they were quite properly engaged in a deadly struggle with one another for complete possession of the terrestrial regions. The natural world, in any modern sense of that term, was a conception quite unknown to popular Jewish thinking at the beginning of the Christian era. By common consent all of life's most treasured experiences, and the solution of its gravest problems, were assigned to the sphere of the supernatural.

While Jews gave a great deal of attention to the plain business of correct living, they were careful to furnish all their religious traditions, practices, and ideals with a full set of divine sanctions. They main-

tained an elaborate system of worship in connection
with their temple at Jerusalem, all in accordance with
what they believed to be explicit instructions from
heaven. Their priests were a special class set apart
by God, and their sacrifices were established by divine
appointment. The contributions made by the people
to the support of their temple were not in the nature of
voluntary offerings inspired by altruism or practised
in the interests of self-discipline. They were taxes paid
by decree of the King of Heaven, and therefore they
were all the more gladly and meticulously rendered.

A conviction that the obligations of religion were God-
imposed seemed to the Jew occasion for genuine gratitude. More than most people in the ancient world,
the residents of Palestine took pleasure in believing
that deity was near at hand. To feel one's self even
temporarily removed from contact with the supernatural was ground for anxiety. On the contrary, when
one was surest of God's presence and favor, life took
on its gayest and most festive character. The Jewish
people truly rejoiced in the Lord, as the great festive
seasons of their religious year amply attest. Back of
all their feasts lay the fundamental notion that these
occasions had been supernaturally ordered, and that
they signified in the experience of the race the realization in some unique fashion of a contact between the
human and the divine.

The Jews had been much more successful than many
of their neighbors in devising a dependable machinery
for securing the regular operation of supernatural
power on behalf of mankind. They did not need to
rely for divine assurances chiefly on some chance happening, like a great miracle; although the performance

of a miracle, when God chose thus to manifest himself, was regarded with high esteem. In ancient times mighty works had been wrought by God and his representatives on the earth. The normal course of life had frequently been interrupted by marvelous displays of divine interference. The origin of the earth, the genesis of the human family, and the whole historic process were given an emphatically supernatural interpretation. And the evidence of God's presence in the affairs of the world was thought to be displayed in a very unusual manner in the history of the Hebrew people themselves. They were the great miracle race.

The supernatural element in ancient Hebrew history was amply exhibited in the Scriptures. Here one read that Abraham, the father of the Hebrews, had been explicitly commanded by God to leave his native country and take up residence in the land of Canaan. His career there and the success of his undertaking had been the special care of the deity. Sacred tradition represented that Jehovah was in constant communication with Abraham, thus sustaining him with promises of victory for his descendants and directing him with reference to his own immediate course of action. In two instances the divine intervention had especial significance. In the one case, it insured for Abraham a line of successors by giving to him and his wife Sarah a child in their old age when they were long past the normal period of fruitfulness. A second time, the divine favor expressed itself in the establishment of the rite of circumcision which was henceforth to be the distinctive mark of the Jewish race.

At many times in the history of Abraham's descendants heaven was believed to have intervened on their behalf. The story of their deliverance from Egypt was shot through with supernaturalism. Moses had received from God a direct command to lead the afflicted people out of their bondage. When the Egyptians offered resistance God smote them with terrible plagues. When finally the Israelites escaped from their masters, the waters of the Red Sea parted, permitting the refugees to pass across on dry land, while their pursuers were engulfed in the waves. Similarly, when after long desert wanderings the Israelites arrived at their destination, the river Jordan held back its waters in order that they might pass dry-shod. While still in the wilderness God had given them for guidance a pillar of cloud by day and a pillar of fire by night, and had delivered to Moses the two tables of stone on which God himself had inscribed the Decalogue. When death from thirst threatened the pilgrims in the desert, water was miraculously produced from a rock, or poisonous springs were made sweet, in consequence of Jehovah's instructions to Moses. Starvation also was averted by the gift of manna from heaven. When the walled city of Jericho blocked entrance into Canaan, its fortifications were miraculously leveled. The Jew believed, on what seemed to him ample evidence, that his title to Palestine had been supernaturally guaranteed.

Subsequent periods of history, particularly times of great crises, continued to display a supernatural ordering of events. In the days of the Judges Jehovah had been very active in raising up leaders and in supervising their exploits. When the time had arrived for the establishment of a monarchy, he had taken care beforehand to provide a miraculously born prophet, Samuel, to give advice and direction to the nation in choosing its first king, Saul. David and his son Solomon had been especially sponsored by God, notwithstanding their manifest human weaknesses. Even when the nation was divided by revolution, and threatened with destruction from conquering armies of Egyptians, Babylonians, or Syrians, the Scriptures did not fail to show a golden thread of supernaturalism still manifest throughout the course of Jewish history. Prophets, who had been called forth to deliver words which God himself had placed upon their lips, encouraged the afflicted people with messages of divine authority. The hero also continued to be the man of miracle. The prophets Elijah and Elisha were famous wonder-workers. The pious Daniel in the den of lions remained unharmed by the ferocious beasts, and even the flames of the roaring furnace could do no harm to Jehovah's faithful ones.

In a setting where all serious thinking about the greatest problems of life moved upon a dominantly supernatural plane, it is not surprising that also the maintenance of good government should have been thought the business of the deity. When properly constituted, church and state were essentially identical institutions for the Jew. He was never a precocious pupil in the school of practical politics. The more devoted he was to his traditional religion, the more difficult was it for him to reconcile himself to the order of things prevailing in Palestine when the country was ruled by the Romans. To one who believed sincerely that this territory was a holy land, which God had promised by irrevocable covenants to deliver to his chosen people for their perpetual possession, Roman domination seemed clearly to represent a temporary

stay of the divine purpose. The oppressed nation
needed and would be granted a supernatural restoration. This was the universal assumption, whether
hope expressed itself in a fanatical outburst of revolu-
tionary zeal like that of a Judas of Galilee, or in the
program of the quietists who patiently awaited action
by God himself, or in the flaming message of a reformer
like John the Baptist calling sinners to repentance in
preparation for an impending Day of Judgment and a
sudden establishment of the Kingdom of God.

For a people so thoroughly supernaturalistic in their
thinking as were the Jews of Palestine at the beginning
of the present era, they were singularly free from indulgence in magic and other gross displays of superstition that often marked the life of their Gentile
neighbor. They were fortunate in possessing an elaborate institutional machinery for safeguarding and perpetuating supernatural power in their present experience. They were spared many of the inconveniences
attending the operation of divine agencies in a Gentile
society where superhuman forces had not been so well
harnessed and so thoroughly subdued to the needs of
an organized community. While miracles played an
important rôle in Hebrew tradition, they were not now
relied upon supremely for guidance in daily living. In
this area of interest the study of Scripture, attendance
upon the synagogue services, the instructions of the
oral law received from successive generations of rab-
binical scholars, all provided a much more sane, normal,
and dependable guide for the shaping of ideals and the
determination of character. But it would be a grave
error to imagine that Jewish religionists in the time of
Jesus had any thought of abandoning supernaturalism

for what a modern world might call an empirically based attack upon the problems of life and conduct.

According to the Jewish way of thinking, super-human care surrounded one from the moment of birth to the hour of death, and continued in the life beyond the grave. Every male child on the eighth day was circumcised in accordance with the covenant that God had made with Abraham in a remote antiquity. The training given to the child in the course of his development was all derived from the body of divine wisdom that had been deposited in the sacred books. The life of the adult conformed to the same body of supernatural instruction, neglect of which was sure to invite God's wrath. Satan and his demons were believed to be just as real and ever present in the affairs of men as were God and his angels. Man had no choice in this matter. He was assumed to be inextricably entangled in the meshes of supernaturalism, from which there was no escape, but which could be made a great source of comfort and profit by so conducting one's self as to merit the divine approval.

II

The Gentiles also looked with high favor upon supernaturalism. In fact, their attachment to this way of thinking was as pronounced as that of the Jews, and in some respects was even more extravagant. There were, however, wide variations of attitudes and opinions on this subject among Greeks and Romans at the beginning of the Christian era. While it was distinctly an age of supernaturalism, the Gentiles were much more keenly aware than were Jews of the rights which naturalism might claim as its own. The work of the ancient Greek physicists had not been completely forgotten. Nor did Roman society lack men of intellectual leadership who vigorously protested against the crude superstitions that still abundantly survived in the popular religions.

In the early stages of Greek and Roman culture, mythology answered all questions regarding the origin of the world and of man. As among the Jews, it was assumed that the world, mankind, and human history were all subject to the domination of superhuman powers. The Gentile deities were legion. In accordance with their own desires they interfered constantly in the affairs of mankind. Escape from their arbitrary power was possible only through attention to more or less elaborate ceremonies performed to avert their wrath or win their favor. They controlled the fertility of the earth; they were responsible for all meteorological phenomena; they hurled the thunderbolts; earthquake, pestilence, and famine were their instruments; sickness and health depended upon their pleasure; the sea was also their domain; in short, the whole range of man's experience upon earth was subject to the arbitrary will of gods and demons.

The rise of a Greek philosophy had tended to undermine popular mythology. Some philosophers expressed doubt about the very existence of gods, and many thinkers proposed not only a purely natural origin for the world and mankind, but also an entirely naturalistic interpretation of the history of human society. It is very true that not all philosophers were thorough-going naturalists, but the tendency of all philosophical thinking was in the direction of reducing the domains of the supernatural. A Plato with his two worlds, the ideal and the real, could not allow to gods that freakish play of their whims permitted to them in the imagery of a Homer or a Hesiod. But in the picture of an ideal world, as the pattern of all reality, Plato had a new supernaturalism and one that might prove even more oppressive just because the processes of its operation had been more thoroughly systematized and stabilized. A dualistic world-view necessarily enthrones the supernatural, and by rendering it philosophically respectable only makes it the more truly tyrannical. Philosophers who adopted a monistic world-view — the Stoics and the Epicureans — were in a more advantageous position to resist superstition. But even they were not always completely successful in eliminating all remnants of the supernatural.

Roman men of culture, like Cicero, entertained a skeptical attitude thought to be in agreement with the scientific bent of a Plato or an Aristotle. But even Cicero was not wholly free from bondage to traditional religion. He admitted that the proofs commonly offered to support the validity of his ancestral religion seemed to him logically quite inadequate, but he added that the customs of the ancestors were not therefore to be abandoned. As an academic question, even the very existence of the gods might be a subject of serious doubt, but any interference with the traditional practices of Roman religion seemed to Cicero a calamity. And there were several occasions in his own experience when he set aside his philosophic doubts and sought solace for his troubled spirit in an appeal to the supernatural.

Among the different philosophical tendencies current

in the Roman Empire, Stoicism was one of the most influential. Its advocates made a vigorous attempt to attain a unified view of the world by eliminating the conflict between natural and supernatural. But their program actually resulted in the adoption of a denatured supernaturalism, by which the area of the natural was virtually supernaturalized. In place of the gods and demons who, according to the popular superstition, played freakishly with the affairs of men, the Stoic substituted a sober and well-behaved divine power called the Logos, or divine reason, which was said to pervade all matter and indeed to constitute the primal material out of which the entire universe was composed. As a consequence of this essentially pantheistic philosophy, the Stoics talked a language which, to the common man at least, meant full allegiance to his religious traditions. Large portions of Cleanthes' famous hymn could have been repeated with approval by the most orthodox member of any of the popular cults.

Most glorious of immortals, O Zeus of many names, almighty and everlasting, sovereign of nature, thee it is fitting that all mortals should address. . . . Thee, all this universe, as it rolls circling round the earth, obeys, wheresoever thou dost guide, and gladly owns thy sway. In thy invincible hand thou holdest as a minister the two-edged, fiery, everlasting thunderbolt, under whose stroke all nature shudders. No work upon earth is wrought apart from thee, O Lord, nor through the divine ethereal sphere, nor upon the sea.

Although Stoicism gained wide popularity in the Roman Empire, it never made any very serious inroads upon the widespread supernaturalism of the masses. Stoics themselves were very sober in their language when they spoke of god and divine providence. Later representatives of the school, like Seneca, Epictetus, and the emperor Marcus Aurelius, continued to use language which the illiterate man could adopt without essentially altering the imagery of the popular superstition to which he was fondly attached. Even in Cicero's day a Stoic philosopher had felt no hesitation in affirming that one might properly regard as manifestations of the divine mind — indeed as gods — the firmament, the sun, the moon, the world itself and all things therein useful to mankind. Also the stories of traditional mythology were not to be rejected outright, but were thought capable of reinterpretation by an allegorical process that enabled one to find them all still true if understood in the Stoic way.

The extremes of superstition alone were subjected to vigorous Stoic criticism. To fear the gods, said Seneca, who are the source of all our good and happiness, is sheer madness on the part of men. No intelligent person would indulge in morbid fancies about the terrors of the future life: "There is no prison house, no lake of fire or river of forgetfulness, no judgment seat, no renewal of the rule of tyrants." [1] Gods are not to be feared, but are to be revered; and there is no escape from their presence. A Stoic poet, Aratus, had said that the godhead of Zeus "fills all streets, all thronging marts of men, the boundless sea and all its parts, whose aid all mortals need, for we are his offspring." And a Christian preacher felt no hesitation in citing this sentiment in support of his own type of supernaturalism (Acts 17: 28).

The most uncompromising critics of current religious beliefs were the Epicureans. They were ardent mis-

[1] *Dialogues*, vi. 19. 4.

sionaries for their cause, and displayed a zeal on its behalf which fell little short of veritable religious enthusiasm. They declared it to be their great mission in life to deliver their fellowmen from the terrible fear which the popular religion of the day had inspired. Their material universe was a purely natural product of space and atoms. While not refusing to believe in the existence of deities, the Epicurean philosophy allowed no place for them in the world of human experience. Man had nothing to fear from divine beings, either in this life or in the hereafter. All dread of the future was removed by denying outright the current notion of the soul's immortality. Also the gods, who, according to Epicurean speculation, were themselves composed of material atoms, were relegated to remote parts of the universe where they dwelt in an ideal state of happiness entirely undisturbed by the affairs of mankind. In Cicero's dialogue on the nature of the gods,[2] the Epicurean spokesman says: "We have no dread of those beings whom we have reason to think entirely free from all troubles themselves and who do not impose any on others. We pay our adoration, indeed, with piety and reverence to that essence which is above all excellence and perfection."

Among the intelligentsia of the Roman Empire, Epicureanism had many disciples, but it was never the faith of the majority, particularly of the common people. This fact is evident from the statements of the Epicureans themselves in their vigorous protest against what they saw in the society about them. The language of Lucretius, the great Roman exponent of the school in the middle of the first century B. C., is

[2] i. 20.

most revealing in this connection. He hailed Epicurus, the founder of the school, as himself almost worthy of worship, because his philosophy delivered men from the terrors which constituted for Lucretius the quintessence of all religion. Epicurus had been a brilliant exception to the general run of men in that he had ventured to withstand religion to her face. Other people were terrified by the story of the gods, by thunderbolts, and the roar of the electric storm. But these things only gave him fresh courage, filling him with a desire to burst the fast bars of nature's portals and bring to men a knowledge of the perfectly natural character of all physical phenomena. Yet more than two hundred years later as Lucretius looked out on the world about him, he saw the worship of the gods spread over great nations; towns were filled with their altars, and society was giving itself up to the performance of well-established sacred rites, rites "now in fashion on solemn occasions and in solemn places, from which even now is implanted in mortals a shuddering which raises new temples of the gods over the whole earth and prompts men to crowd them on festive days." [3] Evidently Lucretius was not disposed, like the modern atheist, to allege that empty churches presage the early demise of all religion.

Pliny the Elder, who died in the year 79 A. D., writing from an Epicurean point of view, penned a memorable chapter criticizing the prevalent beliefs regarding the deities then in vogue throughout the Roman Empire. His comments are especially valuable as indicating the popular state of mind. Believing that the sun is "the mind of the universe, nature's chief regulator and di-

---

[3] *Nature of Things*, v. 1161 ff.

vinity," Pliny deemed it a sign of human weakness to
seek to give shape and form to the deity. If, indeed,
there is any god at all he is "all sense, all sight, all
hearing, all life, all spirit, and wholly self-contained." [4]
This language made its appeal to the few, who, ever
since the time of Xenophanes of Colophon in the sixth
century B. C., here and there raised their voices against
the absurdity of creating gods in man's image. But
this was still a widely popular way of making deity
real and vivid to the eyes of mortals.

Pliny thought it still greater folly to pursue a custom
of more recent origin, which not only made gods in
human shape, but affirmed a multitude of divine coun-
terparts for the virtues and vices of men, thus adding
to the supernatural powers such divinities as Chastity,
Concord, Thought, Hope, Honor, Clemency, Fidelity.
Conscious of its own infirmity, human nature in its
weakness had created a deity for every experience or
emergency that might be encountered in the course of
life. Thus innumerable divinities with a variety of
names arose, even diseases and plagues being deified in
consequence of man's anxiety to propitiate these enemies. In this way Pliny explained the presence of a
temple to Fever erected at the public expense on the
Palatine Hill and one to Orbona, near the temple of the
Lares, and an altar dedicated to Evil Fortune on the
Esquiline. "Hence we may understand how it comes
to pass that there is even a greater population of the
celestials than of human beings, when each individual
makes a separate god for himself, adopting his own Juno
and his own Genius." [5]

[4] Pliny, *Natural History*, ii. 7. 14.
[5] The criticism of Cicero, following Platonic ideals, had been somewhat
milder (*Laws*, ii. 11. 28).

In a similar manner Pliny accounted for another form of supernaturalism that had won favor among the Romans. This was the worship of the emperor, which in Pliny's opinion took its start from the help which the first emperors rendered to mankind, and the consequent disposition on the part of their subjects to honor them with deification. It had been customary among the ancients to reward heroes with divinity in return for their services to their contemporaries, and Pliny saw this disposition perpetuated in the rise of the Imperial cult.

To assist man by man is to be a god; this is the pathway by which the Roman princes attained deity and which is now pursued by the greatest ruler of all time, Vespasian Augustus, along with his sons, who has come to the relief of an exhausted empire. This was the most ancient mode of remunerating those who deserved it, to ascribe to them divinity. For the names of all the gods, as well as of the stars that I have mentioned above, have been derived from their services to mankind.

This pragmatizing of theology may have suited Pliny, but the average man was an absolutist who tended to stress without reserve the superhuman even in the case of a man-made divinity.

Pliny was troubled by still another type of allegiance to supernaturalism now increasingly manifest among the Romans. This was the avidity with which they turned for help to strange cults, especially those that came out of the Orient. Many people were becoming "slaves to foreign rites. They carry on their fingers the gods and the monsters whom they worship. They condemn and they invent various foods, they impose on themselves dreadful ordinances, not even sleeping quietly. They neither marry, nor adopt children, nor indeed do anything else without the aid of their sacred rites."

Still another divinity, the goddess of Fortune, seems to have enjoyed much popularity in Pliny's day.

All over the world, in all places, and at all times, Fortune is alone invoked and addressed. She is the one accused, she is the one blamed, she is the one who fills our thoughts. She alone is praised, she alone is blamed, and is loaded with reproaches, wavering as she is, conceived by the generality of mankind to be blind, wandering, inconstant, uncertain, variable, and often the protectress of the unworthy.

Thus blind chance, of which men are the victims, is by them in their ignorance and superstition exalted to the dignity of a god. But even in this the limit of human frailty is not reached, for many persons reject the goddess of chance and give their allegiance to Destiny which they associate with the influence of the stars. People of this temper—

suppose that God once for all issues his decrees and never afterwards interferes. This opinion begins to gain ground and both the learned and the unlearned vulgar are falling into it. Hence we have the admonitions of thunder, the warnings of oracles, the predictions of soothsayers, and things too trifling to be mentioned, as sneezing, and stumbling with the feet, reckoned among omens.

According to Pliny, this way of thinking, even though it had been adopted by the emperor Augustus, was the *reductio ad absurdum* in religion. But the great masses of the population in the Empire were of a different opinion. They were engrossed in the rites of traditional polytheism, or were seeking help from new divinities, and were daily sinking deeper and deeper in the mire of gross superstition.

Epicurean skepticism was quite unable to save the ancient world from its bondage to supernaturalism. Preachers of this strenuous gospel of doubt continued for centuries to raise their voices in protest against the ever-increasing superstition of their times. But they were always more or less conscious of representing only the minority, and their most serious utterances often betrayed a pathetic note of futility. The message which the aged Diogenes inscribed on the wall of the portico in Oenoanda about the year 200 A. D. contains in itself, perhaps quite unconsciously, a prophecy of the failure that awaited the whole Epicurean cause:

If it were one or two or three or four or five or six or as many as you like of such, but not too many, who were in evil plight, I might have visited each individual and tendered them the best advice as far as in me lay. But the vast majority of men suffer from the plague of false opinions and the number of victims increases, for in mutual emulation they catch the contagion from one another like sheep. [6]

III

The first Christian preachers viewed the religious activities of the Gentiles with horror and disgust. In the early years of the missionary enterprise, the representatives of Christianity were men of Jewish heritage and training who shared with their Palestinian kinsmen a very strong prejudice against heathenism. It was no novelty for the Christian Paul, brought up under the tutelage of Judaism, to declare that the use of material objects to typify the deity was evidence of a senseless and darkened mind. All the wisdom of Greek philosophy was of no avail for a people who changed the glory of the incorruptible God into the

[6] *Fragment*, ii, col. 3 f (William).

likeness of a mortal man or represented deity even in the form of birds and four-footed beasts and creeping things (Rom. 1: 21–25).

Although sharply condemning Gentile idolatry, Christians had no sympathy whatever with Epicurean skepticism. They were not enemies of supernaturalism, but accounted themselves its best friends. They could not follow the Epicureans even in denying to the Gentile gods power to interfere with the affairs of men. While Paul spoke rather disdainfully of the "dumb idols" and declared an image to be "nothing," he possessed a very lively sense of the reality of the demons who, in his opinion, were responsible for the idolatrous customs of the heathen (I Cor. 8: 4 ff.; 10: 20; 12: 2). Christians believed the Gentile gods to be very active demonic powers, and as such a serious menace to human welfare. They were the lords of "this present evil age," the "powers of the air" whose leader, Satan, dominates the lives of those who walk "according to the course of this age" (Gal. 1: 4; Eph. 2: 2). Successful fortification against their machinations was possible only when one enjoyed protection by that superior supernatural being, the Lord Jesus Christ.

Jesus and his immediate disciples looked at the world through Jewish eyes. They pictured a three-tier universe, with God and angels inhabiting the heavens above, with Sheol containing its proper dwellers in the world below, and with man occupying the middle domain, where both good and evil spirits were constantly active. The rain, the sunshine, the revival of nature's life in the springtime, the flowers that adorned the fields, the storms that beat the waters of the Sea of Galilee into violence, and various other striking displays of vital force in the physical environment were ascribed to the activity of an other-worldly agency, either demonic, angelic, or divine. Nature as such was given no inalienable rights of her own. At any moment she might become the medium through which supernatural forces made their presence manifest. With this inheritance from its Palestinian ancestry, Christianity went into the Gentile world, not as a friend of Epicurean naturalism, but as its deadly foe.

A supernatural interpretation of human history was also taken over by Christianity from Judaism and transplanted on Gentile soil. The notion of an inspired scripture was perpetuated among Christians with quite as much zeal and confidence as among Jews themselves. The account of the beginnings of the earth and of mankind as told in the sacred books of the Jews found full acceptance in the new religion. Also the scriptural story of God's founding of the Hebrew nation, together with the full miraculous display depicted in the history of the chosen people, entered completely into Christianity and was there rebaptized with a new supernatural authority attaching to the notion of a confirmatory revelation in connection with the founding of Christianity. It was not called a new religion, but a further manifestation of the true revelation already given to the Hebrew race. Thus Christians appropriated the Jewish Bible in its entirety. And since among Jews these writings were already universally revered as the divine authority for everything in their religion, Christians could easily believe that they also possessed in these documents an inexhaustible fund of supernatural wisdom.

The early Christian preachers taught Gentiles even

the supernatural interpretation of politics that had been inherited from Judaism. Paul was no more concerned to induce the Thessalonians to turn from idolatry to the service of the true God than he was to inculcate in them an attitude of waiting for the coming of the Son of God from heaven to reward believers at the impending Day of Judgment (I Thess. 1:9 f). Christian missionaries endeavored, and with a considerable measure of success, to persuade their Gentile hearers that an ideal order of society would soon be realized through the descent from heaven of a new ruler in the person of the risen Jesus, who would bring to an end all present political authority, and establish in a renovated Palestine, with Jerusalem as his capital, a new Kingdom of God on earth. For almost two centuries, this Jewish type of apocalyptic expectation remained a prominent item in the message of Christian preachers. It required repeated disappointment and many years' experience of hopes deferred to effect the abandonment in Christian circles of this inherited Jewish imagery.

Christians went even beyond their Jewish predecessors in claiming for themselves the favor of heaven. To the supernatural assurances furnished by Scripture, advocates of Christianity added many new displays of heavenly power on behalf of their cause. This expansion of confidence in the divine favor was made easier and more imperative when the new religion was compelled to separate itself from the synagogue. The customary operations of an established institution might still serve in the opinion of Jews to insure for them the continued protection of heaven that had been made available for their ancestors by the more direct action of God in ancient times. But Christians, excommunicated from the synagogue, needed to tap new sources of revelation, and hence to make a more immediate appeal to the supernatural. As yet the adherents of Christianity lacked an adequate institutional equipment, such as the organized Jewish community possessed, for securing present divine help. Hence they looked directly to God to display his favor on their behalf in new and unusual ways. Even in Palestine Christianity surpassed Judaism in this respect, and when the advocates of the new movement expanded their field of operations to include the Gentile world they found still further occasion to develop this phase of their enlarging experience.

Christian leaders believed themselves to be in possession of unusual miracle-working power. They justified their claim on the ground of an especial endowment, resulting from their attachment to the risen Jesus, who had been exalted to a position of authority at the right hand of God in heaven. Paul listed "miracles" and "gifts of healings" among the proper functions of a Christian community and represented that God himself had ordained this form of activity (I Cor. 12: 10, 28 f). Ability to work miracles through the power of the Spirit was convincing evidence of the superior character of the gospel preached by Paul to the Galatian Christians (Gal. 3: 1–5). When the genuineness of his claims to apostleship was called in question by his opponents, he affirmed that in truth "the signs of an apostle were wrought among you in all patience by signs and wonders and miracles." In this he could say that he had not fallen behind "the very chiefest apostles." Apparently in Paul's day power to perform miracles was assumed to be an apostolic credential (II Cor. 12: 11 f).

When the author of Acts wrote a history of early Christianity, for a Gentile reader named Theophilus, the validity of the new religion was defended by an extended appeal to the supernatural. The writer noted that the earliest assembly of disciples had received specific instructions from the risen Jesus. The message was not a repetition of teachings delivered during Jesus' earthly career; it was the utterance of one who now belonged in the supernatural sphere with God and the angels. A still further display of heaven's favor awaited the group of reassembled disciples. At Pentecost when tongues of fire fell upon them they were miraculously endowed with power to speak many different languages to the promiscuous throng gathered at Jerusalem. Again, at Peter's command a lame man sprang up and walked. When arrested and charged with violating the Old Testament law against magical practices, the disciples were only the more firmly determined to test the supernatural authority of their new faith. They prayed for boldness of speech and continuance of power to perform healing and signs and wonders through the name of Jesus. Their prayer was answered by an earthquake, while they experienced a new sense of inspiration from the Holy Spirit.

To the early Christian historian, the new religion seemed now to possess a two-fold divine authentication. It carried forward all the prestige of supernaturalism connected with the history of the Hebrews. But God had called them and preserved them throughout the centuries for a more ultimate purpose. All the while he had kept in view the founding of Christianity, and it was not difficult for its representatives to believe that they now were in an especial measure the chosen people of God. As the new Israel they felt themselves equipped with a superior endowment of heavenly power. Although as yet they lacked an elaborate institution for safeguarding their more recent supernatural acquisitions, they had full confidence in their future because of God's immediate interest in their welfare. If their organization was so imperfect that Ananias and Sapphira by an impaired contribution could hope to win false credit for generosity, God himself stood ready at hand to smite down the deceivers in their tracks. While such special displays of heaven's interest in the new society were believed available, it was quite unnecessary for the historian to concern himself with the disciplinary aspects of early church organization.

Throughout its early history the new religion, as described in Acts, continued to display many miraculous features. Its first martyr, Stephen, in the hour of his execution witnessed a vision of Jesus on the right hand of God in heaven. Presently, Saul of Tarsus was halted in his mad career by the voice of Jesus speaking out of heaven to the persecutor on the way to Damascus. In the meantime, missionaries in Samaria encountered the sorcerer, Simon, himself no mean wonderworker, but he was overcome with admiration for the "signs and great miracles" wrought by the Christians. The welfare of the recently converted Saul was also insured at Damascus through a preparatory revelation made to one Ananias, who was thus divinely instructed to initiate the recently converted persecutor into the new Christian way of life.

Peter, too, in his activities beyond Palestine continued to play the rôle of miracle worker. At his word a sick man of Lydda, bedridden for eight years, was restored to health. At Joppa, Peter displayed still greater supernatural powers. So efficacious were his prayers and so powerful was his command that he restored the deceased Tabitha to life even though she had been so long dead that her body had been prepared for the tomb. When a broader outlook upon his missionary task was needed, again heaven came to Peter's assistance. In a vision he beheld a vessel containing all manner of beasts let down from the sky, and heard a voice say, "What God hath cleansed, make not thou common." Later, when cast into prison by Herod Agrippa, Peter experienced a miraculous deliverance. God sent an angel to loose the chains of the faithful Christian and smite the Jewish king with death.

Paul also was depicted as a man full of divine power. When he encountered a representative of Satan, in the person of the sorcerer Elymas, immediately the apostle was able to smite the heathen miracle-man with blindness. The preaching of Paul and Barnabas in Iconium was said to have been accompanied by "signs and wonders, done by their hands." At Lystra when Paul commanded a lame man to stand on his feet, although the invalid had been a cripple all his life, immediately he leaped up and walked. The expansion of the missionary enterprise from Asia into Europe was a direct result of heaven's intervention. In a vision Paul was visited by the man of Macedonia, in answer to whose appeal Paul heard the call of God to preach the gospel in Europe. In this new territory, Christian and heathen supernaturalism were immediately pitted against one another. Paul demonstrated the superiority of the former by commanding the demon to come out of a soothsaying girl at the mention of the name of Jesus Christ. And just as Peter had been miraculously released from the prison of Herod, so Paul and Silas were granted a marvelous deliverance from the jail at Philippi.

Heaven's favor for Paul was especially in evidence during the shipwreck and subsequent happenings on the way to Rome. Instructed by an angel of God, the apostle was able to cheer his companions and promise them ultimate safety, if they obeyed his commands. When they were cast upon land, Paul's prestige was further demonstrated by his complete immunity from the venomous sting of a viper. Normally, when bitten he ought to have swelled up and fallen down dead immediately, but he shook the creature from his hand into the fire without injury to himself, while the astonished onlookers exclaimed that he was a god.

Supernaturalism rendered its most conspicuous service to Christian history in connection with the story of Jesus' career. The Christian preachers, who felt themselves endowed by heaven to perform wonderful works and who believed the new religion to be especially favored by God, could hardly have avoided crowning their hero, Jesus, with the halo of miracle.

In the several gospels now preserved in the New Testament, each writer gave lengthy consideration to the supernatural features of Jesus' portrait. Even the oldest gospel, that of Mark, was thoroughly permeated by this interest. As there described, Jesus at the very outset of his public activity heard a voice from heaven declaring him to be the beloved Son of God. Immediately he entered upon his battle royal with Satan and the evil demons.   In the pursuit of his task, he raised people from their sickbeds, he restored sight to the blind and power of speech to the dumb, and gave the palsied ability to walk.   He was also superior to all physical forces about him.   He could instantaneously multiply a few loaves and fishes until they constituted a superabundance of food for a large multitude.   He walked on the sea as easily as on land, the winds ceased at his rebuke, and all nature obeyed his voice.   Even the dead heeded his summons to life and rose up at his command.

Subsequent gospel writers excelled even Mark in the use of supernaturalism to interpret the career of Jesus. They showed him to be not only a worker of miracles, but a distinctly superhuman being in his own person. Accounts of his birth depicted the interest of deity in his physical generation.   He had not been born as ordinary human beings, but as the very Son of God, his mother having been impregnated by the Holy Spirit.   He grew to manhood as a child of heaven, displaying a wisdom superior to that of mortals, and he departed from earth in the triumph of a divine being whom the powers of the lower world were unable to hold in subjection.   Other Jews went to Sheol and there remained until the Judgment Day, but the gates of Hades were unable to resist Jesus.   Having broken through the bars of the tomb, he came forth miraculously to show himself to his disciples and in their very presence to rise to heaven.

Christians claimed supernatural sanctions not alone for the past history of their movement, but also for their present crystallizing institutions.   To join the Christian church meant not simply a voluntary attachment to a new religious association. It involved also participation in a new type of experience, where contact with the divine played a much more important part than did the merely human choices and associations that were involved. At least among the Gentiles in the time of Paul, membership in a Christian society carried with it a feeling of divine renewal entitling the convert to be called "a new creation" in Christ (Gal. 6: 15; II Cor. 5: 17). Baptism signified, if it did not indeed effect, a union with Christ that was no mere figure of speech, but a very real experience in the emotions and convictions of the disciple. He could say with confidence that he possessed within himself the spiritual presence of Christ, even the very Spirit of God. Christian living meant an actual participation in the life of deity. On uniting with the church the natural man gave place to the spiritual man, a supernaturally regenerated person, who was now a veritable sanctuary in which the Spirit of God resided (I Cor. 3: 16).

When more attention was paid to the formalities of Christian organization, the church itself was believed to be a divine foundation. Not only were its rites authorized by heaven but their very performance meant the operation of supernatural power. Sanctity attached to both the Old and the New Testaments, not simply because they came from God but also because they were now sacrosanct in their own right. Similarly the ordinances of baptism became a revered sacrament, with chief stress upon its character as a divine rite miraculously operating to effect salvation. In the course of time it was possible for a Christian to declare, as did Clement of Alexandria,[7] that "on being bap-

[7] *Instructor*, i. 6. 26.

tized we are illuminated; being illuminated we are made sons of God; being made sons of God, we are perfected; being perfected, we become immortal."

The tendency toward supernaturalism showed itself again in connection with the church's religious meal. At first it had a distinctly memorial and anticipatory significance. It served to remind Jesus' friends of the last supper eaten with him before his crucifixion, and it was repeated in anticipation of the future messianic banquet to be celebrated with his followers when presently he would return in triumph to set up his new kingdom. It was thus that they tried to "proclaim the Lord's death till he come" (I Cor. 11: 26). But already in the time of Paul, at least among Gentile Christians, a more sacramental feeling had begun to attach itself to the observance. In the Corinthian church, drinking the cup of the Lord paralleled drinking the cup of demons (I Cor. 10: 21). Just as one was in danger of taking demonic spirits into the body through participation in heathen feasts, so apparently it was possible for a Christian to gain a divine increment for his present earthly existence by partaking of the sacred elements at the Lord's Supper. In time it became an actual eating of the flesh and drinking of the blood of the Son of Man. Since this Lord whose presence was recognized in the Christian meal had himself triumphed over death, and thus possessed an immortal body, his disciples believed that their own bodies could be made immortal by eating this supernatural food. Hence Christians in the second century confidently affirmed that the bread and wine of the Eucharist constituted a real medicine of immortality, and that man's own flesh would rise from the grave because it had been nourished on the immortal body and blood of Christ.

Likewise the officials of the church gradually acquired more adequate supernatural credentials and were assigned more distinctly sacramental duties. Paul had said that apostles, prophets, and teachers were appointed by God to serve the congregation. They were not elected by the church, but were designated by the Spirit for specific tasks, and their divine appointment was evidenced by their several abilities to minister to the needs of the membership. Practical as was this test of their authority, their equipment was distinctly supernatural. At this time there was, however, no intimation that they had been charged with the administration of sacraments. But ere long it became the supreme duty of the clergy to mediate divine help to mankind through the performance of sacred ceremonies in which the officials of the church represented Christ in his divine dealings with men. By the first quarter of the second century a Christian bishop himself wrote that Jesus Christ is the mind of the Father, "even as the bishops that are settled in the farthest parts of the earth are the mind of Jesus Christ. . . . Plainly therefore we ought to regard the bishop as the Lord himself." [8]

Pursuing the ways of its Jewish and Gentile predecessors, Christianity early learned to foster supernaturalism and to claim for itself superiority over all rivals in this domain. Thus it made itself thoroughly at home in a miracle-loving age.

[8] Ignatius, *Ephesians*, 3–6.

CHAPTER II

THE VISIBILITY OF SPIRITS

THOSE ancients who drank deeply at the fountain of supernaturalism placed much confidence in the reality of the spirit-world by which they felt themselves surrounded. Gods, angels, demons, and the souls of men seemed accessible to mortal eyes and audible to human ears. Man believed in an other-worldly order of existence because from time to time he met its representatives in his own world. A skeptical Thomas might be mildly reprimanded for lack of faith, but in the end he was granted an objective demonstration that dissipated all his doubts. In this area of experience one walked by sight no less than by faith.

There are certain basal assumptions that must be conceded to the ancients in order to understand their belief in apparitions. The possibility of seeing and conversing with a god depended upon a conviction that divine beings possessed, or could assume when necessary, a shape like that of a man, a beast, or some other familiar object. Communication with human ghosts was possible only when one imagined that man was composed of two separable entities, the spirit and the body, and that the former had a substantial existence apart from the latter. No one who rejected this fundamental presupposition could ever hope to see a deceased friend. But when the soul was thought to be as real, even though not so tangible, an entity as the

body, why should it not wander forth to communicate
with kindred spirits when the body reposed in sleep or
lay still in death? Even more easily might not divinities, who were never by necessity confined within the
prison-house of flesh, transport themselves hither and
thither at will?

I

A belief in apparitions was fundamental to early
Christianity. The appearances of Jesus after his death
constituted the most distinctive supernatural credential of the new religion. Whether addressing Jews or
Gentiles, in the last resort the Christian preacher staked
everything upon his conviction that Jesus had been
seen in the days following the crucifixion. Paul knew
of several such incidents that had occurred even before
he himself had his similar experience on the way to
Damascus. The first appearance had been to Peter,
but others had followed, apparently in rapid succession. Jesus was next seen by the twelve, and again
by an assembly of some five hundred people, the greater
number of whom were still alive in Paul's day. James,
the brother of Jesus, had also witnessed an appearance,
and finally the group called Apostles enjoyed a similar
privilege (I Cor. 15: 5–8).

Apparitions of Jesus were a favorite subject with
early Christian writers. To each of the evangelists
these appearances seemed a particularly happy climax
to the earthly career of the Galilean prophet. Various
people were said to have seen the risen Jesus. While
the accounts did not always agree in detail, they abundantly attested the general acceptance of the opinion
that Jesus had shown himself to several of his former

acquaintances. At one time it was a group of two women, who, visiting the tomb and finding it empty, met Jesus face to face as they were leaving the scene. Later their experience was repeated by the eleven faithful disciples, who returned to Galilee and witnessed an apparition at the appointed rendezvous in a certain mountain. On another occasion, Jesus appeared to two of his former friends while they were making a journey to a town called Emmaus. On returning to Jerusalem, they learned that in the meantime he had been seen by Peter. Then suddenly while they were still talking of recent events, he appeared again to the entire company. According to another version of the story, as narrated in the Gospel of John, Jesus was first seen by a certain Mary only, who on first sight mistook him for the gardener. Later, on the same evening, he appeared to the reassembled group of disciples and took his departure while the doors were still closed. Then eight days afterward he visited them again in order to dispel the doubts of Thomas, who had been absent on the former occasion. Still later he showed himself to several of his former friends on the shore of the sea of Tiberias.

Other accounts placed greater emphasis on the display of Jesus' new heavenly splendor. Even though some of the apparitions had been so real that he ate material food and pointed to the scars on his body, there were also occasions when he manifested himself in the likeness of an angel of light. The heavens received him before the very eyes of his disciples. Similarly, Stephen, in the hour of martyrdom, saw this celestial figure enthroned in glory. Also the apparition to Paul, as described by the apostle himself, was a phenomenon of the heavens, a revelation from God

(Gal. 1:16). In a corresponding vision, Ananias of Damascus had been instructed to welcome the repentant persecutor (Acts 9:10–17). Likewise the seer of the Book of Revelation beheld Jesus, not in the lowliness of his restored earthly life, but in the splendor of his heavenly existence.

The importance attached to visions, and particularly to the reappearance of an actual historical person in the weeks following his death, is difficult for the modern man to appreciate. Belief in apparitions is no longer general among educated people. Nowadays one is inclined to smile at ghost stories and to ridicule spiritism. But a very different attitude prevailed in the setting where Christianity arose. The situation of the first Christians can be understood only as one remembers the readiness of people in that ancient world to believe in the reality of visions. The founders of Christianity saw in these supernatural occurrences a supremely valuable evidence of the validity of their cause. On the basis of a conviction that Jesus had been seen, they formulated their fundamental dogma. As Paul expressed it in concise language, the secret of eternal salvation lay in one's willingness to testify that Jesus is Lord and to believe sincerely that God had raised him from the dead (Rom. 10:9). Whatever secondary arguments might be adduced in support of this faith, such as citations from prophecy or references to Jesus' own predictions, ultimately assurance rested on the experience of the eye-witnesses. For those followers of Jesus who had left Calvary convinced that God had forsaken their leader, the event of outstanding importance was the testimony by one of their own group that he had seen Jesus alive again.

The early Christians themselves ascribed no such exceptional character to the appearances of Jesus as the modern reader is wont to do. While a vision of Jesus was an event of great importance for his disciples, an apparition as such was not unusual in their world. Nor did they, in recounting the history of their movement, restrict interest in this subject merely to appearances of Jesus. The larger spirit-world was also accessible to the representatives of the new religion. In those days people saw and heard many wonderful things, and under the magnifying glass of prevalent supernaturalism such experiences were much cultivated and were highly prized.

Paul, who labored heroically with certain of his converts to suppress extravagant emotionalism, was happy in being able to boast of his own capacity for visions and revelations from heaven. With much fervor he recalled an incident that had happened fourteen years earlier in his life. He had been caught up into the third heaven, whether accompanied by his body or not he was unable to say, but the experience remained for him a highly cherished memory. He had gazed on Paradise itself, and had been told things too sacred for the ears of earthly men to hear. This was among those "visions and revelations of the Lord," which more than once it had been the apostle's privilege to enjoy (II Cor. 12: 1–4).

Primitive Christian tradition was literally crammed with apparitional imagery. Many persons saw visions and heard messages from their environing spirit-world. Closely associated with the appearances of Jesus were apparitions of angels, seen by visitors to his tomb. Similar phenomena were believed to have been manifest throughout his entire career. Even the way for the forerunner, John the Baptist, had been prepared by the apparition of an angel to his father, Zacharias. An angelic messenger announcing the birth of Jesus had also shown himself to both Joseph and Mary. Again, through the visit of an angel, Joseph was instructed regarding the journey to Egypt and the later removal to Nazareth. Also, on the night of Jesus' birth, an angelic choir singing the first *Gloria in Excelsis* had appeared to the waiting shepherds.

Apparitions occurred in connection with less spectacular events than the birth and resurrection of Jesus. At the time of his baptism the Holy Spirit in the form of a dove visibly descended upon him out of the sky. Satan also confronted him in the wilderness, and after the departure of the Tempter, Jesus was attended by ministering angels. The readiness of his companions to believe in the reality of a ghost is assumed in the account of their mistaking Jesus for an apparition when he came walking toward them on the water. In the same vein is the statement that Herod, on hearing of Jesus' wonderful works, believed that he was John the Baptist returned from the dead. Christians felt no difficulty in assuming the reality of the heavenly visitors, Moses and Elijah, in the company of Jesus on the Mount of Transfiguration. It was reported also that an angel had appeared and strengthened him during his night of agony in the Garden of Gethsemane. The same faith in the possibility of apparitions made it seem entirely proper for Jesus to remark, when arrested, that if he so desired God would send twelve legions of angels to defend him against his enemies.

In respect to apparitions, Jesus himself was hardly

more highly favored than were the members of the
early church. In the opinion of ancient Christian
historians, such experiences had continued to be of
common occurrence. The favor of heaven showed itself in visible form when tongues of fire were seen to
light upon the disciples at their first pentecostal assembly. It was also reported that the early preachers had
been liberated from prison by an angelic visitant after
they had been arrested for advocating the new religion.
Again, Philip the Evangelist had been instructed by an
angel to take a road south from Jerusalem toward
Gaza, where he would meet the man from Ethiopia.
Saul the persecutor was halted on the Damascus road
by a vision of Jesus, and Ananias was similarly instructed to receive and minister to the new convert.
Cornelius was visited at noonday by an angel of God,
while Peter had a corresponding experience on the
housetop at Joppa. When Peter had been thrown into
prison by Herod Agrippa, an angel of the Lord came to
him and led him forth to safety. His friends assembled
in Jerusalem at the time were quite ready to believe,
when Rhoda announced Peter's arrival, that it was
only a phantom of Peter that she had seen. The account of the experience with the man of Macedonia and
the angel who assured Paul of escape from the perils
of the voyage to Rome further supplemented what
Paul himself had said about "visions and revelations."
Also John of Patmos reveled in visions of angels and
other heavenly phantoms, and the outstanding feature
of the common Christian hope was an expectation of
seeing Jesus return on the clouds accompanied by a
host of angels.

With this elaborate apparitional equipment, Christianity presented itself first to Jews, and later to Gentiles. It offered men new assistance from heaven on the assurance that Christian eyes had peered anew into the world of spirits. But in that day the claim of Christianity cannot have seemed so strikingly phenomenal as it might seem in modern times. In this particular respect, the new religion was not radically different from its competitors. The best it could hope to maintain was that the visual displays of supernatural favor on its behalf carried greater validity than did the similar credentials with which both its Jewish and Gentile rivals were already equipped. In fact, one suspects that Christian belief in the visibility of spirits derived no slight impetus from the similar views already in vogue among the Christian's neighbors.

II

In Hebrew tradition the visibility of spirits was an easy inference from the universally accepted belief in the existence of God, hosts of angels, Satan and hordes of demons, and souls of deceased men. The Sadducees only were skeptical about the immortality of the soul, but their influence on popular opinion was negligible. On the other hand, the Scriptures bore ample testimony to the possibility of spirit-visions and to their importance in the history of the Hebrew race.

Numerous appearances of the deity were reported in those ancient writings that constituted for later Judaism an infallibly inspired account of past events. Here one learned that God himself had visited the Garden of Eden in person to talk with Adam and Eve (Gen. 3: 8 ff.) Later he appeared also to Abraham, calling him forth to a new career and establishing with him a covenant to insure the prosperity of Abraham's descendants (Gen. 17: 1 ff). Even Abimelech, the king of Gerar, was protected from the consequences of Abraham's deceit by a direct visitation from God (Gen. 20: 3 ff). He appeared also to Isaac, warning him to avoid the land of Egypt and reassuring him of success for the Hebrews (Gen. 26: 6). The experience was duplicated in the career of Jacob. On one occasion he met the deity in a wrestling bout and suffered permanent lameness as a result of his boldness, but he could console himself with the thought that he had seen God Almighty face to face and had not lost his life (Gen. 32: 30; 48: 3).

The new prosperity attending Abraham's descendants after their departure from Egypt offered still further occasion for God to show himself to the faithful and deliver instruction to their leaders. One scene was particularly picturesque. Four of the chief men among the Israelites — Moses, Aaron, Nadab, and Abihu — together with seventy of their elders, were given an audience with the deity, whom they saw in person. The pavement under his feet was like a sapphire, transparent as the sky itself. With impunity they ate and drank in this awful presence and God laid no avenging hand upon the nobles of the children of Israel (Exod. 24: 9–11). At least twice, Solomon also met God face to face (I Kings 3: 5; 9: 2). A vision of the deity had been experienced by the prophet Isaiah in connection with his call to duty (Isa. 6: 1–5). Presumably Jeremiah also had seen Jehovah, who put forth his hand to touch the prophet's mouth (Jer. 1: 9). And Ezekiel testified that he had looked through the open windows of the heavens and there beheld visions of God (Ezek. 1: 1).

Along with many specific references to apparitions of God, the Jewish Scriptures contained statements opposed to the notion that deity ever assumed the form of man or met mortals on their own level of reality. To see the face of God was possible only for the angels who dwelt in his presence. No man could have this experience and live. Only when temporarily transported to heaven in a state of ecstasy could the human eye expose itself with safety to the scorching rays emanating from the divine countenance. Exceptions to this rule were rare, in the opinion of certain authors. While Moses had been so honorable a person that God declared a willingness to talk with him "mouth to mouth," to a prophet he would make himself known only in a vision and would speak to him only in dreams (Num. 12: 5–8). Other stories betrayed greater wariness on the part of both man and God in their approach to one another. Sometimes the deity, even when conversing with so superior an individual as Moses, mercifully concealed his features behind the flames of a burning bush, or veiled the brightness of his face with his hand.

In later Judaism it was believed that God, instead of presenting himself to mankind in human form, was accustomed to show his favor for his people by apparitions of angels, or by some unusual display in nature designed to demonstrate unmistakably the presence of divine power in the physical sphere. Supernatural beings of secondary gradation were still free to show themselves to men. Even Satan, in the shape of a serpent, had visited the Garden of Eden; and from the language of Job one infers that the Adversary was wont to walk manlike to and fro in the earth. But evil spirits designedly kept themselves obscure, or masqueraded as angels of light, preferring to carry on their inimical activities among men in as deceptive a fashion as possible. Good spirits were less reserved. While apparitions of God were no longer available, visions of angelic intermediaries became only the more frequent and the more easy of attainment. Thus men still knew that divine help was near, and they tested their knowledge by the sight of their eyes.

The Jews made relatively little, however, of human apparitions. They were confident that every individual survived death, but their traditional religious thinking had left the soul of the dead man little or no liberty to wander abroad upon the earth after the decease of the body. Their ancient Scriptures gave only the faintest intimation that once upon a time the Hebrews may have shared with their neighbors in Canaan a respect for the dead which amounted virtually to deification (I Sam. 28: 13; Isa. 8: 19). But by the beginning of the Christian era orthodox Jewish thinking employed very different imagery to picture the state of the dead in Sheol.

The lower world, like a ravenous beast, stood ready with gaping jaws to gulp down the immortal part of man immediately the spirit was released from the body. A prophet had remarked that Sheol opened its mouth without measure, and a wise man had said that Sheol and Abaddon were never satisfied (Isa. 5: 14; Prov. 27: 20). Apparently it mattered little what became of the body. When news of Joseph's disappearance was brought to his father Jacob, the bereaved parent immediately assumed that his son was in Sheol and would there await the father's coming, notwithstanding the

fact that Jacob imagined the boy to have been devoured by wild beasts (Gen. 37: 33–35). Similarly,
Samuel told Saul that on the morrow he would meet
the king and his sons in Sheol, although the prophet
with his supernatural knowledge must be assumed to
have known beforehand that the bodies of Saul and
his sons would the next day be hanging on the walls of
Bethshan. Whether a corpse was buried or unburied,
the immortal counterpart of the man descended immediately to the lower regions (I Sam. 28: 19; 31: 10,
12).

In a heathen environment, where dead ancestors
were worshiped and men fondly turned to them for
direction in critical moments of life, Jewish teachers
had thought to preserve the purity of their religion
by pronouncing emphatically against the practice of
necromancy. The Deuteronomic legislation decreed
that the Hebrews when settled in the holy land should
have no one in their midst who was a "consulter with
a familiar spirit, or a wizard or a necromancer" (Deut.
18: 11). The Scriptures also provided that any man or
woman that had a "familiar spirit," which means any
one attempting or claiming ability to consult the spirit
of the dead, should be punished with death (Lev. 20:
6, 27). In the face of these scriptural injunctions, the
pious Jew was not disposed to expect or to seek communications from the deceased, nor is it surprising that
the followers of Jesus should have incurred hostility
among their devout Jewish contemporaries by claiming to have had communication with Jesus after his
death (Acts 4: 1–7).

In sharp contrast with the ease of entrance into
the lower world was the difficulty of exit. No provision

was made for any return from Sheol. People dwelt there behind firmly secured barriers which in later imagery were watched over by supernatural guardians. Once a spirit had passed behind those fast-closed doors, there was no hope of return. David felt it entirely proper to agonize in prayer to Jehovah for the restoration to health of a sick child, but once the child had died, David ceased his petitions. Not even Jehovah could bring back the spirit that had departed. The only consolation remaining to David was a belief that ultimately he would go to be with the child, but the child could never return to him (II Sam. 12: 22 f). In the development of its official religion Judaism barred ever more securely the gates of hell.

The desperate situation of the Jewish dead was somewhat relieved in later times by the development of a doctrine of ultimate resurrection. The Scriptures reported teachers in Israel who had declared that the oppressed and slain should be revived, dead bodies would arise, the earth would cast forth the dead, and no more cover her slain (Isa. 26: 19–21). This hope was certainly a possession of orthodox Jewish piety at the beginning of the Christian era, but it lent no stimulus to belief in apparitions. Sheol still remained the firmly barred prison-house of spirits until the Day of Judgment. Whether the shade remained in Sheol or was transferred, under the influence of contemporary astral thinking, to a paradise with God in heaven, the ghost was offered little or no opportunity to show itself upon earth.

Had not the disciples of Jesus been "unlearned and ignorant men" (Acts 4: 13) — Galilean peasants and fisherfolk — they might have had more scruples against believing that Jesus had actually appeared to Peter. Probably they did not at all realize how improbable such an experience would seem to one properly schooled in orthodox Jewish thinking regarding Hades and the impropriety of seeking communication with the dead. The disciples' preparation for an experience of apparitions had not come to them from their Jewish schooling, or even as they themselves emphatically affirmed, from any expectation which Jesus might have endeavored to arouse in their minds. After they had seen him, they felt convinced that he, with his supernatural foresight, must have predicted this future manifestation of himself. But they, taken completely by surprise, apologized for their unpreparedness by alleging their former stupidity.

The readiness of Jesus' followers to experience and accept as real the apparitions of a deceased friend can hardly be understood from purely Jewish antecedents. The Scripture, in the story of Samuel called up before Saul by the Witch of Endor, offered only a very remote parallel to their experience. But Christians seem never to have had the faintest thought of comparing their experience with that of Saul. Their state of mind was more like that of their ancestors in the primitive days of contact with popular Canaanitish notions when necromancy was in vogue. But in the Palestine of the first century A. D. many new forces were at work tending to give reality and importance to the experience of apparitions. When seeking to persuade their contemporaries that Jesus had been seen alive again after his crucifixion, the Christian preachers found a much more congenial atmosphere for the cultivation of this imagery in the Gentile world. And it is not improbable that Gentile belief in apparitions ought to be taken more largely into account as a means of explaining how the friends of Jesus themselves had found it possible to attach transforming significance in their own lives to this experience. Already for two centuries or more Palestine had been overrun by conquerors who brought with them the cultures and popular ways of thinking that were current in the world at large. The pious and educated Jew might successfully guard against these insidious influences from without, but the common man was less well protected.

III

Among the Christians' Gentile contemporaries, there was some difference of opinion regarding the possibility of beholding a ghost. The majority of persons accepted the phenomenon as true beyond all shadow of doubt, but among the more educated classes there were some skeptics. Epicureans, for example, who affirmed that the soul did not survive the body, were unable to believe in the existence of any ghosts either of dead or of living men. Nor could gods be seen, since they dwelt far from the abodes of men. On the basis of this philosophy there was no possibility of apparitions, either human or divine.

The successors of Plato, while fully believing in the reality both of gods and of disembodied human souls, hesitated to accept popular notions about apparitions. In Platonic opinion the soul was a pre-existent entity, not at all dependent for its survival upon union with the body. Ideally, however, it was wholly incorporeal in its native state, and being thus absolutely bodiless, was entirely lacking in apparitional quality. Only those souls which contained bodily impurities could be seen. The spirit of the man who had given himself over to sin became heavy with an earthly element which rendered it visible and made it desire to cling to this world of sense. Plato had described it as "prowling about tombs and sepulchres in the neighborhood of which, as they tell us, are seen certain ghostly apparitions of souls, which have not departed pure, but are cloyed with sight and therefore visible." [1] This is the imagery which Milton reproduced:

> The soul grows clotted by contagion,
> Imbodies, and imbrutes, till she quite lose
> The divine property of her first being.
> Such are those thick and gloomy shadows damp
> Oft seen in charnel vaults and sepulchres,
> Ling'ring and sitting by a new-made grave.
>
> (*Comus*, 467 ff.)

Men with Stoic leanings found it somewhat easier to believe in the visibility of human spirits. In their opinion, the soul of man was a portion of the divine essence pervading the universe. Hence, whether in the body or out of the body, the soul possessed a real material existence. It was thus easily conceivable that the soul of the living man might now and then go on a journey to some distant friend and return during the hours of sleep. After death, so long as the soul maintained its identity, it possessed the same qualities of visibility. The older Stoics, however, had allowed the soul only a limited period for the enjoyment of personal immortality. Ultimately it would lose its identity and be absorbed into the primal divine essence whence it had originally come. Accordingly, apparitions of de-

[1] *Phædo*, 81 D.

ceased men were possible at most for only a short time after their death. But later Stoics yielded more completely to the inclinations of the populace, and allowed the soul a longer period of independent subsistence.

During the first century of the Christian era, there was a growing disposition, even among the more educated Gentiles, to take seriously belief in apparitions. At the very time when the gospel writers were recording the appearances of Jesus, and other apparitional phenomena connected with the history of the new religion, literary men among the Greeks and Romans, who hardly knew of Christians or knew them only to despise their simplicity, were concerning themselves very seriously with this problem of the visibility of the spirit-world.

Plutarch may fairly be called the best educated man among the Greeks at the close of the first century A. D. He was widely read in history and philosophy. Being a Platonist in his philosophical leanings, he was a sharp critic of both Epicurean naturalism and popular religious superstitions. But in his opinions regarding the possibility of seeing departed spirits he was among the orthodox. Nor would he concede that he was here indulging himself in a weakness. He believed that the intelligent man had full warrant for such faith. In the second chapter of his life of Dion, whom he placed side by side with the Roman Brutus, he argued for the respectability of spiritism:

It has been maintained that no man in his senses ever saw a ghost, that these are the delusive visions of women and children or of men whose intellects are impaired by some physical infirmity, and who believe that their distressed imaginations are of divine origin. But if Dion or Brutus, men of strong and philosophic minds, whose understandings were not affected by any constitutional infirmity, if such men could place so much faith in the appearance of specters as to give an account of them to their friends, I see no reason why we should depart from the opinion of the ancients.

Among the Romans, Plutarch's contemporary, the younger Pliny, although more inclined toward Stoic ways of thinking, was also much interested in the question of the reality of ghosts. In a letter to the Consul, Licinius Sura, he wrote:

I am extremely desirous to know whether you believe in the existence of ghosts, and whether they have a real form, being a sort of divinity, or whether they are only the visionary impression of a terrified imagination. What particularly inclines me to believe in their existence, is a story which I heard from Curtius Rufus. When he was in humble circumstances and unknown in the world, he attended the governor of Africa into that province. One evening, as he was walking in the public portico, there appeared to him the figure of a woman of unusual size and of more than human beauty. As he stood there, terrified and astonished, she told him she was the tutelary power that presided over Africa, and had come to inform him of the future events of his life. He should go back to Rome to enjoy high honors, return to the province of Africa, vested with proconsular dignity, and there he should die. Every circumstance of this prediction actually came to pass.[2]

This, and several other incidents of the same sort, led Pliny to believe in the reality of apparitions.

While a Plutarch and a Pliny were attempting, in the interests of intellectual self-respect, to prove their faith by citation of evidence, the common people were giving themselves over without reserve to an ever-increasing belief in the visibility of spirits. The fancy of every Greek youth had been nourished on the imagery of

[2] Pliny, *Letters*, vii. 27.

Homer, whose poems might be called not only the Bible of the Greeks, but also their principal primary and high-school textbooks.   There one learned in childhood that deceased heroes might reveal themselves to their living friends, and that the renowned dead still existed in the lower world where they might on occasion be consulted by the living when an Odysseus was permitted to visit the nether regions.

The story of Patroclus's appearance to Achilles to plead with the latter for proper funeral rites must have made a deep and abiding impression on the Greek imagination.   The spirits of the underworld had refused to accept Patroclus into their fellowship until the usual burial ceremonies had been performed over his body.   Then he would descend to Hades, never to return.   But lacking the honors of full release from the body, the restless spirit was still abroad, and Achilles marveled at the lifelikeness of the apparition.   He sought to lay hold upon the ghost, but it eluded him, and with a faint cry disappeared again beneath the earth.   Reflecting upon this experience, Achilles significantly remarked: "Ah me, there remaineth then even in the House of Hades a spirit and a phantom of the dead, albeit the life be not any wise therein.   For all night long hath the spirit of hapless Patroclus stood over me, wailing and making moan, and charged me everything that I should do, and wondrous like his living self it seemed." [3]

Among the Romans the same theme was given classic expression by Vergil.[4]   Æneas on a visit to the lower world met his father, whose frequent apparitions had induced the son to undertake his perilous journey to

[3] *Iliad*, xxiii. 64 ff.
[4] *Æneid*, vi. 695 ff.

Hades. There he pled in vain with the shade: "Suffer me to clasp thy hand — suffer me, my father, nor withdraw thyself from our embrace." With tears streaming down his cheeks, Æneas attempted three times to throw his arms about his father's neck, but each time the ghostly substance of the shade escaped his grasp, for it was "light as the winds and fleet as the pinions of sleep." Its existence, however, was none the less real even though, like the apparition of Jesus to Mary Magdalene, it might not be profaned by the touch of mortal hands (John 20: 17).

In popular Roman thinking, ghosts from the infernal regions were constantly breaking through to the upper world to walk once more upon earth. Rites were assiduously observed in order to quiet these spirits and render them friendly. Although feared, they were reverenced, and no one imagined that safety could be secured by burying the dead more deeply or binding ghosts more securely in the lower world. In fact, the ascent of spirits was made more easy by the opening of the *mundus*, as it was called, a circular pit in every city consecrated to the infernal powers. That ghosts should appear was taken for granted. The important matter was to make sure that they were kindly disposed in their attitude toward the living. Popular superstition undoubtedly supported the legend mentioned by Ovid.[5] Once when the Romans were engrossed in warfare they neglected the proper gifts to the *manes*, but with menacing consequences. Many persons were struck dead and terrifying apparitions were seen. The tombs having given up their dead, crowds of ghosts went howling through the streets of the city and the fields of the country-side.

[5] *Fasti.* ii. 549 ff.

The great popularity of belief in apparitions throughout the whole of the Mediterranean world during the years of Christianity's early history is overwhelmingly attested by multitudes of stories, frequently repeated and widely scattered in both Greek and Roman writings. Even the philosophers, it was assumed, had been compelled to believe in ghosts. The account of Athenodorus's experience in the haunted house at Athens seemed absolutely convincing. It had been told to Pliny the Younger on what he believed to be adequate authority. Athenodorus was a Stoic who went from Tarsus to Athens where he noticed the advertisement of a house for rent at a very low price. He learned that prospective tenants were frightened off by a ghost accustomed to haunt the place; but he, being a philosopher, paid no attention to the story. He rented the house, and when busy with his studies late at night he suddenly heard the clanking of metal and the rattling of chains. At first he tried not to admit to himself that he heard these noises, but they grew louder and approached nearer, until finally the ghost entered the very chamber in which he was sitting. It looked just like the descriptions of it given by those who had reported its previous appearances. It beckoned to him to follow it out, but at first he disregarded its request. It then rattled its chains over his very head and to this act he responded by accompanying the apparition into the courtyard where the specter disappeared. In the morning he informed the magistrates regarding the experience, and an excavation made in the yard on the spot where the apparition vanished revealed the chained skeleton of a murdered man. When the bones had been collected and publicly burned the ghost ceased to appear. Evidently we are to assume by implication that the philosopher's doubts about the reality of apparitions were also dispelled.[6]

Ghostly visitors served many other purposes than merely to secure proper burial for their mortal remains. Sometimes they seem to have shown themselves in order to emphasize the horrible character of certain recent events. Even the Epicurean skepticism of the elder Pliny was not sufficient to restrain him from remarking that the colossal wickedness of the emperor Nero had peopled the dwellings of the Romans with ghosts.[7] Most Romans were more credulous than Pliny, and would have been quite ready to accept Christian tradition when told that at the time of Jesus' crucifixion tombs had been opened in the vicinity of Jerusalem and many bodies of the deceased saints had come forth out of the tombs and entered into the city itself, where they showed themselves to many persons (Matt. 27: 52 f).

Not all apparitions were terrifying. Many of them served the interests of genuine affection and loving memory. Children returned to console bereaved parents, the grief of lovers was assuaged by apparitions of prematurely deceased companions, and the longing for communion with friends was answered by many a spectral visitation. So numerous were these occurrences in Gentile tradition that even a representative selection of illustrations is quite beyond the range of possibility in the present connection. Certainly persons accustomed to this imagery would find no difficulty, and perhaps much satisfaction, in picturing Jesus ap-

[6] Pliny, *Letters*, vii. 27.
[7] *Natural History*, xxx. 2 (5).

pearing after death to his distracted friend Peter, or
to his own brother James, or to the faithful women
whose devotion and affection sought to express itself by
carrying gifts to his tomb.

IV

The ancients were familiar not alone with specters
from the infernal regions, the heavens also yielded them
visions of supernal beings who appeared with an authority and majesty truly divine. While Jewish reserve
with reference to apparitions of God was shared by the
earliest Christians, the latter possessed in their traditions regarding the appearances of the heavenly Jesus
a type of imagery that easily paralleled Gentile readiness to believe in visions of an actual divinity. The
Christians preached a Jesus who, after death, had
appeared to his disciples, and who in their very presence
had ascended visibly to heaven (Acts 1: 9–11). The
Christian martyr in the moment of death had been
vouchsafed an apparition of this same heavenly being
standing on the right hand of God (Acts 7: 55 f). To
Saul, the persecutor of the new cause, this divine being
showed himself from heaven in a blinding blaze of light.
The Christian preacher was fond of repeating the story
(Acts 9: 3–9; 22: 6–14; 26: 12–18). No type of appear-
ance could be more emphatically divine in its features.
For Christians such visions of the Son of God, the
Righteous One, were virtually equivalent to the Old
Testament imagery of God's own appearing among men.
A Christian, perhaps in deference to contemporary
Jewish scruples, could affirm that "No man has ever
seen God," but immediately he could assert that God
has been exhibited by the only begotten Son, who is in

the bosom of the Father (John 1:18). Both in his human form while on earth, and in his post-resurrection appearances, Jesus had made deity available for human eyes. This way of thinking proved offensive to Jewish sensibilities, as the failure of Christian preaching to Jews amply attested. But such imagery was not at all strange or unwelcome among Gentiles.

Greek tradition was exceptionally rich in suggestions of the visibility of deity. The whole Greek heritage of literature, sculpture, and painting presented a multitude of divinities, usually in very picturesque fashion, before the eyes of mankind. Gods were accustomed to assume not only human form, but sometimes they took the shape of animals, or other material semblances, in order to make their presence real among men. The Homeric deities were almost as much at home on earth as they were on the summit of Olympus. Greek legend was rich in stories of occasions when gods had appeared among men to satisfy the pleasure of the deity, to avenge a wrong, or to perform a marvelous deed of kindness. The author of Acts knew right well that his Gentile readers would readily understand the implication of his remarks about what had happened to Paul and Barnabas at Lystra. The magical power of Paul's words to heal the lame man and the beauty of Barnabas's form inspired even the barbarian peoples who spoke the language of Lycaonia to believe that two Greek deities had appeared in their midst. Barnabas, they said, was Zeus, and Paul was Hermes (Acts 14: 8–18). At the time this was perfectly orthodox thinking for people in that region.

Popular notions about the visibility of deity had long been resisted by certain Greek philosophers, and some

Romans had also taken up the protest against anthropomorphism. Xenophanes was remembered as its radical critic in ancient times. By piecing together the fragments of his writings, preserved in the quotations of later authors, one is able to recover his opinions. Apparently he had protested that Homer and Hesiod attributed to the gods all those actions which are shameful and disgraceful among men, namely, theft, adultery, and mutual deceit. Mortals delude themselves into thinking that the gods are born, wear clothes, and have a voice and form like men. Indeed, if oxen and horses and lions had hands, or could paint with their hands and make images as men do, horses would paint and shape their gods like horses, oxen like oxen, each after their own likeness. So the Ethiopians picture their gods as woolly-headed and pug-nosed, while the Thracians represent theirs as blue-eyed and red-headed. All of this seems to Xenophanes absurd. On the contrary he would affirm that there is only one God, the greatest among gods and men, who is not like mortals, either bodily or mentally. The deity is all eye, all mind, all ear, and without effort dominates all things by the intellectual power of his mind. He always remains in one place, never moving, for it is not seemly that he should wander from place to place. He is the whole expanse of heaven.

The polemic against anthropomorphism was championed by a few of the later philosophers. The followers of Plato, in particular, were insistent upon the transcendence of the deity. Plato himself favored the opinion that God does not mingle at all with men but that all intercourse and speech which men have with the deity, whether when they are awake or asleep, is carried on through Love. Indeed, Love is himself a god, who "walks not upon the earth, nor yet upon the skulls of men, which are hard enough, but in the heart and souls of men; in them he walks and dwells and has his home." [8]

The Stoics also, at least in their more strenuous moods, did not take kindly to the notion of specific apparitions of deity. They were content to see the immanent divine presence in all nature about them. As Seneca expressed it, God is the universal intelligence who could be perceived only by thought. He is hidden from our eyes, yet he directs all things in the universe, and is in fact himself the greater and better part of his works. One who would appreciate the true greatness of deity will admit that he is all in all, at once within and without his works. And if you ask what is the difference between the divine nature and the human, the proper reply is that in man the better part is spirit, while in God there is nothing except spirit.[9] In later times the Stoic emperor Marcus Aurelius conceded that gods might be seen with the human eye. But the emperor insisted that they were to be honored for their works, even though they remained unseen. "I have not even seen my own soul," he said, "and yet I honor it. So it is in respect to the gods. From what I constantly experience of their power, I know that they exist, and I venerate them." [10]

However much philosophers might endeavor to transcendentalize and intellectualize the concept of deity, popular interest moved in the contrary direction. The

[8] *Symposium*, 195; cf. the criticism of Homeric anthropomorphism in *Republic*, 379 ff.

[9] Seneca, *Natural Questions*, i. *Prologue*, 13 ff.

[10] xii. 28.

most effective religions of the day all brought the deity near to humanity. Often he was said to have been originally a man, like one of the Greek heroes, or a demi-god who had once lived heroically on earth. In former times these divinities had been seen by everybody, and although now they had passed in triumph to the skies, they still manifested themselves in visible form when the occasion might so demand. Yet a respectful attitude of caution was maintained. To look upon the gods was a special privilege, not to be indulged in too frequently. Pausanias cites two instances in which persons who had made bold to look upon the goddess Isis had suffered death, and he concludes "thus it appears to be a true saying of Homer, that it is ill for man to see the gods in bodily shape." [11] Every one also knew the legend about Semele, the daughter of Cadmus, who had asked Zeus that he show himself to her in the majestic splendor of his Olympian glory. When finally he yielded to her demand she was consumed by the fiery flames of the lightning that shot forth from this god of thunder. The undimmed effulgence of a Zeus was as great a menace to Greeks as was the unveiled brightness of Jehovah's countenance to the Hebrews.

Also picturesque historical characters, like an Alexander the Great, arose to the status of gods and reappeared on earth. According to his biographer, Arrian, after Alexander's death his supernatural personality had been demonstrated by oracular responses, visions, and dreams experienced by various people.[12] On the

[11] x. 17 f, 32. But compare the joy of Apuleius over a vision of the great Osiris, *Metamorphoses*, xi. 30.

[12] *Anabasis*, vii. 30.

authority of those who claimed to have witnessed the phenomenon, an actual *parousia* of the deified Alexander was accepted without question by Dio Cassius.[13] According to this story, a spirit exactly resembling the Macedonian prince in form and dress had shown himself in upper Moesia and Thrace accompanied by a retinue of four hundred attendants equipped with thyrsi and fawn-skins. Lodgings and provisions had been furnished the visitants at public expense. Neither governors, soldiers, procurators, nor heads of provinces had dared to offer opposition either by word or by deed. The apparition proceeded "as if in daylight procession prescribed by proclamation," and after passing to the regions beyond Bithynia, where certain sacred rites were performed, it finally vanished.

The Romans had their own tradition, although modeled after the Greek, relative to the visibility of deceased heroic personages. Romulus figured in popular belief as a divinized hero, who had later manifested himself on earth. Cicero referred to the incident in a distinctly skeptical vein when he asked for the opinion of his brother Atticus, whose home was near the spot where Romulus was reported to have been seen alive again after his decease.[14] Also Livy seemed somewhat shocked at the readiness with which people accepted this story, but he knew that it had long been the custom to salute Romulus as a god, to implore his favor with prayers, and to honor him with a cult. According to popular belief, Romulus had been snatched away to heaven during a severe thunderstorm. When the disturbance subsided, his throne was found empty.

[13] lxxix. 18.
[14] *Laws*, i. 1. 3.

Also a certain Proculus Julius declared to the people that Romulus, suddenly descending from heaven, had appeared at daybreak and had said: "'Go tell the Romans that the gods so will that my Rome should become the capital of the world. Therefore, let them cultivate the art of war, and let them know and hand down to posterity that no human power shall be able to withstand the Roman arms.' Having said this, he ascended up to heaven." [15] Thus an apparition served to give the Roman Empire its divine commission. On the authority of heaven, Rome was to go into all the world, making subjects of all nations.

Other visitors from heaven were less intimately associated with a previous earthly career, but the reality of their appearance and the help which they rendered were no less highly appreciated. The trick Pisistratus played upon the Athenians, when he dressed up a woman of unusual size and represented her as Athena in visible presence leading him into the city, was easily perpetrated upon a credulous populace.[16] Both Greeks and Romans were fond of claiming the interest of deity in their racial and political welfare. Particularly at critical moments in history had messengers from heaven appeared upon the scene. Poets were fond of describing how gods participated in wars and slaughter. The Athenians pictured divinities fighting on their side in the battle of Marathon.[17] Also the destruction of the Gauls at Delphi was thought to have been accomplished most manifestly by "the hand of the god and the visible interposition of divinities." [18] Among Romans too

[15] Livy, i. 16.
[16] Herodotus, i. 60.
[17] Herodotus, vi. 105 and 117.
[18] Pausanias, viii. 10. 4; cf. Herodotus, viii. 38 f, 65.

the same faith prevailed. In Cicero's book on the nature of the gods,[19] one of the characters remarked on the belief that Castor and Pollux had been seen fighting in the Roman army on horseback in the war with the Latins. Indeed, he concluded that deities had often appeared in forms so visible that they compelled everybody who was not entirely senseless and hardened in impiety to confess the presence of the gods.

At other times the purpose of an apparition was to demonstrate the favor of heaven for some distinguished human individual. Plutarch sponsors the tradition that the famous Roman dictator, Sulla, had been visited in a dream by the Cappadocian goddess, Ma, who "stood by him and put into his hand thunder and lightning, then naming his enemies one by one, commanded him to strike them." Encouraged by this vision, Sulla marched on victoriously to Rome. Frequently in the case of great men, apparitions had served to show that they were a care of the gods. Suetonius tells of an appearance at midnight to Augustus's mother in the temple of Apollo when the deity in the form of a serpent visited her, thus insuring the divine ancestry of the future emperor.[20] Even a philosopher might be similarly accredited. The mother of the noted Pythagorean teacher, Apollonius of Tyana, had a like experience. Shortly before the birth of her child, Proteus, who announced himself to be the god of Egypt, appeared to the mother and said that she was to bear a second Proteus, a teacher to be more distinguished for wisdom than even the god himself had been.[21]

[19] ii. 2.
[20] *Augustus*, xciv.
[21] Philostratus, *Life of Apollonius*, i. 4.

Quite ordinary people were sometimes directed in a vision to perform some heaven-assigned task. In one instance, an apparition instructed a Roman rustic to inform the Senate that the divinity was displeased with the president of the games. At first the humble peasant feared man more than god, and, like the Jonah of Hebrew story, was disobedient to the heavenly vision. He also failed to heed a second warning, and suffered the sudden death of his son. Even after a third vision he still hesitated, and consequently was smitten by a serious illness. Finally, when carried on a litter to the Senate, he discharged his unpleasant but inescapable task, whereupon he immediately recovered his strength and returned home completely restored to health.[22]

Demonic powers also claimed a place for themselves in the world of vision. Even though the demon was merely the spirit of a dead man, when it entered the sphere of the supernatural it assumed the prerogatives of a divinity. In one such instance an actual cult had shaped itself around a much dreaded figure that was popularly reputed to be the ghost of one of the sailors of Odysseus. Pausanias tells the story in all serious-ness.[23] When the Trojan warrior came to the small town of Temesa in southern Italy, the natives killed one of his drunken sailors for violence done to a maiden of the town. Odysseus passed on without giving any thought to the incident. But the ghost of the mur-dered man took revenge upon the natives by killing many of their number. Not until they were advised by the Pythian priestess to build a temple to the ghost and make provision for his satisfaction did he cease his

[22] Cicero, *Divination*, i. 26.
[23] vi. 6. 3 f.

depredations. But finally the boxer Euthymus, appearing upon the scene, girded himself for a conflict with the specter, who was so real that a mortal could actually engage him in a physical combat. The demon was driven into the sea, never to return, but his form was well remembered. Pausanias himself had seen a portrait, said to be a copy of an old painting, in which the ghost was represented as of a horrid black color with a most dreadful appearance, and "the writing on the picture gave him the name of Lycas." The vision of Lycas descending headlong into the sea was as real for the Gentile reader of the Gospel of Luke as was the Christian picture of Satan fallen as lightning from heaven (Luke 10: 18), or the imagery of demonized swine plunging to death in the lake of Gennesaret (Luke 8: 26-39).

Notorious characters, like the infamous Nero, also readily assumed the rôle of divinities in apparitional imagery. When the author of Revelation spoke of "the beast that was and is not and is about to come up out of the abyss" (17: 8), his contemporaries would have no difficulty in recalling the popular legend that had already connected itself with this most vicious of emperors. Even during his lifetime, if Plutarch — who was a contemporary of John of Patmos — is correctly informed, Nero's enormities had led the Roman people to suspect that he was "no human creature, but some penal or vindictive supernatural power that had seized the Empire." [24] And after his death there quickly arose the belief that he would return to take vengeance on his enemies. When Suetonius [25] was a

[24] Plutarch, *Otho*, ii.
[25] *Nero*, lvii.

young man, an impostor who claimed to be Nero had appeared among the Parthians and many people were quite ready to accept his pretensions. A Christian could concede such honors to Nero without any hesitation, because Christians could set over against the heathen's faith the bolder and more triumphant hope of a reappearance of their own hero, the Lord Jesus Christ, who would conquer and hurl down to eternal perdition the Neronic monster with all his demonic attendants.

CHAPTER III

MEDIA OF REVELATION

THE supernatural world impinged upon the life of people within the Roman Empire in a great variety of ways. Not everybody's physical eye was sufficiently sensitive to register visions of those gods, angels, demons, and ghosts that were commonly believed to visit the haunts of mortals. Although the reality of apparitions might be accepted without question, communications with the supernal regions were by no means limited to this single area of experience. Even among Christians there were many persons who had never been privileged to see an angel, much less to witness a vision of the risen Jesus. Nor did apparitions, numerous as they were, furnish mankind with an adequately full disclosure of divine wisdom and inspiration for every contingency in life. It was necessary to tap other and more readily accessible sources of help. These were not wanting. At the time of Christianity's rise the inhabitants of the Roman world were accustomed to seek and find divine guidance in many different quarters. The media of revelation were varied and abundant.

I

Many people were expert in reading the signs of the times. For Gentiles, as well as for Jews and Christians, the heavens declared the glory of God, and one saw in the revealing features of nature's face knowledge of the

67

divine forces behind all phenomena. Cicero put into
the mouth of the Stoic Lucilius words that were acceptable to large numbers of persons in that age: "What
can be so plain and evident, when we behold the heavens
and contemplate the celestial bodies, as the existence
of some preëminently intelligent divinity by whom all
things are governed." [1]

Nature was thought to reveal the presence and the
will of divinity in many striking ways. In summarizing
the argument used by an older Stoic, Cleanthes, to
prove the existence of God, Lucilius specified four principal kinds of divine revelation that stand written for
every man on the face of nature. In the first place,
there is that foreknowledge of future events which God
has entrusted to certain individuals. The augur, if
a genuine performer, is a chosen instrument of deity.
And the proof of his genuineness is to be seen in the
numerous occasions when his predictions have been
proved true by succeeding events. Hence one concluded that "God shows us signs of future happenings,
and if we are occasionally deceived in the results, it is
not to be imputed to the nature of the gods, but to the
conjectures of men."

The second type of revelation was the manifest kindness of providence displayed in nature. In the salu-
brious climate of the Mediterranean area, in the fertility of the earth and the variety of its products, the
intelligent man would recognize the expression of the
divine favor for humanity. An Epictetus would render
unstinted praise to the deity for such every-day blessings as agricultural instruments, hands with which to
toil, mouths for eating, stomachs for digesting food,

[1] *Nature of the Gods*, ii. 2.

and the repose of sleep. Since God is the father of all men, his care is sufficient for them: "Shall kindred to Cæsar, or any other of the great at Rome, enable a man to live secure, above contempt, and void of all fear whatever; and shall not the fact of having God for our maker and father and guardian free us from griefs and terrors?" [2]

The terrible side of nature was also useful to man in his efforts to read the will of the gods. Thunder, tempests, storm, snow, hail, devastation, pestilence, earthquakes, hideous noises, showers of stones and rain like drops of blood, were voices of the deity. The shaking of the earth, accompanied by sudden openings that sometimes engulfed living beings, monstrous births of men and beasts, and meteors shooting across the heavens, were all divine forebodings of impending calamities.

In the fourth place, the stable and orderly side of nature was no less significant for divine revelation. No intelligent man, it was thought, could regard as the result of mere chance the regularity with which the heavenly bodies followed their courses, the beauty of sun and moon, and the glory of the starry night. Such perfection could have come into being only through the operation of a supreme divine intelligence. Here was an open book of revelation ready for every man to read. In the opinion of Seneca, contemplation of the heavens offered the human soul its best opportunity for acquiring knowledge from the deity. In the pleasure to be derived from soaring in thought to the heights of heaven there to discover nature's inmost secrets, the soul found the proof of its divine origin. In this quest it

[2] *Discourses*, i. 9 and 16.

was "emancipated, prepared for the knowledge of heavenly things and rendered worthy of entering into communion with God." [3]

The philosopher might be able to find a satisfactory revelation of God by reflecting upon the beneficence of a kindly providence and the magnificence of an orderly cosmos. But the average man felt ill at ease in so rarefied an atmosphere. When he wanted to know the meaning of nature — and he always desired this knowledge — he was prone to consult a professional augur in the hope of discovering hidden meanings in portentous happenings. It was a generally accepted belief that the gods, since they knew in advance everything that would take place, could forecast the consequences of any decision that an individual might make. Also the divinities were assumed to be friendly and ready, when duly consulted, to intimate by omens, dreams, auguries, or other revelatory signs, the line of conduct that one should pursue or avoid. He who chose to obey the revealed will of the deities would never have occasion to regret his decision, but disobedience would be attended by inevitable punishment. [4]

There were numerous forms of divination very generally practised among the Greeks and Romans. The divine mind was found revealed in the flight of birds, in the action of lightning, in the entrails of the sacred victim, and in many other signs known to the professional diviner. A very simple form of divination was practised by the use of lots, a custom common to Jews, Christians, and pagans. The Jews called the sacred stones used for this purpose Urim and Thummim, and

[3] *Natural Questions*, i. *Prologue*, 6.
[4] Xenophon, *Banquet*, iv. 48.

one who wished to inquire of the Lord besought the priest to manipulate the sacred emblems. Christians, too, when they desired divine guidance in selecting a successor to Judas, put forward Joseph and Matthias and gave the lots for them, at the same time praying to God that he would thereby indicate his choice. When the lot fell upon Matthias its decision seemed a matter of divine revelation (Acts 1: 15–26). The early Christians rarely resorted to the lots, but they appealed freely to other portentous happenings in proof of heaven's interest in their welfare.

Tradition among both Jews and Gentiles recorded vast numbers of portents by which heaven had foreshadowed coming events. It was a widely established belief that no momentous occurrence ever had or ever would come to pass without appropriate warnings from the deity. Jewish opinion on this subject was given most striking expression in the description of premonitory signs to precede the end of the world. The stars would deviate from their course; the moon would shine in the daytime and the rays of the sun would suddenly burst out in the night; fire would fall from heaven or break forth from the ground and terrible earthquakes would occur; the seasons would be altered and the year shortened; rain would cease, and drought and famine would result; terrible apparitions would be seen in the heavens — open books which all might read, flaming swords, and battling giants; on earth rocks and trees would drip blood, stones would cry out and all nature would be out of joint. These and a vast number of similar phenomena would reveal to man the approach of the final catastrophe.

Even less terrible events were preceded by appropri-

ate portents in which the divine will was made known
to those who had eyes to see. Josephus lists the prodigies that had foreshadowed the fall of Jerusalem in 70
A. D. There was a star resembling a sword which stood
over the city, and a comet that continued a whole year.
At the feast of the Passover immediately preceding
the war at three o'clock one morning for half an hour
so great a light shone around the altar and the holy
house that it appeared to be bright daytime. At the
same festival a heifer, as she was led by the high priest
to be sacrificed, brought forth a lamb in the court of the
temple. The eastern gate of the inner court, though
so heavy that it required twenty men to close it, opened
of its own accord about midnight. A few days after
the feast, before sunset, chariots and troops of soldiers
in their armor were seen running about among the
clouds. Most terrible of all, four years before the out-
break of the war, Jesus, the son of Ananus, began to
shout Woe, woe, to Jerusalem, a cry which he kept
up for seven years and five months without growing
hoarse or being tired, nor did he cease until killed by a
stone from one of the engines shortly before the fall
of the city. Reflecting upon these signs, Josephus remarks, "Now if any one consider these things, he will
find that God takes care of mankind and by all ways
possible foreshadows to our race what is for their preservation." [5] Likewise among the Greeks and the Romans, portents were highly rated as indications of the
deities' will in connection with momentous events.
Livy recounts a formidable array of prodigies preceding
the defeat of the Romans by Hannibal. It was reported from Sicily that several darts belonging to the

[5] *War*, vi. 5. 3.

soldiers had taken fire, and in Sardinia the staff of a horseman who was going his rounds upon the wall burst into flame as he held it in his hand; the shores had blazed with frequent fires; two shields had sweated blood; at Præneste red hot stones had fallen from the heavens; at Arpi shields were seen in the sky, and the sun fought with the moon; at Capena two moons rose in the daytime; the waters of Cære had flowed mixed with blood; in the territory of Antium while the grain was being gathered bloody ears had fallen into the basket; the heavens appeared cleft asunder and a great light had shone forth; the statue of Mars at Rome had sweated at the sight of images of wolves; at Capua the heavens were seen on fire and the moon appeared to be falling amidst rain; while other prodigies of less magnitude had also been observed.[6]

A series of similar warnings had, it was said, been experienced by Julius Cæsar prior to his assassination. A few months earlier, in some building operations at Capua, a brass tablet had been found with an inscription upon it declaring that a descendant of Julius would be slain by the hands of his kinsmen and his death avenged by fearful disasters throughout Italy. Shortly before his death he had been told that the horses which, upon his crossing the Rubicon, he had consecrated and turned loose to graze without a keeper, abstained entirely from eating and shed floods of tears. The soothsayer Spurinna also noted ominous appearances in the sacrifices. Cæsar had dreamed that he was soaring above the clouds and his wife had dreamed that her husband had been stabbed and had fallen upon her bosom. Such were the ways in which the deity endeav-

[6] Livy, xxii. 1.

ored to convey warnings to Cæsar. Moreover, after the tragic event the displeasure of the gods was made plain through further portentous happenings. The sun, being unwilling to view the horrid crime, turned away its light, and continued to shine with dimmed splendor. It failed to show its ordinary radiance at its rising and its heat was much diminished during that whole year. On the other hand, the divine favor toward Cæsar himself was shown by the elevation of his soul to the heavens, where it shone brightly in the form of a new comet for seven nights in succession.[7]

In a similar vein Dio Cassius referred to signs preceding Domitian's assassination, remarking that "no occurrence of such magnitude is without previous indications." Domitian in a dream beheld the assassin approaching him with a sword; he also dreamed that Minerva, whose statue he kept in his bedchamber, threw away her weapons, mounted a chariot drawn by black horses, and disappeared in an abyss. But, most wonderful of all, Proculus, a prophet, had foretold in Germany the very day on which the event was to occur. Even when brought into the presence of the emperor and threatened with death to himself, he reiterated the prophecy; and the event happened as predicted in spite of the emperor's precautions.[8]

Christians also made much of portents as an indication of the divine will. In the first place, they took over Jewish ideas regarding the terrible events to precede the end of the world. It is this imagery which underlies Jesus' language as reported in the thirteenth

[7] Suetonius, *Julius Cæsar*, lxxxi; cf. Vergil, *Georgics*, i. 466 ff; Josephus, *Antiquities*, xiv. 12. 3; Plutarch, *Cæsar*, lxiii ff; Strabo, *Fragment* 14 (Müller, III, 494).

[8] Dio Cassius, lxvii. 16.

chapter of Mark, where he warns the disciples that they shall hear of wars and rumors of wars, there shall be earthquakes in divers places, also famines; "for those days shall be tribulation such as there hath not been the like from the beginning of the creation which God created until now, and never shall be." In Peter's sermon recorded in the second chapter of Acts the very language of the Old Testament is cited: "I will show wonders in the heaven above and signs on the earth beneath; blood and fire and vapour of smoke. The sun shall be turned into darkness and the moon into blood before the great and notable day of the Lord come" (Acts 2: 19–21; Joel 2: 28 ff).

These predictions of events yet to be revealed were supplemented by the citation of portents in the past. The latter type of thinking was especially congenial to Gentiles, who gave their attention, not so much to the miraculous events yet to be disclosed, as to those which were daily happening or which were reported by tradition. The Christian preacher on Gentile soil was able to meet this demand. The star of Bethlehem which had guided the Magi bespoke the interest of heaven in the birth of Jesus; the will of deity regarding him had been uttered verbally from heaven at the baptism and again at the transfiguration; his entire career had been a display of mighty works and wonders and signs which God did by him in the presence of men; and finally, at his death, the sun hid its face, the earth quaked, the veil of the temple was torn in two, the rocks were rent, the tombs were opened, and many bodies of the dead saints came forth. Thus Christianity proved to be not at all inferior either to Jewish or to pagan faith in the use of portents as a medium by

which the will of the deity had been communicated
to men.

II

The sacred book was an important source of supernatural wisdom for many persons in the ancient world.
Among Jews inspired scripture had early attained a
position of unique respect; it was taken to be a verbally
accurate record from which the revealed will of God
in all things could be learned. This is a fact too well-
known to call for further comment. But the use of
sacred books as a source of revelation among Gentiles
is perhaps less familiar. By the beginning of the
Christian era there were in circulation, particularly in
the eastern Mediterranean lands, large numbers of
writings containing formulas whose divine potency was
supposed to be efficacious over a wide range of human
experience. These books contained recipes for casting
out demons, for healing all sorts of diseases, for insuring
safety in various undertakings, and for rendering assistance in every imaginable emergency.

Knowledge of effective formulas was coveted by many
adventurers, although the practice of magic, except
by properly authorized persons, was often severely cen-
sured and sometimes strictly forbidden. In an ideal
society Plato would impose the penalty of death upon
a prophet or diviner who resorted to the use of "magic
knots or enchantments or incantations," while a private
magician would be liable to punishment according to
the measure of the injury which had resulted from the
practice of his art.[9] The efficacy of magic seems to have
been universally conceded. It was thought possible

[9] *Laws*, xi. 933.

to obtain formulas of adjuration or petition that, when correctly repeated, would force even the gods to do one's bidding.[10] Many persons must have been severely tempted to seek the acquisition of such books as were supposed to yield this superhuman wisdom.

Among the Romans in early times careful provision was made for the effective use of proper formulas. When a Decius desired to know the correct word to recite in a very critical situation he consulted the pontiff who directed him to say, "Janus, Jupiter, Father Mars, Quirinus, Bellona, Lares, New Gods, Native Gods, Gods who hold power over us and our enemies, Infernal Gods, I pray, I adore, I entreat and beseech your favor, that you grant strength, victory, and prosperity to the Roman people of the Quirites, and that you visit upon the enemies of the Roman people of the Quirites terror fright, and death." [11]

It was the business of the pontiff to keep himself fully informed as to what formula was to be employed on any required occasion. Not only success in war, but farming and health were safeguarded by the recital of magical phrases. One treated a sore on the body by placing the hand in a prescribed manner upon the afflicted spot and reciting, "Depart, whether produced to-day or aforetime, whether created to-day or afore-time. This plague, this pestilence, this pain, this tumor, this inflammation, these goitres, these tonsils, this bunch, these swellings, this scrofula, this blotch, I call forth, I draw out, I exorcise by means of this magic from these limbs and marrow." [12] In private hands an

---

[10] Lucan, vi. 430 ff.
[11] Livy, viii. 9; cf. Pliny, *Natural History*, xxviii. 2 (3). 12.
[12] Marcellus, *Remedies*, xv. 11.

instrument of this sort was easily misused, and it was not a simple matter for the law to control one who possessed this supernatural skill. It is not surprising that books containing a great variety of magical formulas should have been much in demand and widely circulated. When Christian missionaries succeeded in persuading the heathen to trust simply in the all-efficacious name of Jesus for full protection from human ills it would have been easily possible to find in these converts' possession magical books for a bonfire like that staged one day at Ephesus (Acts 19: 18 f).

The numerous magical papyri that have been exhumed from the rubbish heaps of the Roman East give point to Pliny's statement that of all the arts known in his day, magic was the most influential and had exerted its baneful influence over the legitimate arts of divination, medicine, and religion.[13] In Pliny's opinion the pernicious practice had come from Persia, where its literature had originated with some "two millions of verses" from the hand of Zoroaster. Democritus is charged with having encouraged the art among the Greeks by alleging that the tomb of Dardanus contained writings for this purpose and in agreement with which Democritus produced a further literature about the time of the Peloponnesian War. Pliny accuses Jews also of contributing to the perverted custom, the persons most responsible having been "Moses, Jannes, and Lotapea." Evidently the high estimate placed upon a sacred book among the Hebrews, as well as among the Persians, lent color to the charge that these peoples were natural adepts in the magic art. This suspicion made it highly desirable for the Jewish philosopher Philo to affirm that

---

[13] *Natural History*, xxx. 1 ff.

holy inspiration could not live in the same house with magic.[14] Nevertheless, evidence is not lacking to indicate that there were expert Jewish magicians. The Essenes had, in addition to the regular Hebrew Scriptures, other secret holy books by the use of which they were reputed to be exceptionally successful in divination.[15] And individual Jews, like Simon in Samaria and Elymas at Paphos (Acts 8: 9 ff; 13: 6 ff), already enjoyed a reputation as successful magicians before Christian missionaries proclaimed among Gentiles the superior efficacy of Jesus' name.

It was an entirely different matter, in the opinion of the Romans, to use sacred formulas under the official direction of the state. The Roman people had long been in possession of holy books that were believed to constitute an infallible source of information for ascertaining the will of the gods. The origin of heathen Rome's sacred canon of scriptures is veiled in obscurity. But where facts were lacking fancy filled the gap. Legend reported that an old woman came to King Tarquin with a collection of nine books of Sibylline oracles, presumably from Cumæ, which she offered to sell for a stated price. The king refused to pay the sum, whereupon she burned three of the books and demanded the same amount for the remaining six. The king again refused, and she burned three more. Becoming alarmed by the woman's unusual conduct, the king consulted the augurs who reported that he had rejected a favor sent him by the gods. Thereupon he purchased the three remaining books at the original price. They were entrusted at first to two guardians, but later the number

[14] *Life of Moses*, i. 50.
[15] Josephus, *War*, ii. 8. 7 and 12.

was raised to ten, and finally to fifteen, who held office for life. No one else had access to this sacred collection of Sibylline books which were kept in the crypt of the Capitoline Temple and might be consulted only by the "Fifteen Men." [16]

When the Capitol was burned in 83 B. C. the precious documents perished. But fortunately Cumæ was not the only home of an oracular priestess. In other places similar oracles had existed for centuries. In ancient times the Greeks appear to have known only one Sibyl. But this number gradually increased with the growth of tradition, as different authors reported various places where local prophetesses giving out inspired utterances were to be found. As early as the fourth century B. C. the Greeks seem to have recognized at least three Sibyls, and the Roman Varro in the first century B. C. spoke categorically of ten,[17] nine beside the Cumæan from whom the original Sibylline books of the Romans were assumed to have been derived. Consequently after their destruction the Senate decreed that a new collection should be made from all available sources and the whole submitted to the priests, who were to sift the genuine from the spurious. Thus a new official document was procured and endowed with all the sanctity of the old.[18]

From time to time the authorities had adopted measures for suppressing any oracular books which were thought unorthodox or which might rival the official collection. Livy cited an occasion of this sort from the days when Hannibal was threatening Rome in 214 B. C. During the unstable conditions caused by the war the

---

[16] Dionysius of Halicarnassus, iv. 62.
[17] Lactantius, *Divine Institutes*, i. 6.
[18] Tacitus, *Annals*, vi. 12.

citizens had been seized by a passion for "superstitious observances." Many rites had come in from foreign countries, and the ancient Roman ceremonies, both private and public, fell into disuse. When the situation became so serious that the ordinary officials were unable to cope with it, the Senate especially commissioned the city prætor to rid the people of these superstitions. He summoned an assembly where he read the decree of the Senate and demanded that all persons who had any books of prophecy or forms of prayer, or any prescribed forms of sacrificing, should deposit such books with him before the calends of April.[19]

This watchful attitude was seen again a few years later (182 B. C.) in the familiar story of the discovery of the books of Numa Pompilius. Some workmen on the farm of Lucius Petillius, digging deeper than usual, were said to have found two stone chests. One proved to be the sarcophagus of Numa, and the other contained his books in two bundles tied up with waxed cords, each bundle including seven books.[20] One set was written in Latin and related to the pontifical law; the other seven books were in Greek and contained the teachings of Pythagoras. When the story of the discovery came to the ears of the city prætor he borrowed the books, and after reading merely the chapter headings he perceived, so he said, that the documents were dangerous, as tending to undermine the established system of religious doctrines. Accordingly, he informed the owner that he had decided to throw these books into the fire, but before doing so would allow him the right of appeal and a claim for damages. The

[19] Livy, xxv. 1.
[20] Livy, xl. 29; Pliny, *Natural History*, xiii. 13 (27).

matter was referred to the Senate, but when the prætor declared under oath that the books ought not to be read or preserved, the Senate deemed the evidence sufficient and ordered their destruction without so much as reading the chapter headings. The prætor was instructed to pay the owner whatever sum seemed to the prætor reasonable, but the owner, tradition says, never received the money.

After the fire of 83 B. C. additions were admitted more freely into the official document, when these were properly attested. But the new oracles had to show Sibylline credentials; otherwise they went to the flames. This was the motive that prompted Augustus in the course of his reforms to destroy the two thousand volumes mentioned by Suetonius.[21] Whether these rival books were in Latin or in Greek, if their authors were unknown or of no great authority, the documents were burned. Only those officially approved were spared, and when enclosed in a gilded box were deposited under the pedestal of the statue of the Palatine Apollo.

Under Augustus' successor, Tiberius, the same care was exercised in admitting books into the Sibylline canon. A member of the College of Fifteen petitioned the Senate to allow a certain writing to be included in the official collection. A young tribune made a motion to that effect, and the matter was passed without comment. But when Tiberius heard of the proceedings he criticized the parties concerned for putting through so important a motion without giving it due publicity. He excused the tribune who made the motion in the Senate, on the ground of his youth and lack of familiarity with ancient usage, and he upbraided the member

21 *Augustus*, xxxi.

of the pontifical college who had first suggested the move. The emperor's hostility was based upon the fact that the author of the document in question was not known, that the consent of the entire college had not been obtained, and that the motion had not been given the proper reading and deliberation in the Senate, but had been passed in a thin house.[22]

Christians from the first entertained the idea of revelation in a sacred book, which they took over from Judaism. The Bible of the earliest Christians was identical with that of their Jewish kinsmen, although it was interpreted to suit the special needs of the new religion. Christians also wrote letters to friends and to churches for the purpose of furthering the new propaganda, and they assembled traditions about the life of Jesus for the edification of different communities; but at first there was no disposition to include these distinctively Christian documents in the category of sacred Scripture. It was not until the second century A. D. that they were assembled into a canon and given a place beside the original collection of Jewish books. And then it was the Romans, with their inherited genius for sifting spurious from genuine, and thus safeguarding orthodoxy, who led in the movement. Ultimately it was not so much the Jewish Palestinian conception of a body of ancient religious books, as the old Roman idea of a Sibylline canon, that came to prevail in the Christian church. Belief in the sanctity of the letter was, to be sure, a Jewish inheritance; but the application of the orthodox test, insistence upon a particular class of authorship, e.g., that of apostles or near apostles, the suppression of such documents as

[22] Tacitus, *Annals*, vi. 12.

did not conform to official standards, and the withholding of the Scriptures from the laity were all a distinctively Roman, rather than a Jewish, inheritance within the early church.

III

Another notable source of revelation was the inspired person, an idea essentially more primitive than that of the inspired book. There were two main classes of such persons: (1) those who were taught of God, and (2) those who were filled with God. Yet these two groups were not always mutually exclusive.

One of the oldest forms in which the divinely instructed man appears is that of lawgiver. Among the Hebrews, Moses had been chosen to receive the law from God and pass it on to the people, even as in earlier times the Babylonian Hammurabi received his famous code from the god Shamesh. But the peoples of the Græco-Roman world were not dependent upon the Semites for the figure of the divinely instructed lawgiver. It was also true of the Greeks that they—

regarded and respected divine in preference to human law. The number of persons was very great who consulted oracles and, being desirous of obtaining the advice of Zeus, hurried to Dodona. And Minos among the Cretans . . . every nine years, as Plato says, ascended to the cave of Zeus, received ordinances from him, and conveyed them to men. Lycurgus, his imitator, acted in a similar manner; for he was often accustomed, as it seemed, to leave his own country to inquire of the Pythian goddess what ordinances he was to promulgate to the Lacedæmonians.[23]

After making these statements, Strabo adds that he cannot vouch for the truth of the tradition, but he con-

[23] Strabo, xvi. 2. 38 f.

cedes that it was popularly accepted, which is the point of interest for us. Among the Romans the Twelve Tables as such were a strictly human creation, but they embodied materials from earlier codes then in existence,[24] and they had been promulgated by leaders who administered justice as impartially "as if from an oracle." [25] Moreover, the actual genesis of Roman law was believed to have been much older, its real founder having been Numa, who was as wise as any man of that age could be in all laws "both divine and human," and ruled the people by "religious devices and divine law." [26]

In Christian teaching, Jesus was the new lawgiver speaking the genuine oracles of God. He was presented to Jews as a second Moses supplementing the older revelation — they of olden times had taught so-and-so, but now the final word had been spoken by Jesus. But when Christianity spread to Gentile lands the figure of the divine teacher, communicating to men wisdom which he had learned from the deity, would not have seemed at all strange. In fact, the form in which the collections of Jesus' teaching were best known in the early days is not that of "laws" (*nomoi*) or "teaching" (*didache*), which would have been the words corresponding to Hebrew usage. On the contrary, they were "oracles" (*logia*), the term used of oracular responses received by the pagan lawgivers and passed on by them to mankind.

Closely related to the lawgiver stood the prophet. He had two chief, though kindred, functions: (1) he

---

[24] Tacitus, *Annals*, iii. 27.
[25] Livy, iii. 34.
[26] Livy, i. 18; Tacitus, *Annals*, iii. 26.

conveyed instruction from God to men, and (2) he fore-told events. That is, he exhorted and he predicted. He differed from the lawgiver in that the latter mediated one specific body of revelation, whereas the prophet's work was more continuous; he brought revelation down to date, so to speak.

The prophet figured very prominently in all the religions of the Græco-Roman world. With his importance for the Hebrews every one is familiar; but among the Greeks, Romans, and Christians he occupied a similarly significant place. Strabo remarks [27] that among various peoples, including Hindus (Indians), Persians, Assyrians, Greeks, and Romans, prophets received so much honor as to be thought worthy even of thrones, because, both during their lifetime and after their death, they were supposed to communicate ordinances and precepts from the gods. They spoke with the authority of deity behind their words, whether it was the Hebrew Isaiah exclaiming "thus said Jehovah," or the Roman Marcius proclaiming "thus spake Jupiter." [28] Frequently, as with the Hebrews, the prophet's activity was connected with the people's political welfare. Thus the famous Greek leader Epaminondas had been incited by the prophecies of Bacis to lead the Messenians in their efforts to recover their lost territory. [29] Both Bacis and a predecessor named Euclus had prophesied with reference to the conflict between the Greeks and the Persians. As late as the second century A. D. the works of several of these prophets were still extant. Pausanias says that there

[27] xvi. 2. 39.
[28] Livy, xxv. 12: *ita Juppiter fatus est.*
[29] Pausanias, iv. 27. 4.

have been the following prophetic men: Euclus, a Cyprian; Musæus, an Athenian; Lycus, son of Pandion; and a Bœotian named Bacis. Pausanias had read the oracles of all of them except Lycus. Unfortunately their writings no longer exist, except in a few alleged fragments. The Greeks also recognized prophetic women, like Deborah of early Hebrew tradition (Judg. 4: 4). To the many well-known Sibylline prophetesses one may add Phænnis, daughter of the king of the Chaonians, and the Peleæ at Dodona, whose fame was known to Pausanias.[30]

The rôle of the prophet among the early Christians was an important one. When instructing the Corinthians regarding the order of preferment among the officials of the new community, Paul remarked that "God hath set some in the church first apostles, secondly prophets, thirdly teachers" (I Cor. 12: 28). Next to the apostles, whose number was limited, stood the prophet as the foremost individual in the Christian community. Also the ability to prophesy was the one spiritual gift toward the attainment of which every Christian should strive — "desire earnestly spiritual gifts, but above all that ye may prophesy" (I Cor. 14: 1). Yet Paul would not admit prophetesses within the Christian community. In fact he vetoed their activity with the injunction, "Let the women keep silence in the churches, for it is not permitted for them to speak" (I Cor. 14: 34). He did not propose to have a Christian Sibyl. But other Christian communities apparently were more tolerant, for we learn from Acts 21: 8 f that Philip, the evangelist who resided at Cæsarea, had four daughters, all of them prophetesses.

[30] x. 12. 5; 14. 6.

The functions of the Christian prophet were essentially the same as those of his predecessors in other faiths. He uttered the divine message both as exhortation and as prediction. His duties in the Corinthian community were clearly indicated by Paul, who contrasted the intelligible utterance of the prophet with the unintelligible mutterings of him who spoke in a tongue:

If therefore the whole church be assembled and all speak with tongues and there come in men unlearned (in the secrets of Christianity) or unbelieving, will they not say that ye are mad? But if all prophesy and there come in one unbelieving or unlearned he is convicted by what you say . . . the secrets of his heart are made manifest through your powers of divine insight and he will fall down on his face and worship God declaring that God is in you indeed.

The prophet spoke whenever a revelation came to him, and if one or more prophets were already in action and a revelation came to a third sitting by, the others were to cease speaking in order that the third might utter his message while the prophetic afflatus was fresh upon him (I Cor. 14:30). It was also the business of the Christian prophet to predict future events. This function is apparent in the case of Agabus, who was among the prophets that came down from Jerusalem to Antioch and announced an approaching famine, which came to pass in the days of Claudius (Acts 11:27 f). Agabus also predicted the fate that awaited Paul on the occasion of his final visit to Jerusalem, when he was arrested and cast into prison (Acts 21:11).

The figure of the Christian prophet mediating the divine revelation, sometimes in hortatory address and sometimes in specific predictions, was in many respects a more natural phenomenon among Gentiles than among Jews. Christians, it is true, had before them constantly in the Old Testament the examples of the ancients, and the Christian conception drew much from that source. But Hebrew prophecy of the ancient type was a thing of the past, although the Jewish preacher was by no means extinct. On the other hand, in the Græco-Roman world the professional exhorter in the form of the Cynic-Stoic preacher, and the professional forecaster of events (the diviner), were to be met on almost every street corner, both alike claiming to have a divine message to deliver to mankind. Christians entered the lists with these competitors and ultimately won from them on their own ground.

The prophet was not merely taught of God; he was also full of deity. When God took a part of the Spirit with which he had endowed Moses and put it on the seventy elders, they also prophesied. Saul became a prophet when the Spirit of God came mightily upon him (I Sam. 10: 10). When Elijah died he passed on this divine gift to Elisha (II Kings 2: 9 f, 15), but Elisha was less successful in transmitting it to King Joash (II Kings 13: 14–19). The prophet, because of his divine equipment, was especially the "man of God." He was "the man that hath the Spirit" which so overmastered him that people said the prophet is a "fool," he is "mad" (Hosea 9: 7). Similarly the great literary prophets uttered their message because the Spirit of the Lord came upon them. When they were thus filled with God, so to speak, they gave vent to the divine urge in the message of revelation spoken and recorded for the guidance of their hearers or readers.

The same type of divine impulsion characterized the

prophets and prophetesses among the Greeks and Romans. The devotees of Dionysus experienced, in the ecstasy accompanying the Bacchic frenzy, the prophetic gift of this deity, "for in all fulness when he floods our frame he makes his maddened votaries tell the future." [31] Speaking of the Cumæan Sibyl, Vergil says, "the prophetess raves with wild outrage in the cave struggling if possible to unburden her soul of the mighty god"; she is actually frenzied with prophetic inspiration. [32] Similarly, Pausanias says of the Sibyl at Delphi that her oracles were uttered under the frenzy and inspiration of the god. [33] Likewise, Euclus the Cyprian, Musæus the Athenian, Lycus son of Pandion, and Bacis the Bœotian "prophesied by the inspiration of god." [34]

Even the philosophers recognized the divinity of prophetic frenzy — a "madness which is the special gift of heaven and the source of chiefest blessings among men." Rationality was a merely human characteristic while prophetic madness was of divine origin. Thus it happened that the prophetesses at Delphi and at Dodona in their normal moments had been of no significance, but when frenzied by divine inspiration they had been the source of inestimable good for both the public and the private affairs of the Greeks. [35] Among the Romans prophetic inspiration was taken for granted, [36] although there were some critics who doubted

[31] Euripides, *Bacchanals*, 298 ff; cf. Pausanias, x. 33. 5.

[32] *Æneid*, vi. 42 ff.

[33] i. 12. 1.

[34] Pausanias, x. 12. 5. The divine equipment of Bacis is more specifically defined as coming from the nymphs.

[35] Plato, *Phædrus*, 244.

[36] E.g. Vergil, *Æneid*, vi. 77 ff; Pliny, *Natural History*, vii. 33; Lucan, v. 165 ff; Tacitus, *Annals*, ii. 54.

whether the verses of the Sibyl had really been uttered under the impulsion of frenzy. The acrostic arrangement and other artifices evident in these poems seemed rather to indicate that they had been the work of a more sober technical skill.[37] But the Greeks in the first and second Christian centuries still believed, even though the oracles were then falling into decay, that prophetic frenzy was a genuinely divine gift to humanity. The revered Heraclitus was cited in support of the Sibyl "who with frenzied mouth utters words unmirthful, unadorned, untricked, reaches with her voice through a thousand years by the agency of god." [38]

When Christians preached the doctrine of the prophet's divine infilling, the idea was not at all a novel one even to their Gentile hearers. The Corinthians would take readily to Paul's explanation of prophecy as due to endowment by a divine spirit. Also in Acts 19:6 one reads that after certain converts were baptized and Paul had laid his hands upon them, they received the Holy Spirit and prophesied in consequence of this new equipment. When predicting the imprisonment awaiting Paul on his visit to Jerusalem, Agabus sealed his own words with the remark, "thus saith the Holy Spirit." The Christian prophet was a possessed person; he was inhabited by a divine potency called the Holy Ghost.

This conception was not at all un-Jewish, but it was so like the Gentile notion of divine possession that the Corinthians seem to have asked Paul how they could distinguish between possession by the Spirit of the Christians' God and the kindred phenomenon of pos-

[37] Cicero, *Divination*, ii. 54.
[38] Plutarch, *Pythian Oracles*, vi; cf. *Cessation of Oracles*, xl.

session by heathen divinities. To this query Paul replied that no man speaking in the Spirit of the Christians' God — who is necessarily the only true God — says Jesus is anathema, and no man can say that Jesus is Lord except through inspiration by the Holy Spirit (I Cor. 12: 3). Paul did not deny that others were possessed, yet they were actuated not by the Holy Spirit but by the inferior inspiration of demons. The Christian prophet, on the other hand, was inhabited by the true divine wisdom. But his heathen competitors had long been accustomed to make a similar claim for their own type of inspiration.

Inspiration was credited to many other ancient persons, particularly to great poets and philosophers, who thus served as media of revelation for their contemporaries and descendants. Homer, above all others, was called the all-wise poet, who was not only himself a spokesman for the divine wisdom but who became a source of inspiration for those who studied and interpreted his verses. To be able to speak understandingly and appreciatively of Homer was not simply an interpretative art, but was itself a continuation of the poet's own inspiration. God, it was said, so takes away the mind of poets that beautiful poems are the utterances of the divine wisdom, the very word of God, spoken for the edification of posterity. The writer who imagines that he can by art, and without any "touch of madness in his soul," enter the sanctuary of the Muse, will find himself rejected.[39] Poetic language owed its beauty to the divine afflatus with which God endowed the poet.[40] The author was like a servant in the sacred

[39] Plato, *Phædrus*, 245; *Theætetus*, 194; *Ion*, 530 ff.
[40] Democritus, *Fragment* 18 (Diels).

mysteries, who stood without, ministering at the altar, and to whom there came from within the sanctuary an inspiration, a flash of truth, like a sudden beam of light shooting out from an invisible fire.[41] In the case of Homer, his inspiration was so great that it was thought as impossible to improve upon one of his lines as it was to detract from the fire of Zeus or the club of Hercules.[42]

All distinguished accomplishments, particularly by the ancients, were attributed to divine inspiration. In this heritage later generations had access to a veritable revelation from God. It was not only in the quality of his poetry that Homer was believed to have exceeded all men. A geographer of the Augustan age affirmed without hesitation that Homer was also the founder of geographical science.[43] It was the custom to speak of distinguished individuals of the past as persons who had been provided with a divine guidance during their lifetime, and because they were thus beloved of the gods, they had been able to render special services to men.[44] A great philosopher was a man who had forgotten earthly interests and had become rapt in the divine. The vulgar man might rebuke him as insane, but that was because the common man was incapable of appreciating the philosopher's inspiration.[45] It was a superhuman energy in man that made possible the accomplishment of all worthy study and all eloquence of speech. No man was ever great without a measure of the "divine afflatus." [46]

[41] Dio Chrysostom, *Oration*, xxxvi. 33 f.
[42] Macrobius, *Saturnalia*, v. 3.
[43] Strabo, i. 2.
[44] Plutarch, *Numa*, iv.
[45] Plato, *Phædrus*, 249; *Timæus*, 72.
[46] Cicero, *Tusculan*, i. 26; *Nature of Gods*, ii. 66.

The Greek doctrine of inspiration survived and continued to be reaffirmed well into early Christian times. Dio Chrysostom gave it emphatic expression. He rated all wisdom emanating from the natural man as relatively worthless in comparison with the utterances of those inspired and prophetic spirits through whom the gods had spoken. All wisdom and truth possessed by mankind regarding the gods and the universe had come, in the opinion of Dio, not from human reason, but from a revelation of the divine will and decrees made known through the medium of prophetic and divine men of old.[47]

Not everybody demanded that all inspired men should have belonged among the ancients. The Stoics maintained that every rational soul had within it a native energy derived from the gods. A soul which kept itself detached from the body, as happens especially in sleep, would have a superior insight and would display a certain divine ardor which is truly inspiration. While such souls were media of revelation, they did not, however, represent any new insert of the divine into the area of the human. It would be more accurate to say that their message was derived from a purified human reason which was by its own nature divine.[48]

There were other persons who believed that inspiration by the deity was a privilege to be enjoyed by a man in his immediate daily experience; he was a conscious vehicle of the divine, like a Pindar, who had said that he merely interpreted what the Muses prophesied,[49] or an Empedocles who affirmed: "I am with you now as

[47] *Oration*, i. 57.
[48] Cf. Cicero, *Divination*, i. 49 ff.
[49] Pindar, *Fragment* 15 (Schroeder).

an immortal god, no longer mortal." [50] There were moments in one's life when the inspirational infilling was felt to be exceptionally real. Combining both Jewish and Gentile sentiments in this area of thinking, the Alexandrian Philo contrasted the relative futility of normal mental effort with those occasions when inspiration, taking violent hold on one, temporarily dethroned the puny human mind.[51] Philo did not blush to narrate that such experiences had happened to him "ten thousand times." He marveled at the manner in which God on occasion filled the soul with wisdom:

Sometimes, when I have come to my work empty, I have suddenly become full, ideas being in an invisible manner showered upon me and implanted in me from on high; so that through the influence of divine inspiration I have become greatly excited and have known neither the place in which I was nor those who were present, nor myself, nor what I was saying, nor what I was writing. At such times I have been conscious of a richness of interpretation, an enjoyment of light, a most penetrating sight, a most manifest energy, in all that was to be done, having such an effect upon my mind as the clearest ocular demonstration would have on the eyes.[52]

For Christians also, inspiration was both ancient and immediate. Moses and the prophets were media of divine revelation no less revered in Christianity than in Judaism. Very early in the history of the new movement it became a uniformly accepted belief that God had spoken quite as authoritatively in the message of Jesus as in the ancient Scriptures. Also in the prompt-

[50] *Fragment* 112 (Diels).
[51] *Care of Divine Things*, liii.
[52] *Migration of Abraham*, vii.

ings of their own pious convictions Christians found a message of revelation for the men of their own generation. When lacking a passage of Scripture or a command of Jesus to cite in support of an opinion, Paul could speak in his own authority as one who possessed the mind of Christ, even the spirit of God (I Cor. 2: 16; 7: 40). When the missionary met forceful opposition, he relied not upon his own feeble words of defense, but upon the language that would be given him by the Holy Spirit (Acts 4: 8; Mark 13: 11; Matt. 10: 20; Luke 12: 12; 21: 15). In displays of emotion within their own communities Christians felt themselves to be media of divine power by which God was communicating through them his will to their contemporaries. Especially in ecstatic utterances did the Christian speak with "God's own voice." [53]

IV

Still another source of divine help highly prized by the Greeks was the activity of beings intermediary between gods and men. This class of inferior divinity was best known by the term demon (*daimon*). The Christian notion that all demons were evil was Jewish rather than Greek imagery. In Greek thinking the demons were primarily kindly, serving the interests of a needy humanity. Their power was higher than that of man himself but lower than that of the mighty gods. Hesiod, giving literary dress to popular mythology, depicted the demons as kindly powers who haunted the earth, traveling hither and yon and wrapping themselves in mist, in order that unperceived they might render assistance to mankind. They were said to be

[53] Ignatius, *Philadelphians*, vii.

the souls of those men who had lived in the Golden Age, and who by their native superior powers were particularly well suited to this intermediary rôle. Thrice ten thousand in number, they served as the watchers of Zeus over mortal men.[54] In the language of the Hymn to Musæus [55] they are

> Demons good and bad that o'er mankind preside;
> Illustrious Providence, the noble train
> Of demon forms, who fill th' ethereal plain;
> Or live in air, in water, earth, or fire,
> Or deep beneath the solid ground retire.

When the Greek philosopher attempted to convert mythological imagery into a more rational picture of the demons' relation to mankind, he selected for emphasis their virtues and helpful activities. He did not deny, however, the existence of both bad and good demons,[56] but he preferred to dwell more extensively upon the benevolent aspects of the intermediaries' functions. Socrates, taking over the imagery of Hesiod, affirmed that the souls of the deceased men of the Golden Age had become "holy demons on the earth, beneficent, averters of ills, guardians of morals." [57] The guardian demon is a daily companion and guide so far communicating his own wisdom and goodness to the object of his care that every virtuous man may properly be called a "demonized" person. According to Democritus, the soul itself is the dwelling place of a divinity,[58] and Heraclitus was authority for the belief

[54] *Works and Days,* 122 ff, 251 ff.
[55] 30 ff (Translation by Thomas Taylor, *Mystical Hymns of Orpheus,* p. 5; cf. E. Abel, *Orphica,* p. 58).
[56] Plutarch, *Cessation of Oracles,* xvii; *Isis and Osiris,* xlv ff.
[57] Plato, *Cratylus,* 397 f.
[58] *Fragment* 171 (Diels).

that the distinguishing mark of man in contrast with other animals is his possession of a demon.[59]

In Socrates' famous discourse on Love, this power is called a great spirit (*daimon*) intermediate between the gods and mortals. It is the intermediate agent that interprets and conveys to the gods the prayers and sacrifices of men, and in return teaches men the truth regarding the commands and rewards of the deities. It spans the gulf which separates the human from the divine. Its mediation insures the effectiveness of the prophet and the priest, of sacrifices and mysteries, and of all other rites which have to do with the relation between God and man. It is the revealing power of the deity, who himself cannot have direct intercourse with man; and the meaning of its work can be understood only by those who are themselves demonic, that is, spiritual. There are indeed many spirits or intermediate powers helping to bridge the chasm between gods and men, and Love is one among them.[60] The pre-existent soul had the privilege of selecting the kind of demon that was to be its guide, but once the choice had been made the soul's ministering companion remained faithfully at its post until, after the death of the body, it conducted its charge once more to the world below.[61]

The guardian spirit that had watched over Socrates throughout his career, and in accordance with whose guidance he had shaped his ideal conduct, was a favorite theme upon many occasions. The demon was said to have led Socrates in all the actions of his life, pre-

---

[59] *Fragment* 119 (Diels).
[60] Plato, *Symposium*, 202 f.
[61] Plato, *Republic*, 617 f; *Phædo*, 107; cf. *Statesman*, 271 f.

siding over and by divine instinct directing his thoughts.
But those philosophers who strove to maintain the
fundamental dualism of Plato, could not allow the
demon to identify itself completely with the personality.
The popular notion that the demon actually dwelt
within man seemed untenable. Rather it was a kind
of divine double that stood above one ministering to
one's needs.[62] Moreover, the gods thus directed the
lives of only the few, and of such as they intended to
raise to the highest degree of perfection and happiness.
Or, perhaps, the demon was a kind of superior soul
with which God had endowed man. It resided in the
head as the rational principle constantly pulling the
soul Godward.[63] At death the souls of such persons,
freed from all union with the body, turned guardian
divinities and presided over other souls still in the flesh.
Thus the transcendental god of Platonism preserved
the sanctity of his isolation while the reality of divine
mediation was not denied. Here the demon served,
much as did the Holy Spirit, or Wisdom, or Logos,
among Jews and Christians with Platonic leanings, to
span the gulf that must of necessity separate the realms
of the gods from the abodes of men.

The Stoics, on the other hand, were free from any
embarrassing scruples regarding the proximity of the
divine and the human. They delighted to believe that
God was not only near at hand but that he actually
dwelt within the pious man's soul, and was indeed its
very essence. They, like later Christian admirers of
Socrates, were ready to identify the demon of Socrates
with the divine Logos itself. Our souls, says Epictetus,

[62] Plutarch, *Demon of Socrates*, xx ff.
[63] Plato, *Timæus*, 90.

are connected and intimately joined with God as being indeed members and a direct portion of his essence.[64] In other words, we are tabernacles of God by virtue of the very souls implanted in us at birth. Every man is naturally so constituted that communion with the divine is possible for any human soul that wills to live in accordance with its own highest capacities. This ideal had been realized by Socrates. The cultivation of virtue is the primary condition upon which one may permanently experience the sense of divine guidance made possible by the native kinship between man and the deity. The virtuous man, to use a phrase of Seneca's, rises to a splendid eminence because the soul is emancipated, prepared for the knowledge of heavenly things and rendered worthy of entering into communion with God. Or, to state the same truth in another way, a holy spirit resides within us, who is our guardian and protector. In matters both good and evil he treats us in accordance with our conduct toward him. No good man is ever without God.[65]

A more concrete visualization of mediating demons was preferred by most persons in the ancient world. Among the Romans each man had his protecting genius and each woman her protecting Juno, a kind of superior divine double that shadowed one throughout life, and survived beyond death to trouble or to bless one's descendants. This intermediate power was not so ever-present and kindly as the demon of Socrates had been, and often it played the part of a veritable evil genius. It had been conspicuously such in the experience of Brutus, to whom it had appeared as an ominous appari-

[64] *Discourses*, i. 14. 1.
[65] *Epistle*, xli; *Natural Questions*, i. *Prologue*, 5 f.

tion shortly before the fatal day at Philippi.[66] In Roman religion the worship of the genius, like the reverence paid to the departed dead, was as genuine an attitude toward the supernatural as was worship of the greater gods. Intermediary beings were popularly regarded in strictly personal fashion whether their home was supposed to be in the lower world or in the upper air. Probably Apuleius advocated a widely popular view of the second century A. D. when he called the divine powers of a middle nature, named demons by the Greeks, messengers between the inhabitants of earth and those of heaven.[67]

The manner in which revelation was mediated by these demonic powers might vary. From the standpoint of a strict Platonist or an older Stoic, one could not permit them any very great freedom to display extraordinary and independent supernatural activities. But, without really abandoning Platonic ways of thinking, one might go so far as to allow that these intermediary beings were responsible for the revelations and miracles of the magician. Also, they could be made the source of revelation for the diviner and the prophet. As Apuleius again remarks, we have reason to believe that everything happens by the will and power and authority of the celestial gods, but that the immediate agency in accomplishing their will is one or another of the many demons who are busy journeying back and forth over the space separating the immortals from mankind.[68] In fact, such knowledge as is communicated through verses of the Sibyls, through predictions

[66] Plutarch, *Brutus*, xxxvi.
[67] Apuleius, *God of Socrates*, vi.
[68] *God of Socrates*, vi.

of the augurs, and through all sorts of portents and dreams, is thought by Apuleius to find its only legitimate explanation in the theory of intermediary agencies.

Dreams seem to have been an especially popular way of establishing communication with the intermediate supernatural powers. Often, it is true, even the greater gods appeared to men in this fashion. But the soul itself, being by nature demonic and destined ultimately to take its own place in this intermediary region of departed spirits, was particularly susceptible to communications of this type. The soul was thought to be much more vigorous and sensitive when the body was asleep, since then it could anticipate something of the spiritual freedom that it would ultimately enjoy when the body lay in the final sleep of death.[69] Sometimes poets expressed this faith in more pictorial fashion. Dreams came from the kindly gates of sleep, as messengers from another world, whose warnings and advice were to be faithfully heeded. It was then that spirits from below roamed abroad. Even Cerberus himself broke his vigil at the doors to Hades, thus giving greater freedom to his wards to visit the earthly scenes of their former activities.[70]

When demons failed to act of their own accord, devices were available for compelling their services. The magician with his spells, charms, and powerful formulas came to the rescue. In this connection he was chiefly significant on account of his assumed ability to obtain revelations from the dead by skill in necromancy. He would, for a fee, bring up from Hades one's recently deceased relative, or an ancient person of re-

[69] Plato, *Symposium*, 203; Cicero, *Divination*, i. 51.
[70] Propertius, v. 7.

nown, from whom one hoped to obtain information about matters lying beyond the range of normal human knowledge. Plato would have jailed all magicians who claimed ability to conjure the dead; he said they would utterly demolish whole houses and states for the sake of money.[71] But the philosopher's skepticism was not shared by the credulous public, ever ready to be victimized by an expert in spiritism. One might poke fun at an Apion when he claimed to have raised the ghost of Homer to inquire about the poet's ancestry;[72] or one might upbraid the folly of him who, thinking the celestial deities lacking in wisdom, resorted to ruthless magicians who were in reality detested by the gods of heaven.[73] But still necromancers were in demand even in aristocratic circles. The practice of the art by a certain Junius had been the undoing of a prætor in the time of Tiberius.[74] Nero had sought the aid of men of this craft in bringing up his mother's ghost in order to allay her anger toward him,[75] and Caracalla had vainly endeavored to obtain a message from enchanted spirits to relieve the diseases and distressing dreams from which he suffered.[76]

The Gentile reader whom the author of Luke addressed would have felt no difficulty in assuming that the deceased Lazarus could have returned to earth to warn the rich brothers of Dives, although Theophilus might have wondered why the request was not made to a professional necromancer instead of to Abraham (Luke 16: 19 ff). But neither Christians nor Jews en-

[71] *Laws*, 909.
[72] Pliny, *Natural History*, xxx. 2 (6).
[73] Lucan, vi. 430 ff.
[74] Tacitus, *Annals*, ii. 28.
[75] Suetonius, *Nero*, xxxiv. 4.
[76] Dio Cassius, lxxvii. 15.

couraged interest in this form of commerce with the supernatural. Saul's example in consulting the enchantress of Endor was not generally followed, and any effort to revive the practice would have been frowned upon by Christians as severely as was resort to the Thessalian witch deprecated by the Roman Lucan. Intermediary agents of the upper world were too abundant and too easy of access for both Jews and Christians to make necessary any extensive practice of the necromantic art.

Philo of Alexandria endeavored to equate Jewish and Gentile belief in the activity of intermediaries by means of his doctrine of angels. According to Philo, those beings whom the Greeks designated by the word demon (*daimon*) had been called angels by Moses. They were invisible souls that hovered about in the air. Some of them were kindly while others were malevolent. As the Gentile spoke of good and evil demons, meaning good and evil souls ever present but imperceptible to normal vision, so the Jew spoke of good and evil angels. To recognize that souls, demons and angels were in reality identical, would, Philo thought, relieve the heathen of the great burden of superstition from which they were suffering. It was God himself who had filled the world with intermediary incorporeal beings, hence their beneficent activities were a phase of his own operations. In minds that had been thoroughly purified by reason God himself presided, but in the minds of those persons who had not yet attained to so high a degree of perfection angels continued to serve as his representatives. Thus Philo sought to preserve the ideal of Jewish monotheism, while recognizing current Gentile belief in intermediaries.[77]

[77] *Giants*, ii–iv; *Dreams*, i. 22 f.

Christians were less troubled by the philosophical problem, but they conceded without question the existence of demons, together with both good and bad angels. In Christian opinion, the activities of evil powers and the kindly ministrations of good intermediate spirits had been extensively displayed in connection with the career of Jesus and the experiences of his followers during the early years of the new religion's history. Angelic mediators of good were especially frequent as helpers and instructors in supernatural wisdom. But angels were secondary to the new intermediary power recognized in the person of the risen Jesus, who continually led and protected his followers. As Holy Spirit, Comforter, divine Logos, he exercised a never-failing care over the faithful. He stood between them and God, serving as their advocate in heaven and their monitor on earth.

CHAPTER IV

HEROIC REDEEMERS

THE kindly presence of supernatural forces working on behalf of mankind was most vividly and effectively depicted in the figure of the ancient hero. He was the ideal mediator between gods and men. Through his activities the hard lot of mortals was relieved and evil destiny averted. He redeemed them from all sorts of limitations, dangers, and misfortunes. He knew the needs of men because he himself had formerly shared human experiences on earth, even to the extent of participating in the agonies of death. But his triumph had been complete even over the grave. After his departure from earth, he passed to heaven where he acquired the status and character of a genuine divinity.

There was much variety in the imagery used to describe the form, the functions, and the credentials of these helpers of mankind. The hero was variously an idealized and divinized Greek, or Thracian, or Phrygian, or Syrian, or Egyptian, or Roman, or Hebrew. Some representations made him simply a man apotheosized after his death. At other times he was a demigod, born of a human and a divine parent. Or he was thought to be an incarnation of deity, only temporarily clothed in a mortal body while on earth. His activities also varied according to the particular tastes and needs of his devotees. He was revered for one or another type of extraordinary service which he had rendered, or was believed capable of rendering, to society or to the indi-

vidual. His popularity was in evidence all about the
Mediterranean long before Christianity arose. Probably no religious impulse among the peoples of the
Roman Empire in the first century of the Christian era
was stronger than the disposition to seek supernatural
aid through the mediation of one or another type of
heroic savior.

I

The Gentile contemporaries of the early Christians
were abundantly supplied with a great variety of divine
helpers. During an earthly career many a highly reputed individual of the past had rendered exceptional
aid to mankind, and after death in the capacity of a
divinity continued to serve still more effectively all who
trusted in him. Sometimes he was pictured on earth
in the rôle of a highly endowed person, who as a patron
of civilization, a founder of cities, a teacher of agriculture, a leader of armies, a skilful physician, a powerful athlete, a brilliant poet, or a profound philosopher,
had proved so superior to the average run of men that
he was from the start marked for citizenship in the
kingdom of the gods. He was an illustration of the
statement by Pliny the Elder that one who renders distinguished service to his fellowmen is rewarded with
deification. The Epicurean might see in this only a
naturalistic explanation of how reverence for imaginary
supernatural beings had arisen. But to the devout man
of faith the traditional belief in a kindly heroic helper
of humanity constituted a very substantial basis for
present confidence in the availability of supernatural
assistance.

The Greeks were much given to the custom of

expressing appreciation for various forms of service rendered to mankind and to society by conspicuous individuals. This appreciation commonly took the form of a shrine erected to the memory of the departed, and the observance of rites that virtually amounted to worship. Herodotus [1] tells us that the Spartans esteemed so highly the blessings conferred upon them by their lawgiver Lycurgus, that after his death they erected a temple in his honor. Also their distinguished general, Lysander, was said by Plutarch [2] to have been the first person among the Greeks to whom cities raised altars as to a god and offered sacrifices. Athletes of exceptional prowess, like Euthymus, who expelled the demon from the town of Temesa, and the famous Theagenes, were similarly honored. There were many places, not only in Greece but in foreign lands, containing images of Theagenes, who was highly revered by the natives, especially for his reputed ability to heal diseases.[3] The physician Hippocrates also was rewarded for his skill in medicine by receiving divine honors like those which the Greeks paid to Hercules.[4]

Poets were honored with altars erected to their memory and with stated sacrifices. In early imperial times Homer was worshiped at various places. His cult was to be found even at distant Alexandria. Smyrna was particularly zealous in claiming to have been the birthplace of the poet. The city contained a temple dedicated to him and his statue was exhibited in a quadrangular portico.[5] Dio Chrysostom, addressing the

---

[1] i. 65.
[2] *Lysander*, xviii.
[3] *Pausanias*, vi. 11. 9.
[4] Pliny, *Natural History*, vii. 37.
[5] Strabo, xiv. 1. 37.

citizens of Borysthenes on the north shore of the Black
Sea, remarked that they made a god of Homer and a
near-god of Achilles.[6] The tomb of Pindar was shown
at Thebes, where tradition said he had in youth received
his earliest poetical inspiration. Also at Delphi the
Pythian priestess had commanded the people to give
him an equal share in all the first fruits offered to
Apollo.[7]

Philosophers enjoyed a like distinction. Aristotle
erected an altar to Plato, and later was himself similarly
honored in his native city of Stagira. By the first century B. C. it had become the custom among some
philosophers to make a deity of Plato,[8] and even
Lucretius could with difficulty resist the temptation to
hail the revered founder of the Epicurean school as
himself a god. It is less surprising that the disciples of
Pythagoras should have converted the house of the
philosopher into a temple where he was worshiped in
consequence of the people's admiration for his character.[9]

Although a hero's name might have perished, devotion to the cause of patriotism like that of the soldiers
who fell at Platæa seemed to the Greeks worthy of
commemorative religious rites. These ceremonies were
still being observed in the time of Plutarch.[10] Once a
year a procession formed at dawn. The trumpeteer,
who led the train, was followed by chariots covered
with myrrh and garlands, after which came a black
bull, who in turn was followed by young men of free

[6] *Oration*, xiv.
[7] *Pausanias*, ix. 23. 2.
[8] Cicero, *Nature of the Gods*, ii. 12; cf. *Atticus*, iv. 16.
[9] Justin, *History*, xx. 4.
[10] *Aristides*, xxi.

birth laden with wine, milk, jars of oil, and precious ointments. Since the soldiers in whose honor the rites were performed had died in the defense of freedom, only persons of free birth were permitted to take part in the rites. The chief magistrate of the place, adorned with a purple robe and carrying a sword in his hand, proceeded through the middle of the town to the sepulchre. He washed and anointed the monument. Then, he sacrificed the bull, at the same time making supplications to Zeus and Hermes. The deceased heroes were invited to the banquet and the libations of blood. Then, taking some wine from a bowl, he said, "I drink to those who lost their lives for the liberty of Greece."

The Greeks also recognized a distinct class of person called "hero." In Hesiod's catalogue of successive ages[11] the fourth had been one when the earth was populated by men of heroic mould worthy of the name of demi-gods. They were the characters of Homeric story, who had fought on the plains of Troy, or before seven-gated Thebes. Long ago they had all passed from earth to the Elysian fields set apart for their special enjoyment. There the fertile soil produced for them three times every year its honey-sweet fruits. These epic heroes included Achilles, Agamemnon, Menelaus, Hector, Theseus, and a multitude of others, who were revered and worshiped.

There were many other heroes reputed to have rendered mankind divine assistance as founders of cities, noble kings, or great warriors. At public expense cities often erected altars and celebrated religious rites in their memory. These customs survived far into Roman times. A particularly striking instance of the practice

[11] *Works and Days*, 150 ff.

was found among the people of Daulis who maintained a shrine in honor of their hero-founder. Notwithstanding different opinions about his identity, his worship was faithfully celebrated every day by the sacrifice of victims. The blood was poured through a hole into the grave, while the flesh was eaten by the people.[12] Where rites were performed in this ceremonious fashion, the hero must have been given a distinctly supernatural significance both for the men of his own day and for successive generations who perpetuated his memory.

Among well-remembered historical persons, Alexander the Great was the chief of heroes, and was much praised for the blessings he was presumed to have bestowed on mankind by forcing Greek culture upon the crude barbarians. His admirers declared that his wonderful deeds could not have been accomplished without the presence in him of supernatural power. At least in Greek tradition, Alexander early assumed the position of an ideal hero who won his way to divine honors through a manifest demonstration of super-human ability during his earthly career. A man of Plutarch's heritage could not have been expected to speak more moderately. In his first oration on the fortune or virtue of Alexander he declared that the hero himself was conscious of having been divinely equipped to mollify the customs of barbarian peoples and to act as an arbiter of all nations. Those whom he could not peaceably persuade, he compelled by force to submit to his rule, and this was done for the common good of humanity. Had not Alexander conquered the barbarians, they would have remained ignorant of Homer and Plato and would never have lived in glorious cities

[12] Pausanias, x. 4. 7.

like Alexandria and Antioch. In short, they would have remained uncivilized had not heaven intervened to bless the world by giving it a conquerer in the person of Alexander.

The uncanny success of Alexander seemed to attest his supernatural personality even during his own lifetime. The kings whom he had conquered so masterfully had themselves been worshiped as gods by their subjects. Must not the victor be an even greater god? His successors, particularly the Seleucids and the Ptolemies, carried on the tradition of the divine king, even though history provided no such magnificent demonstration of their ability to benefit mankind. Just as the Hebrew king was an anointed one of God, the Seleucids and the Ptolemies were epiphanies of deity — gods manifest in the flesh. Their divinity no longer needed to be proved by superhuman deeds performed in their service to men. One's exalted position in society as a ruler of peoples accustomed to regard the king a descendant of the gods was a sufficient basis for popular faith in his divinity. The monarch was a deity in his own right.

Extravagant adoration of the prince occurred even among the Greeks themselves. In his *Banquet of the Learned* Athenæus quoted from Duris the Samian a hymn that had been addressed by the Athenians to Demetrius in the year 302 B. C. It associated the ruler with the great mother-goddess Demeter, and greeted them both as the —

greatest and most beloved of the gods come to the city. For here the occasion has brought together at the same time Demeter and Demetrius. She, indeed, comes to celebrate Kore's sacred mysteries. But he is here, joyful as

befits a god, and handsome and smiling. What an august
occasion, with all his friends about him, and he himself in
their midst, as if his friends were stars and he the sun!
Hail to thee, child of the most mighty god Poseidon and of
Aphrodite. Other gods remain far off or have no ears, or
are non-existent, or give no heed to us; but thee we see in
actual presence, not in a graven image of wood or stone, but
in very truth. We address our prayer to thee. First grant
us peace, most Beloved One, for thou art Lord.[13]

The Romans followed the example of the Greeks in
deifying persons who had wrought nobly for the welfare
of their contemporaries. The spokesmen who are
brought forward by Cicero to represent different schools
of thought all take for granted that Romans are familiar
with the custom of paying divine honors to historical
personages distinguished for service to mankind and
society. When an Epicurean is speaking, he places the
deification of men side by side with the Syrian deification of a fish and the Egyptian consecration of beasts of
every kind to the honor of divinity. But it is admitted
that in the case of the Greeks they deified only men,
not only certain mortals but also demi-gods like Hercules, Asklepios, and the twin brothers Castor and
Pollux. Among the Romans there is the same custom.
They have deified not only Romulus but many others
who, as citizens newly admitted into the ancient body
of the gods, are imagined to have been received into
heaven. And the speech closes with the caustic remark,
"these are the gods of the illiterate." [14]

Outside of Epicurean circles, the attitude toward this
prevalent custom of deifying men was more sympa-
thetic. One asked with much force, Where is a more

[13] Athenæus, vi. 63.
[14] *Nature of the Gods*, iii. 50.

perfect type of manhood to be found than in those persons who regard themselves born for the help, the protection and the preservation of others? This Stoic sentiment was applied even to Hercules himself. While he has gone to heaven, that honor was the reward of virtue, and would never have been won by him, had he not during his stay among men paved his own way to glory.[15] Accordingly, it seemed altogether proper that those persons who had rendered important service to the public should be exalted to heaven by the universal consent of their fellows. In Cicero's treatise on the laws, a good deal of emphasis was laid upon the propriety of worshiping not only the older heroes like Hercules and Romulus, but even abstract deities representative of such virtues, as intelligence, valor, piety, fidelity. Since it was thought fitting that temples should be consecrated in their honor, men who exemplified these virtues in their own lives deserved a similar reward. In Scipio's dream this conviction was forcibly expressed: "A certain place in heaven is assigned to all who have preserved or assisted or improved their country, and there they are to enjoy an endless duration of happiness."[16] The unparalleled achievements of Alexander the Great were not unknown to Latin writers, who sometimes affirmed that Alexander, by virtue of his mighty deeds, could never be equalled, much less surpassed, by any rival.[17] But Livy was of a very different opinion. After listing a series of distinguished names in early Roman history, he declared that every one of these men possessed mental powers and ability entirely the

[15] Cicero, *Tusculan*, i. 14.
[16] Cicero, *Republic*, vi. 13.
[17] Apuleius, *Florida*, vii.

equal of those possessed by Alexander. And he was quite convinced that had Alexander been ruling the East in the Augustan age, he would have found the Roman Empire invincible.[18] While Livy believed that the stability of the Roman Empire depended upon the proper observance of religious rites, he was not disposed to deify even the great men of his day. But many of his contemporaries readily fell into line with the Greek and Oriental custom. It was assumed that distinguished individuals were not only possessed of a "genius," but were in some unusual sense a divinity. On this account they were able to render exceptional service to mortals, and their suitable reward was elevation after death to a place among the gods, if indeed during their lifetime they were not entitled to a reverence like that paid to the deities.

The deification of Romulus, the idealized founder of Rome, was well-nigh universally conceded.[19] The magnitude of Julius Cæsar's accomplishments was heightened by contrast with his untimely end. If while Cæsar was still alive Romans feared his power, when death removed the menace admiration for his accomplishments quickly blossomed into heroic deification. Even his surviving contemporaries could declare the deceased Cæsar worthy of deification on account of his great achievements in the conquest of the Gauls.[20] In the next century there was no hesitation about giving him a place beside the deified Alexander. Appian, in his

[18] ix. 17.
[19] E.g. Cicero, *Tusculan*, i. 12; *Nature of the Gods*, iii. 15; *Laws*, ii. 8; *Commonwealth*, ii. 10; Dionysius of Halicarnassus, ii. 63; Livy, i. 16; Florus, i. 1; Tacitus, *Annals*, iv. 38; Plutarch, *Romulus*, xxviii; *Numa*, ii; Ovid, *Fasti*, ii. 479 ff.
[20] Diodorus, i. 4.

Roman history,[21] remarked without fear of offense even to the intelligent reading public of his day that Cæsar was a man "most fortunate in all things, and super-human, and capable of mighty deeds," whose soldiers had properly paid him divine honors after his death, as a like reverence had been rendered to Alexander.

The peace which came to the Roman world with the establishment of the Empire by Augustus, and the long continuance of his régime, inspired the recognition of a new hero in the person of the emperor. Even during his lifetime his subjects were not slow to concede him this distinction. No one will take too seriously the compliments which Vergil and Horace were wont to pay their imperial overlord, but one can be quite sure that they were not the only persons in the Empire to imagine that the beneficent régime of Augustus had been made possible through the presence of a very unusual man in office, and that the service which he had rendered justified belief in his divinity. The implications of Horace's language were perfectly apparent, when he wrote praising men of resolute mood who stood undaunted even though the heavens should crumble and thus by a display of strength won for themselves a place among the gods. Nor is he likely to have given offense to any of the emperor's subjects when in this connection he named Augustus beside Pollux, Hercules, Dionysus, and Romulus.[22]

In the East, where appreciation of rulers more readily expressed itself in the imagery of deification, the language of the Priene inscription was not at all extraordinary. It was quite fitting to call Cæsar the common

[21] *Civil Wars*, ii. 149 and 151.
[22] *Odes*, iii. 3.

good of all men and to hail his birthday as the beginning of a new age for the world when heaven had adorned life "most perfectly by granting us Augustus whom Providence filled with virtue for the benefit of mankind sending him to be a savior for us as well as for our descendants, bringing all wars to an end, and setting up all things in order." His subjects regarded it a privilege to be able to call him "savior and benefactor," indeed "savior and god," "son of god," "god Augustus, overseer of every land and sea."

When Augustus died, exaltation to heaven was his inevitable destiny, just as it had been the reward of Alexander the Great. Although Suetonius was hopelessly credulous, there is no reason to suppose that he did not represent the popular opinion of his day. He affirmed it to be common belief that even the soul of Julius Cæsar had risen to heaven and was there to be seen in the form of a comet which blazed in the sky for seven days together during the first games that Augustus celebrated in honor of his martyred predecessor. The glorification of Augustus was still more apparent. It was reported that a man of prætorian rank had upon oath declared that he saw the spirit of Augustus ascend from the funeral pyre to heaven. Later writers felt the propriety of adding that this ascension had happened after the same manner in which the ascent of Romulus had been attested by the eye-witness, Proculus. Thus Augustus, the latest savior of the Roman people, had gone to heaven to receive a suitable reward for his services to humanity, and witnesses could be cited in support of this popular faith.[23]

[23] Suetonius, *Augustus*, c.; Dio Cassius, lvi. 46.

II

The interest attaching to the earthly activity of the heroic redeemer varied widely in different settings and under diverse conditions. The display of supernatural power in connection with his life on earth showed itself in a variety of manifestations with many shadings of impressiveness. Sometimes this period of his existence was only a prelude to his apotheosis, when as a heaven-exalted divinity he became truly significant for mankind. In other instances, a good deal of attention was paid to the events connected with his earthly career. If he was assumed to have been of strictly human ancestry, the element of supernaturalism showed itself in his wonderful accomplishments, effected through the special favor of heaven, or in his native ability to perform superhuman feats. Even the more legendary demigods were subjected to the same pragmatic test.

Euripides, with his rationalist leanings, had called Demeter and Dionysus the two chief deities of Greece because they were the gods of bread and wine.[24] In time, this sentiment of Euripides became popular orthodoxy. Diodorus, who filled his pages with uncritical rehearsals of current tradition, declared that among all the deities, Dionysus and Demeter were most deserving of reverence, because their benefits to the human race had been the greatest. The one had discovered the most pleasant drink and the other the most strengthening food. Also Dionysus was credited with having traveled all over the world to teach people the blessings of agriculture. Even the distant land of Egypt had received his ministrations. And because Greeks and

---

[24] *Bacchanals*, 272 ff; cf. Isocrates, *Panegyric*, xxviii.

barbarians alike had shared his favor and bounty, all mankind rendered him immortal honors. Evidently Dionysus was now modeled after the likeness of a beneficent divine Alexander.[25]

The Egyptian deities, Isis and Osiris, were portrayed in similar imagery. Their title to worship was based upon the wonderful benefits that they had conferred upon humanity during their period of residence on earth. Osiris had traveled over the whole world, acquainting crude peoples with the amenities of civilization. Isis, too, had spent her time in the exact administration of justice and had surpassed all other rulers in bestowing blessings upon one's subjects. Not the least of Isis' distinctions had been her skill in finding out medicines for the recovery of men's health. She was believed to have had ability even to raise the dead and by this means made her own son Horus immortal. Consequently, both she and Osiris after their death were numbered among the gods, and rightfully received honors equal to those which had been accorded even the greatest of the deities.[26]

Another hero much revered for his therapeutic activities was the Greek Asklepios, called Æsculapius by the Romans. In Homeric story he was a physician in the service of the Greek army, but long before the beginning of Christian times a wealth of legend had gathered about his name. While on earth he had displayed marvelous ability to heal diseases, and had even restored the dead to life. By this act he had incurred the anger of Zeus, who, fearing lest mortals would escape their divinely decreed destiny, hurled a thunderbolt at Ask-

[25] Diodorus, iii. 4.
[26] Diodorus, i. 2; Plutarch, *Isis and Osiris*, xxvii.

lepios. But the great healer could not be cheated out of his proper reward. Through the intervention of Apollo, Zeus was persuaded to place Asklepios among the stars. Henceforth men rendered him divine honors and continued to enjoy his healing ministrations, now only augmented in consequence of the hero's ascent to heaven. But the reality of his earthly career was not forgotten. He was credited with the invention of probes, bandages, purgatives, and dental instruments that continued in use even after his decease. Several places contended for the honor of showing his tomb, and at each he was duly worshiped.[27]

Among the reputed benefactors of humanity, Hercules enjoyed especial honor. He had been compelled to labor hardest to win immortality. Like the Jesus of Christian tradition, Hercules had withstood the tempter before entering upon his life work. On arriving at manhood he had been approached by two figures personifying virtue and vice, who appeared to him in a vision as he sat alone in a solitary place. Vice offered him a life of ease and pleasure, while virtue invited him to undertake hardships in the service of others, remembering that the gods grant nothing to mankind without labor and care.[28] Hercules chose the thorny pathway, and the gods allotted him such toils as no one before had ever endured. But he successfully performed one feat after another, his crowning accomplishment being a descent to the lower world and a safe return. There he had delivered from their torment the afflicted Theseus and Ascalaphus and had overcome barehanded the three-headed monster that guarded the gates of hell.

[27] Cicero, *Nature of the Gods*, iii. 22. 57; Diodorus, iv. 71.
[28] Xenophon, *Memorabilia*, i. 1. 21–22; cf. Cicero, *Offices*, 1. 32.

So mighty a hero fittingly immolated himself on Mount
Oeta and was caught up from the funeral pyre in a cloud
to Olympus. Euripides was versifying popular belief
when he wrote of Hercules: [29]

He hath burst from earth's dungeons, hath rifted the chain
　Of Pluto's deep prison!
Thou art worthier to rule than the churl-king slain,
　O my King rearisen!

Hercules's fame as a victor over the power of death
was known far beyond Greece. His "awakening" or
"arising"— the Greek expression is the same as that
used for the notion of resurrection, whether of Jesus or
of others, in the New Testament — was celebrated at
various places. In fact the Jewish historian Josephus
affirms, on the authority of a certain Menander who
had translated the Phœnician records into Greek, that
Solomon's friend King Hiram of Tyre had built a temple
to Hercules and had instituted the ceremonies of his
arising.[30] Presumably the arising was from a funeral
pyre prepared for the occasion. In Tarsus, Paul's native
city, a similar ceremony was still observed at the time
of Dio Chrysostom. In his first oration to the people
of Tarsus, he remarked upon the fact that they counted
Hercules to be the founder of the city, for whom they
made a very handsome funeral pyre.[31] Greek writers
identified the Tyrian Melkart and the Tarsian Sandan
with the Greek Hercules.

Great heroes like Hercules and Dionysus, and others
of lesser distinction, commanded the faith of people all
about the Mediterranean in imperial times. They were

[29] *Madness of Hercules*, 187 ff (Translated by A. S. Way).
[30] *Antiquities*, viii. 5. 3.
[31] *Oration*, xxxiii. 47.

trusted, not only because of the reality of their historic careers attested by alleged tombs shown at many places, but because in the art and theology of the cults one learned of the heroes' triumph over death and ascension to the sky. It was said that one needed only to examine the sepulchres that were shown in Greece, and to recall, if one has been initiated in the mysteries, the teachings inculcated in those ceremonies, in order to perceive how extensively men believed in gods who had been raised from the dead and exalted to heaven.[32]

The picture of a triumph over death was a conspicuous feature in those widely popular and highly revered mysteries connected with the name of the mother-goddess Demeter, and her daughter Kore (Persephone). Tradition told of the mother's grief when her daughter was carried off to the lower world by Pluto, the king of the nether regions. In her bereavement the mother refused to nourish the life of nature, and only when Kore was restored did dormant vegetation revive. Even though it was decreed that the daughter must spend half of each year in the lower world, the assurance that after the death of winter her return would guarantee nature's resurrection, signified a perpetually recurring triumph of life over death. It is not surprising that the goddess who successfully completed her yearly pilgrimage to Hades and back to earth, thus insuring the preservation of life in this world and a kindly reception for her devotees when they too descended to the abode of the dead, should have been gratefully designated "Savior Kore" at different places in Greece.

Dionysus (Bacchus) was conspicuously a dying and rising god among the Greeks. He was widely famed,

[32] Cicero, *Tusculan*, i. 12 f.

not only for deeds performed during an earthly career, but also for his significant victory over death. The tomb of Dionysus was shown at Delphi, beside the oracle of Apollo, and the sepulchre is said to have borne the inscription, "Dionysus, the son of Semele, lies buried here." At Delphi his devotees celebrated with sacred rites his awakening in the springtime. Plutarch addressed his treatise on the Isis mysteries to a certain Clea, who had herself headed the Bacchanalian rites at Delphi, where the devotees, driven by divine frenzy, raised loud shouts and went through strange motions in honor of Bacchus. Also they conducted a secret service in the temple of Apollo, the function of which was to wake up the god.

Indeed, in Plutarch's day at Delphi Bacchus seems to have been quite as much at home as Apollo. The theology of the Dionysiac cult, written partly in verse and partly in prose and used in the chants connected with the rites, represented that the god was by nature incorruptible and eternal, yet he also typified the principle of change and transformation in life. His interpreters spoke of certain "destructions and disappearances and diseases and new births which are riddles and fables pertaining to the aforesaid transformation, and they sing the dithyrambic song filled with sufferings and allusions to some change of state that brought with it wandering about and dispersion." [33] The fifty-third of the so-called Orphic hymns was addressed to this annually arising Bacchus, who slept through the winter in the abodes of the lower world, and was roused to life again by the rites of the spring festival.

Orpheus, in many respects the double of Dionysus,

[33] Plutarch, *The E at Delphi*, ix (389 A); cf. *Isis and Osiris*, lxix (378 F).

was widely reputed in tradition to have suffered a violent death after which he ascended into heaven. When Pausanias was sight-seeing in Greece he was told various traditions about the death of this hero. The honor of possessing his mortal remains was claimed by different places, where his tomb could be seen, and the urn containing his bones was shown as a sacred relic. A shepherd lying down on the grave at noonday was himself so filled with the vitality of the dead god that he broke out into beautiful music while he slept, and the people from the country-side, desisting from their labors, gathered to listen to the song of the sleeping shepherd.[34]

Outside of Greece the dying and reviving divinity was a very conspicuous figure. At the eastern end of the Mediterranean the Syrian divinity, Adonis, was widely worshiped with rites of lamentation and rejoicing, celebrated in memory of his death and his rising again to life. His grave was to be seen in a cavern of the rock at Ghineh near Byblos. Above it was a carving depicting Adonis in conflict with the wild beast by which he was slain and Aphrodite mourning for the deceased. There were variant traditions regarding the manner of his death, but they all agreed in representing that the youthful god had died by violence and had been loudly lamented by grieving women whose sorrow was later turned into joy by Adonis' restoration to life.

Although Byblos in Syria was the principal seat of Adonis-worship, the popularity of the cult at Alexandria as early as the beginning of the third century B. C. is attested by Theocritus's poem on the festival of

[34] Pausanias, ix. 30.

Adonis. The poet draws a vivacious picture of the preparation for this feast in the palace of Ptolemy II, and vividly portrays the acclamations and excitement connected with the celebration. This Easter song depicts a holy marriage between Adonis and Aphrodite interrupted by the death of the bridegroom. Loud wailing attends this disaster. But the agony of funeral ceremonies is relieved by the anticipation of his return to life. Adonis is hailed as the one who above all others has power to journey back and forth between the nether regions and the world of mankind. In this he is said to transcend in ability even the greatest of the Greek heroes. The song closes with the refrain:

> Adonis sweet, Adonis dear,
> Be gracious for another year;
> Thou'rt welcome to thine own alway,
> And welcome we'll both cry to-day
> And next Adonis-tide.[35]

The mysteries of Adonis were still popular in the second century A. D. when Lucian visited Byblos and participated in the ceremonies which he described in his treatise on the Syrian goddess. He was skeptical regarding the truth of some of the legends, but of course the rank and file of the worshipers were more credulous. The annual festival was celebrated in the springtime, when the neighboring stream swollen by the melting snow from the Lebanon brought down to the sea large quantities of red mud, which made the waters seem colored by blood. The faithful called it the blood of Adonis, shed in his conflict with a wild boar. Then it was that his devotees "beat their breasts

[35] Theocritus, xv. 143 f (Translated by J. M. Edmonds, *Greek Bucolic Poets*, p. 195).

and wail every year and perform their secret ritual and make signs of mourning through the whole country-side. When they have finished their mourning and wailing they sacrifice in the first place to Adonis as to one who has departed this life. After this, they allege that he is alive again and exhibit his effigy in the sky." [36]

To the north of Syria, in Phrygia, very similar rites were celebrated around the hero-divinity, Attis, whose cult was closely associated with that of the great mother of the gods, Cybele. There were different legends regarding the manner of his death. One tradition represented that he had died in conflict with a wild beast and the other that he had sacrificed his own life. But in either event, mourning for his demise was a conspicuous motif in the tradition. The grief of Cybele, Attis lying dead in his coffin, and his restoration to life, were vividly depicted in the art of the cult and may be seen to-day in many archæological remains. In the time of the emperor Claudius (41–54 A. D.) the rites of Attis were elaborately celebrated at Rome. The principal features of this great drama were, first, the felling of a pine tree sacred to Attis, a rite typifying the death of the divinity. This symbol of the god was swathed in grave clothes and treated like a corpse to represent the dead Attis. On the following day, the devotees abstained from food and mourned the decease of the deity. Following the funeral ceremony, the initiates kept their mysterious vigil which was presumed to confer on the mystic the life of a new Attis. Then suddenly sadness turned to joy; when the god arose from his sleep in death, his followers gave vent to great jubilation.

Egypt gave the ancient world the very old and widely

[36] Lucian, *Syrian Goddess*, vi.

popular hero-divinity, Osiris. He too had died in conflict with a hostile power. The goddess Isis, with whom his name is closely associated, was overcome with grief. There is a luxuriant growth of legend connected with his death and her suffering. But ultimately both she and the slain Osiris came off victorious over their enemies, and attained to a position of superior authority in the realm of the supernatural. In the time of Diodorus [37] the tomb of Isis was shown at Memphis, although she was now believed to be the greatest of the divinities and the mistress of the cosmos. The devotees of Isis and Osiris, who were to be found all about the Mediterranean world at the beginning of the Christian era, reverenced these Egyptian divinities particularly for the assurance which they gave of a blessed immortality. They mediated salvation, both to the dead in the world beyond the grave, and to the living when beset by difficulties in the present world. The healing of disease and the comforting of the afflicted were distinctively their tasks. Probably Plutarch's treatise on these divinities was an accurate summary of popular feeling toward them throughout the Roman Empire in the first century A. D. Undoubtedly he expressed common opinion when he said that the efforts of Isis ceased not with her own struggle to satisfy her quest for the recovery of her slaughtered brother Osiris, but were a perpetual benefit to humanity because of the sacred ceremonies which had been established in consequence of the activities of these divinities. Isis had "consecrated at one and the same time both lessons of piety and consolation in suffering for men and women when overtaken by misfortune and she, together with

[37] i. 2. 22 and 27.

Osiris, having been translated from the rank of good demons up to that of gods . . . received not inappropriately the united honors of gods and demons everywhere, both in the regions above earth and in those underground, possessing the supreme power." [38]

Last of all, Persia made its contribution toward the imagery of a hero-redeemer. The religion of Mithra constituted one of the most vigorous rivals of Christianity during the second and third centuries. The central figure in this cult was a glorious hero who while on earth had participated in many gigantic conflicts. But, triumphing over all obstacles, he passed victoriously from earth to heaven where he faithfully watched over the welfare of his devotees. The monuments of the cult depicted his career in vivid fashion. Since Mithraic religion was much concerned about the struggle between good and evil in the world, Mithra devoted himself to the ideals of deliverance and redemption. Pictured as a figure miraculously born from a rock, he burst upon the world with redeeming light like that of the sun itself. He and his heroic associates brought their earthly career to an end in a last supper, commemorated by disciples in memory of his triumph. Afterward Mithra ascended to the heavens victorious over the last great enemy, the ocean, which vainly endeavored to swallow him up. From his position among the immortals, he continued to mediate supernatural help to his devotees until in future he should return to earth to raise the dead and finally annihilate all the forces of evil.

[38] Plutarch, *Isis and Osiris*, xxvii (361 E).

III

The supernatural credentials of the heroic redeemer were found not alone in the memory of his earthly service to humanity, or even in the fact of his exaltation to heaven after death; he was also provided with appropriate supernatural antecedents. Pindar explained the genesis of distinguished individuals on the theory that they were reincarnations of souls who, after nine years of incarceration in Hades, had won their release from Persephone, the goddess of the lower world. When their atonement had been thus accomplished, they were permitted to return to earth. Persons who possessed these souls became "illustrious kings, and men swift in strength and superior in wisdom, and therefore they are called holy heroes among men." [39]

To explain the hero by giving him a soul superior to that of the average man was a notion adopted by Plato,[40] from whom it passed on to the Romans. In its Latin form the doctrine was promulgated by Vergil in describing the experiences of Æneas on a visit to the lower world. There he was shown preëxistent spirits who, when they return to their "allotted place in life," will distinguish themselves in public affairs and make the Roman world glorious. Among these persons stand out conspicuously Romulus and Augustus.[41]

In later times, when Christians were endeavoring to explain the distinctiveness of Jesus on the theory of a preëxistent divine Logos incarnate in his earthly manifestation, heathen theologians were still advocating the old doctrine of preëxistent souls. One of the Her-

[39] *Threnoi, Fragment* 113 (Schroeder).
[40] *Meno*, 81.
[41] *Æneid*, vi. 756 ff.

metic treatises represented Isis giving instruction to her
son Horus on this important theme. When Horus
asked how it came about that kingly souls appeared
on earth, his mother replied that the king is a creation
of the gods, who send down to earth a superior soul
destined for this noble calling. The king is least among
the gods, but first among mortals. While on earth
he is not a full deity, yet he is to be distinguished
from other mortals by the godlike element resident
in his person.[42]

While philosophers were struggling with the problems of preëxistence, the man on the street depicted in
more picturesque fashion the supernatural credentials
of the heroes in whom he trusted. Evidences of
divinity were thought to be more readily perceivable
in the miraculous displays connected with the earthly
career of a hero. It was not so easy for the common
man to discover the superior excellence of an incarnate
soul, as it was to convince himself that he had witnessed
a miracle, or to imagine that such deeds had been seen
by others. For people of this temper and with these
limitations, legend was a far better instrument than
philosophy for accrediting heroic redeemers.

All the great heroes of tradition had performed
wonderful deeds, nor were these always wrought simply
for the sake of humanity. Such displays might very
properly occur with no other motive than that of
attesting the supernatural ability of the performer.
Similarly, in Christian circles the Gospel of Mark depicted the miracles of Jesus chiefly as mighty works
accomplished on behalf of humanity, while in the
Gospel of John the hero wrought miracles primarily

[42] W. Scott, *Hermetica*, I. 497.

for the purpose of showing forth his divine glory. It was commonly believed in the Roman Empire that the gods accredited their favorites by special displays of miraculous power. It was very fitting that a distinguished emperor or philosopher should show himself able to perform superhuman deeds. Such exhibitions of power were an evidence that the person had been appointed by heaven to mediate divine assistance to the people of his own age.

An appropriate illustration of this attitude is the story told to prove that Vespasian had been selected by heaven to restore order to the Empire after the chaos following the death of Nero. According to the popular legend, before news of the death of his rival, Vitellius, had reached Vespasian, the ability of the latter to heal sick people had been attested by the god Serapis. He had instructed certain persons that they could be cured by a visit to Vespasian, who had at first been modestly hesitant in attempting any such feat. But when finally he put his ability to the test he was not a little surprised to discover that he could perform miracles of healing. Still more significant was a vision which he had in the temple of Serapis, whither he went to consult the god about the affairs of the Empire. Although every one else had been excluded from the temple, suddenly there appeared before him a certain Basilides who, he afterward learned, was eighty miles away at that particular moment. But the divine import of the incident was discovered in the word "Basilides." Since this proper name resembled the Greek word *basileus*, meaning king, it was inferred that the deity had signified by the vision his choice of Vespasian to be emperor. So the story ran, and it seems to have been readily believed even by men of culture in Vespasian's own day. Tacitus, who is always cautiously incredulous on such matters, accepted the report of healings wrought by Vespasian on the ground that they were "attested by eye witnesses at the present day, when there is no longer any advantage to be gained by falsehood." [43]

Political heroes were not the only outstanding individuals accredited by miracles; sometimes distinguished teachers were provided with similar credentials. It was not sufficient for a miracle-loving age that the philosopher should speak human wisdom; he had also to be linked in some special way with the supernatural. While the followers of Plato, Aristotle, Epicurus, and the Stoics were usually too sober-minded to make miracle-mongers out of their great teachers, the Pythagoreans were somewhat less reserved. The biographers of Pythagoras told of occasions when he had exhibited superhuman powers, as befitted one who was a "divine entity." [44] Later representatives of this school were even more conspicuous for their supernatural abilities. Apollonius of Tyana, whose activity covered the latter part of the first century A. D., was especially distinguished in tradition for both his divine wisdom and his great miracles. He was said to have predicted with infallible accuracy the approach of an earthquake or the advent of a pestilence. He healed numerous persons of various diseases and frequently demonstrated his complete mastery over demons. He called up from Hades the ancient Achilles who communed with Apollonius on terms of friendship, even as Jesus of

[43] Tacitus, *History*, iv. 81 f; Suetonius, *Vespasian*, vii.
[44] Diogenes Laërtius, viii. 1. 21.

Christian faith had been visited by Moses, Enoch, and Elijah on the Mount of Transfiguration. He brought dead people back to life, and after his own decease he reappeared to the disciples.[45]

A story of supernatural birth was a particularly favorite way of accrediting heroic redeemers. Among the Greeks the supposition of divine parentage was a very common means of accounting for the extraordinary powers of a hero. Sometimes the word "hero" was explained as derived from *eros*, meaning love. Heroes, therefore, were demi-gods born of the love of a god for a mortal woman or of a mortal man for a goddess.[46] Most persons took the imagery very realistically. Just as the Jews read in their Bible that gods in mingling with men produced a giant race (Gen. 6: 1–4), so the Greeks in the Homeric scriptures were told that Poseidon had visited a certain earthly woman, admonishing her "to be glad in our love, and when the year comes round thou shalt give birth to glorious children, for not weak are the embraces of the gods." [47] And in due time she bore Pelias and Neleus, who both grew to be "mighty men, servants of Zeus." And in the same connection Odysseus declared that the powerful Hercules was a son of mighty Zeus.

The traditional mother of Hercules was Alcmene, herself well-descended among mortal women, and so virtuous that Zeus knew it would be impossible to seduce her. Therefore he assumed the form of her husband in order to produce from her a divine child. Popular reverence for Hercules demanded that both

---

[45] Philostratus, *Life of Apollonius, passim.*
[46] Plato, *Cratylus*, 398.
[47] *Odyssey*, xi. 248 ff.

the mother and the god should have been prompted by the sincerest of motives in begetting their noble son. Again it is Diodorus who is a convenient spokesman of popular opinion.[48]   He writes that when Zeus visited Alcmene, he "tripled the length of the night, and by the amount of time spent in the procreation of the child signified beforehand the superior strength of his progeny. This act of intercourse was performed, not at all on account of erotic passion, as was the case with other women, but only for the sake of procreation."   The same sentiment was expressed with a much finer artistic touch by Euripides:

> Hail to the couch where the spousals divine
> With the mortal were blended.
> Where for love of the lady of Perseus' line,
> Zeus's glory descended.[49]

Dionysus too was reputed to have been the son of Zeus, and already in the time of Euripides [50] his mother Semele was famed as one who "gave birth to a god" (*theon tekein*), the prototype of the later Christian title *theotokos*, applied to the mother of Jesus.   The twin brothers Castor and Pollux, much beloved for their interest in the welfare of mariners, were also illustrious sons of Zeus.   They had been born to be the "saviors of mortals" and of their frail barks when driven before the winds of winter on a pitiless sea.   In the hour of his peril the sailor invoked them as "children of Zeus," beseeching them to calm the storm and send salvation.[51] But these sons of deity, it must be remembered, were

[48] iv. 9.
[49] *Madness of Hercules*, 796 ff (Translated by A. S. Way).
[50] *Bacchanals*, 335.
[51] *Homeric Hymns*, xxxii.

particularly insistent upon righteous conduct. They refused to help those who worked abominations, but to him who loved faith and righteousness, they brought salvation from all distress.[52]

Asklepios, beloved for his healing ministrations, possessed also a sufficient supernatural authentication in the tradition of his descent from Apollo. It was in the land of Epidaurus, which contained his celebrated sanctuary, that his mother had given him birth. Although she exposed the babe, he was presently discovered by a shepherd, who immediately recognized that the brilliant light shining from the infant's face indicated that the hand of God was manifest in the occurrence. Quickly the fame of the child spread abroad over every land and sea, as one having all power to heal the sick and even to raise the dead.[53]

It was inevitable that the famous athlete, Theagenes, should have been accounted the son of Hercules who it was said had visited his mother, taking on himself the likeness of her husband. Tradition also reported that the fame of the child for Herculean strength had been demonstrated even when he was only nine years of age. One day, returning from school, he had wrenched loose a large bronze image in the market-place and carried it home on his shoulder. Manifestly, divine blood flowed in the veins of this mighty boy.[54]

Belief in the supernatural ancestry of famous historical personages like Alexander the Great was inevitable in a world where divine generation was so popularly accepted to explain the genesis of heroic personages.

[52] Euripides, *Electra*, 1350 ff.
[53] Pausanias, ii. 26. 4.
[54] Pausanias, vi. 11. 2.

Even had not the theory of divine parentage for Oriental and Egyptian kings already existed, the Greek imagination might easily have devised for Alexander a similar tradition. It was only appropriate that Zeus, the chief of the gods, should have been the father of Alexander, the greatest of princes. Neither the skepticism of a Livy nor the ridicule of a Lucian could shake popular faith in the divine descent of this mighty hero.[55] Even the Athenians, as observed above, learned to call Demetrius the son of Poseidon very soon after Alexander's death. The Seleucid rulers in Syria and the Ptolemies in Egypt were still more easily hailed as gods descended from gods and themselves fathers of gods.

The less imaginative Romans were none the less ready to ascribe divine parentage to their kings and great men. Romulus was commonly believed to have been the son of the god Mars and the virgin priestess Rhea Silvia, as was also Remus.[56] A still better known historical character, Scipio Africanus, like Alexander, was popularly rumored to have been a man of divine extraction. The tradition is said to have arisen from his custom of visiting the Capitoline Temple of Jupiter for a period of meditation and quiet before transacting any business, either of a public or a private nature.[57] Also, Pompey seems to have tried to increase his prestige during the period of the civil wars by making out, on the strength of two successful naval encounters, that he was the son of Poseidon, god of the sea.[58]

Augustus and his successors in the imperial office could hardly have escaped, even had they so desired,

[55] Livy, lx. 18; Lucian, *Dialogues of the Dead*, xiv.
[56] Livy, i. 4; Florus i. 1.
[57] Livy, xxvi. 19.
[58] Appian, *Civil Wars*, v. 100; Pliny, *Natural History*, ix. 16 (22).

the ascription to them of a supernatural origin. Even before Augustus was established in power, Vergil had embodied in his fourth *Eclogue* the popular belief that it was Rome's destiny to be ruled by a child born under the special favor of heaven. And once the régime of Augustus became established, it was not difficult to see in his person the fulfilment of this heathen Messianic hope. Apollo, it was said, had been his father. Suetonius [59] narrated an incident found in older records describing the manner in which the god had visited Augustus's mother, and how both the father and the mother before the birth of the child had been marvelously instructed by visions and dreams. Even the terrible Nero was said in some quarters to have been a son of Zeus and Hera. [60]

Those persons who objected to the crass imagery implied in the belief that men were literally begotten by divinities visiting human mothers, were still disposed to explain the abilities of striking individuals by connecting their genesis in some other fashion with the supernatural. Sometimes even philosophers did not escape the doubtful honor of an alleged divine parentage. Plato's nephew, Speusippus, so the story goes, had sponsored the tradition that his uncle was a son of Apollo, who warned the husband of the mother not to approach her until the divine child had been born. [61] Literal divine parenthood was not, however, a generally acceptable mode of thinking in philosophical circles. The Stoic could say that the wise man is the "son of God," using the expression with reference not to a physical

---

[59] *Augustus*, xciv.
[60] *Sibylline Oracles*, v. 140; cf. Suetonius, *Nero*, vi.
[61] Diogenes Laërtius, iii. 1; Plutarch, *Symposiacs*, viii. 1. 2.

generation but to an especial endowment of Logos resident in the individual's personality.[62] The disciples of Pythagoras knew a story which made him a son of Hermes,[63] but this was not universally believed. The Pythagoreans were hesitant about locating the superiority of any person in the realm of the flesh, yet they believed that the wisdom of Pythagoras was of superhuman origin, and that in him there dwelt a divine soul. His later biographer Iamblichus thought that the soul of Pythagoras had been sent to mankind from the realm of Apollo, where previously it had been an especial attendant of the deity. Its incarnation had also been effected in accordance with the divine counsels. This belief seemed to be substantiated by the tradition that Pythagoras had been born from a virgin and had shown himself master of all kinds of wisdom.[64] Similarly, in the case of Apollonius of Tyana, while one tradition gave him a supernatural birth, reporting him to have been the son of Zeus, others made him affirm himself to be simply the son of Apollonius. He bore his human father's name. The divine part in him was not his body, but his soul; he was an incarnation of the Egyptian divinity Proteus.

Among the intellectual men of the Roman Empire in the first century of the Christian era, the propriety of supposing that the seed of divinity could mix with mortals seems to have been seriously discussed. While Plutarch thought it is quite proper to call Apollo the father of Plato, he knew others who said that it was repugnant to the incorruptibility of the deity to be con-

---

[62] Epictetus, *Discourses*, i. 9. 1.
[63] Diogenes Laërtius, viii. 1. 4.
[64] Iamblichus, *Life of Pythagoras*, ii.

cerned with the generation of mortals. But Plutarch himself was convinced that there was no impropriety in assuming that deity might visit women who were wise and pure. Plutarch was ready to adopt the opinion of the Egyptians, whom he cited to the effect that one must not suppose that god in person had intercourse with a mortal woman, but that the act was accomplished through the agency of a "spirit of god." [65] Thus it had come about that from the philosopher in his lecture hall to the most illiterate man on the street, the Gentile world exalted the notion of divine ancestry in one form or another as a most desirable credential attesting the supernatural worth of a heroic redeemer.

IV

The Jews had many heroic figures among their religious traditions, but they hoped for the future manifestation of a still greater mediator of supernatural assistance. He would be a divinely anointed one, a "Messiah," chosen by God to inaugurate a new age of perfection and happiness for the much afflicted Hebrews now subject to Roman domination and threatened with defilement from the ever-increasing pressure of heathenism upon Palestine. Outstanding individuals had rendered great service in the past. Abraham, Moses, Elijah, David, Solomon, prophets, wise men, and the Maccabean princes who had successfully championed the cause of liberty against the Syrians, were names never to be forgotten. Heaven's favor for these men had been demonstrated by their ability on occasion to

[65] Plutarch, *Numa*, iv; *Symposiacs*, viii. 1. 3. In Plutarch the generative agent was "spirit of god" (*pneuma theou*) and in Matt. 1: 20 and Luke 1: 35 it was "holy spirit" (*pneuma hagion*), but the child was a "son of God" (Luke 1: 35; cf. Matt. 1: 23).

work miracles, to mediate divine laws, to wage a successful war against formidable foes, or to furnish unusual wisdom for use in the ordering of life's program. But the need was still very great; the ideal mediator of divine help was yet to appear.

The coming deliverer, who would bring full salvation to the Jewish people, was himself variously represented. By some persons it was thought that he would be a prince raised up from among the people to restore them their political independence after the model of the idealized kingdom of David. He would in fact be a lineal descendant of David, especially anointed by Jehovah for his new heroic task. At other times the future Messianic hero was transcendentalized. He would be not a man of earth descended from the family of David, but an angelic being preëxistent in heaven with God. This savior would suddenly appear with an army of angels to redeem Israel from all enemies. Indeed, God himself might directly intervene to save his people and transform their holy land into a suitable abode for them and their deity. In that event Jehovah in person would be the heroic redeemer of Israel.

The Christian movement from its very inception made extensive use of heroic imagery. It adopted from Judaism the expectation of a triumphant Messiah to descend from heaven, and it affirmed that the crucified and risen Jesus was that transcendental figure. It is indeed true that previously, so far as we know, no Jew had ever imagined that a deceased man was to be identified with the Messiah who would suddenly come from heaven to establish the kingdom of God. For this particular phase of their heroic imagery the friends of the crucified Jesus found no precedent in Judaism.

But in their picture of a helper existing in heaven with God and awaiting that critical moment in history when it would be the divine good pleasure to bring to completion the redemption of mankind through the revelation of a savior from the sky, the followers of Jesus were depicting the redeemer in eminently Jewish fashion.

Those friends of Jesus who believed that he had appeared alive again after the crucifixion, no doubt thought themselves in a position to interpret authoritatively the hope of a redeemer for the Jewish people. But their interpretation proved unacceptable to large numbers of Jews. Gentiles, on the other hand, showed greater readiness to attach themselves to the new movement and to find in its heroic figure satisfaction for their needs. As early as the year 50, Christianity had become a vigorous Gentile propaganda. From this time on there was a continually growing interest in presenting Jesus as a savior for the Roman world at large. This is the period in which the movement's missionary literature, as contained in the letters of Paul, the four gospels and other books preserved in the Greek New Testament, had their origin. During these years Christians were declaring, whenever the opportunity offered, that Jesus was the only savior in whom men could find a complete and adequate redemption. Paul never wearied of insisting that faith in Jesus as the hero who had died, arisen from the dead, and ascended to heaven, whence he would presently descend to officiate at the judgment of all mankind, was the only hope of salvation for every man, whether he be Jew or Gentile.

The hope of a salvation to be attained through trust

in the accomplishment of a deceased historical individual, later apotheosized through the divine favor, sounds strange on the lips of one who could boast of the progress he had made in youth as an adherent of Hebrew religion. Certainly he found nothing there to suggest that salvation was to be attained through the death of a man who would subsequently be elevated to the dignity of a god. But this is exactly the phase of religion which Paul admitted he did not discover in Judaism. He believed that he could find ample warrant in the Hebrew Scriptures for his new faith. But on that point he was radically at variance with the vast majority of his fellow Israelites. Gentiles, however, had been much better prepared by their traditions to give his message a favorable reception. They had been accustomed to look for help to heroic redeemers of a similar type, and they were quite ready to hear the testimonials that could be offered on behalf of the new savior.

Paul had said comparatively little about the heroic features of Jesus' earthly career, except to call attention to the manner of his death and his subsequent exaltation to heaven. Yet Paul's hero had not been simply a man while on earth, but an anthropomorphic manifestation of an angelic being who previously existed in heaven with God. His former status had been one of practical equality with God. Thus for Paul the Christian hero was a god-man, not a man-god, and his apotheosis following the crucifixion had been simply reinstatement into a position of dignity which was equal, if not superior, to that previously occupied by him in heaven. But as a divine being upon earth, according to Paul's way of thinking, Jesus apparently

had carefully suppressed any indication of those heroic prerogatives which one might have expected him
to display. On the contrary, Paul affirmed that Jesus
had lived like the veriest bondservant, exhibiting an
ideal humility, and had been content to wait until he
passed the gates of death for the further demonstration
of his divine authority (Phil. 2: 5–11).

Other Christians gave greater attention to the display of redemptive powers by Jesus during his earthly
career. The author of Acts provided his Gentile patron,
Theophilus, with an epitome of missionary preaching
put into the mouth of Peter, according to which the
heroic elements in Jesus' career began to show themselves from the moment of his baptism. On that occasion God had anointed him with the Holy Spirit and
with power. Immediately Jesus began traveling about
to perform a saving work by healing the sick and driving
demons out of all who were possessed. If Theophilus
had been accustomed to hear of the beneficent labors
of a Hercules or a Dionysus or an Asklepios, he now
had opportunity to learn of one who had shown himself still more effective in performing service for mankind. When his earthly career was ended, he arose
from the grave and showed himself to his followers,
who were now going about the world bearing witness
both to the fact of his service for mankind while he
was himself upon earth and to the still more significant
fact of his triumph over death and elevation to heaven
(Acts 10: 37–43).

Each gospel writer devoted himself extensively to
the heroic activity displayed by Jesus during his earthly
career. He taught mankind supernatural wisdom, he
healed sick bodies by his divine power, and his word of

command struck terror into the heart of evil demons. Some of the evangelists were able to furnish additional evidences of his claim to attention. In Matthew and in Luke readers were told of supernatural displays connected with the announcement of his birth. To a Gentile familiar with saviors accredited by divine parentage, Jesus, born of a mother who had been impregnated by the Holy Spirit, might now well seem a formidable rival to all other heroic saviors. A reader of the Fourth Gospel would learn further that Christianity's hero was not only an incarnate god but that while upon earth he had made every possible effort to display among men the glory which he had had with his Father before the foundation of the world. One who shared characteristic philosophical shyness toward the notion of literal divine parentage for the hero's flesh, could believe when reading the Gospel of John that Jesus had been distinctive because he was an incarnation of the divine Logos (Word), while physically he had been a true son of Joseph. His uniqueness lay entirely in the realm of his spirit; he was truly a god manifest in genuinely human flesh.

Before the close of the first century, Jesus had been presented to the Gentiles in a fairly complete heroic rôle. In the opinion of his disciples he was not simply another divine helper to be trusted for some special type of service but he was the one all-sufficient redeemer who must supplant all rivals. Christians affirmed that there was no other name under heaven known to mankind by which one could obtain genuine salvation. If redemption was to be had at all it must be secured through his mediation. And since he tolerated no rivals and no associates, it was necessary that

his disciples demonstrate his ability to render mankind
the full quota of services that had previously been
credited to his predecessors. In this endeavor Christians ultimately proved successful. But, difficult as
their task may at first have seemed, they had no need
to teach Gentiles for the first time the desirability of
trusting in heroic redeemers equipped with divine
power to render supernatural assistance to needy humanity. The more exacting task of the Christian
preacher had been to transform the rather forbidding
imagery of a Jewish Messiah, presently to institute a
terrible Day of Judgment, into the more friendly and
elaborately adorned figure of a Gentile savior who had
mediated divine help to mankind during his own earthly
career and who now from his position of power in the
heavens insured both a present and a future salvation
for his devotees.

CHAPTER V

SUPPLIANT HUMANITY

THERE was a great wealth of divine help available for men living in the ancient world. But the supernatural powers had to be properly approached, firmly laid hold upon, and effectively harnessed in the service of a seeking humanity. For many centuries before the Christian era, the various peoples around the Mediterranean basin had industriously devoted themselves to the task of building up an adequate machinery for man's use in dealing with the gods. Business with the supernatural was conducted on a large scale and with great energy. The Christian movement was able to learn from its heathen competitors many a lesson in the organization and technique necessary for an effective approach to these sources of superhuman help universally assumed to be available for mankind.

I

The Gentiles were very diligent in rendering worship to their deities. Christians commented upon this fact, although they thought the procedure to be wholly senseless and demonic. Yet they half admired the exemplary fidelity with which the heathen every day on arising from his sleep rushed to worship his idols. He sometimes traveled long distances to attend services, and undertook no kind of work without first consulting the deities.[1] The Epicurean Lucretius had been

[1] *Apostolic Constitutions*, ii. 60.

pained to observe that the temples were visited by multitudes of people and that the solemn ceremonies of many different religions were ardently performed by the credulous populace. In the centuries following the establishment of the Empire by Augustus, a traveler in any part of the Roman world found himself confronted on every hand by a great variety of different cults. People of all classes were zealous suppliants of one and sometimes of several divinities.

The faithful worship of the gods was advocated by many a Gentile preacher. The Greeks had been taught that every man should offer sacrifice according to his ability, approaching the deities in a holy and a pure manner. Suitable burnt offerings and propitiatory libations were to be rendered at the proper seasons. In the evening before going to sleep incense was to be burned, and also again in the morning when the holy light of day brought back new life to mankind. Homer could be cited in support of the belief that men when they had sinned and transgressed might avert the wrath of heaven by prayers and sacrifices, by libations and the savory odor of burnt offerings.[2] In a spirit that suggests the temper of the Hebrew prophets, Hesiod had admonished the Greeks to perform faithfully customary religious rites in order that the gods "may entertain toward thee a propitious heart and spirit, that thou mayest buy the land of others and not others thine." [3]

Admirers of Socrates made him a model religious person. It was said that he always conducted himself most piously in accordance with the laws of his country,

[2] *Iliad*, ix. 493; cf. Plato, *Republic*, 364.
[3] *Works and Days*, 335 ff.

particularly in matters of religion. He prayed earnestly to the gods, but always left it to them to answer his requests according to their own knowledge of what was best. Their will, not his, should prevail. He sacrificed as elaborately as his circumstances would permit, believing that the gods took greater pleasure in the meager offerings of the devout man than in the more abundant gifts of the less pious rich. But most important of all, in whatsoever manner the gods indicated their will to Socrates, he is said to have obeyed absolutely the behests of the deities.[4] Socrates also taught that man should appeal to the gods not only at critical moments, but in all the affairs of life. If the farmer desired a successful year, he should supplicate the gods for a good harvest, for increase of his flocks, for the warding off of disease from horses and sheep and cattle, and for protection from all other dangers threatening his crops and his stock.[5] The Greeks recognized the desirability of calling upon the gods to safeguard all the concerns both of the individual and of society in all its varied activities.

The Romans were even more noted than the Greeks for diligence in sacred things. Already in the second century B. C. a Greek observer, who thought himself exceptionally free from superstition, remarked upon the devotion of the Romans. They were commended for their scrupulous fear of the gods and were said to have made pious considerations supreme both in private and in public business.[6] The Romans themselves admitted that conspicuous examples of impiety had not

---

[4] Xenophon, *Memorabilia*, i. 3. 1–4.
[5] Xenophon, *Economics*, v. 19.
[6] Polybius, i. 505 f.

been wanting even in positions of great responsibility during the course of their history. But neglect of sacred ceremonies had always proved a sure forerunner of disaster, while assiduous observance of religious rites had always been rewarded with success.[7] An irreverent Claudius might throw the sacred chickens into the Tiber when they refused to eat, but he paid the penalty of his impiety by suffering the destruction of his fleet, and the navy of his colleague Junius met a like fate because its leader had refused to heed the auspices. The pious man could say without fear of contradiction that every one knew the city of Rome had been built by auspices, and that all things had been conducted by auspices during war and peace both at home and abroad.[8] Similarly, the philosopher would have every one take for granted that the gods are lords and directors of all things, and hence all happenings are in conformity with their superior judgment and divine will. They are most highly deserving of respect from the human race, for they observe what sort of person one is, how he acts, what designs he entertains, with what motives and sincerity he performs religious rites, and they take account of both the righteous and the wicked.[9]

In the imperial age, when the religions native to Greece and Italy were being extensively supplemented by the rapid expansion of foreign cults from Asia and Egypt, the importance of worship both for the life of the individual and for the welfare of the state received only further emphasis. Time and again, in critical periods, both private citizens and the government

[7] Cicero, *Nature of the Gods*, i. 2; ii. 3.
[8] Livy, vi. 41.
[9] Cicero, *Laws*, ii. 7. 15.

showed great concern regarding the matter of divine protection. On different occasions the worship of new gods had been introduced into Rome as a means of giving renewed energy to the failing power of the state. The stories about the formal acceptance of such cults may often be questioned, but the interpretation put upon these alleged events is perfectly apparent. An illustration of an importation from abroad was the introduction into Rome of the worship of the Phrygian goddess Cybele in the year 204 B. C. The Carthaginian invasion was threatening, a severe plague had devastated the army, and numerous showers of stones had led the authorities to consult the Sibylline books. The answer directed, as tradition tells the story, that the invasion of Italy by a foreign foe could be successfully met, if the Phrygian goddess were brought to Rome. Following elaborate negotiations and preparations, with much solemnity her worship was introduced into Rome where she was provided with a temple on the Palatine. It was popularly believed to have been in reward for this new manifestation of Roman piety that threatening disasters had been averted and Hannibal had been defeated.[10]

While it is true that in general foreign religions were accepted with reserve and strange rites were kept within bounds, there was a manifest feeling among the Romans that in the past they had been able to secure no small measure of benefit through the official adoption of new cults. In this way a very real supernatural increment had been added to that body of divine guarantees with which the political career of Rome had begun, and by which it was continually sustained.

[10] Livy, xxix. 10-14.

Safeguards for the individual were no less in need of divine reënforcements from without. Many an honorable Roman, when stricken by grief for the loss of a child, or when overtaken by illness that seemed likely to prove fatal, not only appealed for help to the gods of his fathers but also turned to the worship of Isis or some other new deity now popular throughout the Empire. Thus he obtained restoration to health, and was given assurances of a blessed immortality to be shared with departed loved ones in the world beyond the grave.

There were in antiquity persons with modernistic tendencies who strove to prevent worship of the gods from degenerating into gross superstition. Plato had set the model for all philosophers in his treatise on the Laws, where he had much to say about the way in which religion should be regulated in an ideal state. If a man did not believe in the gods, but conducted himself righteously, he might be tolerated. But for the impious man, who took advantage of his disbelief to work harm to his neighbors, harsh treatment was prescribed. The safest procedure was to throw the offender into prison. Religion was so important a matter in Plato's eyes that all sacred rites should be under the care of the state. When a man wanted to worship, instead of setting up in his own house private religious ceremonies, he should take his sacrifice to the priests and priestesses, who know how properly to perform the rites. Only for purposes of prayer might private assemblies gather. Religious ceremonies on their more formal side were too sacred and important to be trusted to the ignorant masses.

By the first and second centuries A. D. the dangers feared by Plato had become greatly magnified. Plato's reasons for advocating control of religion by the state were the ease with which gods and temples could be established by persons incompetent to handle sacred affairs. When overtaken by sickness or menaced by some danger, people were especially prone to rush into the presence of the gods, where they performed religious rites without proper knowledge. Under stress of circumstances they hastily offered up prayers and sacrifices, and they promised statues to gods and demi-gods and sons of gods without due regard for the proprieties. When their sleep was troubled by terrifying apparitions, they found "in altars and temples the remedies of them, and filled every house and village with them, placing them in the open air or in any chance place, and with a view to all these cases we should act as the law decrees." Also when private sanctuaries were thus permitted, people with evil designs made them a cloak for their own wickedness. They imagined that they could live an evil life and yet have their own gods to whom they raised temples and altars in private houses and whom they propitiated secretly with sacrifices and prayers. Thus they vainly supposed that they could enjoy the favor of heaven. But as a matter of fact, they were "bringing guilt from heaven upon themselves and also upon those who permit them, who are better men than they are, and the consequence is that the whole state reaps the fruit of their impiety." [11]

Later philosophers among the Greeks and Romans followed Plato's example in criticizing the superstitions of the ignorant without, however, denying to the individual freedom to worship the gods according to the dictates of his own conscience. Yet they endeavored

[11] *Laws*, 909.

by their instructions to purify and elevate the conception of worship as they found it current among the masses of humanity. Cicero, like Socrates, insisted that purity of soul was necessary for approach to the gods. He advocated that all costliness be banished from the temples and that men when they entered into the sanctuary, which they ought always to do with frequency, should keep the divine image before their eyes. Nor should they ever forget the fear of the punishments awaiting offenders. The worshiper should remember that evil men could not propitiate the deity with gifts; the favor of heaven could not be bought. It could be secured only by a pure heart and sincere motives. While the gods were forgiving, Cicero was as emphatic as Paul in maintaining that sin should not be committed in order that grace might abound. It was, however, the duty of everybody to frequent places of worship. Pythagoras was thought to have been right when he said that "piety and religion are at their best in our souls when we give attention to divine ceremonies." To which Cicero added that "all persons will be more truly pious according as they frequent the religious sanctuaries. For there some believe they have the images of the gods before their eyes and not only in their minds." [12]

Cicero's summary of laws relating to worship scarcely permits of further condensation.[13] The requirements are that (1) the worshiper must be pure and devout; (2) wealth must not be displayed in the temples lest the poor man feel out of place; (3) no private gods are to be allowed, but new and foreign deities may be wor-

[12] *Laws*, ii. 11. 26.
[13] *Laws*, ii. 8 f.

shiped if they have been officially recognized; (4) the ancestral temples are to be maintained, along with traditional agrarian rites and worship of the household gods; (5) one is to revere not only the celestial deities but also heroes and deified virtues; (6) all work is to cease on sacred days so that even the slaves will have leisure to participate in religious ceremonies; (7) well-trained priests are to conduct the rites with strict accuracy; (8) each deity is to have his appropriate sacrifices and his own priests, while the pontiff is to serve all of the deities and the flamen a particular god; (9) the vestal virgins are to watch the holy fire and to seek instructions from the public priests; (10) one class of public priests is to preside over sacred rites while the other is to interpret the utterances of the prophets and diviners; (11) also there are to be public augurs whose duty is to interpret the will of Jupiter, and of other gods, from the auspices; (12) the priests who deal in auguries are to watch over the public welfare and give warnings and advice regarding the wishes or purposes of the gods; (13) the divine will in matters of war and peace is to be interpreted by two special priests, called *fetiales;* (14) Etruscan soothsayers are also to be recognized; (15) mystery ceremonies performed at night and participated in by women are all to be suppressed except the ancient rites of Demeter; (16) pardonable sins are to be expiated by the aid of the priests; (17) songs and music on the harp and flute are, with some restrictions, to be permitted in honor of the gods; (18) the devotees of Cybele are alone to be allowed the privilege of taking up private collections; (19) stealing from temples, the violation of oaths, and incest are crimes to be severely punished; (20) the wicked man must not try to bribe the gods; (21) vows are to be strictly kept; (22) extravagance in the consecration of personal property is to be avoided, but private consecrations are not to be revoked; (23) religious rites in honor of the dead are to be observed without an undue display of wealth and lamentation.

The desirability of a sane and intelligent attitude in worship continued to be emphasized among the Greeks and Romans all through the period when Christianity was slowly gaining ground in the Roman world. The deity was to be worshiped with the mind and the conscience fully active during the ceremony. Fear, magic, and absurd practices ought, so the reformers said, to find no place in the life of the suppliant when approaching the deity. Persons who entertained these perverted ideas and feelings needed first to be educated by the philosopher, in order that they might know more truly wherein the realities of genuine religion consisted. Plutarch was spokesman for a goodly number of the intelligentsia of his world when he remarked that much of the worship to be seen in connection with many contemporary cults was simply base superstition. He was not surprised that its silly gestures, its charms, its magic, its processional gyrations, its beating of drums, its foul expiations and uncleanly purgations, its barbaric and inhuman penances and self-defilements at the temples and the like, had given occasion to some persons to assert that it were better there should be no gods at all than that there should be any that would accept such worship and take pleasure in such rites.[14]

The effort to refine worship in the fire of intellectualism was not carried so far by Plutarch, and those

[14] *Superstition*, xii.

of like mind, as to advocate the abolition of traditional rites, or even the giving up of popular religious notions. Worship was still the indispensable means by which suppliant humanity could hope to obtain a hearing with the deity. A century earlier Seneca had said, citing Aristotle as his authority, that the most reverent moment in a person's life was the hour of worship. The temple was to be entered with all fitting gravity, the eyes were to be lowered and the toga to be drawn over the face, and every token of modesty to be exhibited when one approached the sacrifice.[15] And Plutarch, severe as he was in his criticism of superstition, was equally antagonistic to atheism. He could not tolerate the man who attended religious ceremonies with a sardonic grin on his face, who made light of what he saw there, and scoffed at sacred things. For the reasonable man, the festivals and banquets at the temples were pleasant and holy ceremonies, which he faithfully attended. Rites of initiation, the Dionysiac celebrations, prayers to the deities, and adorations, all properly belonged to the program of the sensible worshiper.[16]

The masses of mankind felt less at ease in the presence of the deity. But they participated no less faithfully in religious ceremonies. They were wont to take the procedure so seriously that they turned pale when the garland was placed on their heads, and prayed with a faltering tongue. Overcome by awe before the altar, they offered their libations with a trembling hand. When the atmosphere of the place was heavy with odors of incense and perfume, the presence of the divine filled them with fear rather than with joy, but a fear

[15] *Natural Questions*, vii. 30.
[16] *Superstition*, ix.

from which there was no escape. So at least Plutarch interpreted the state of mind of those persons who seemed to him so benighted that they were unable to take his intellectual attitude toward the ceremonies of worship. Doubtless he described their feelings in language chosen by himself with a view to its service for his argument. But whether the people whom he criticized had a false or a correct opinion about the nature of worship, one thing at least is clear. They were all suppliants before the deities. It was only the Epicureans, and they were relatively few in number, who did not place their destinies upon the knees of the gods.

While a Plato, a Cicero, or a Plutarch evidently thought it desirable that all men should worship God in a uniformly decorous manner, as a matter of fact society demanded a wide range of religious ceremonies to meet the needs of many different types of persons mingled within the syncretistic life of that day. Different individuals chose to journey heavenward by different routes, and there was a sufficient abundance of rites and ceremonies to permit every man a liberal choice of means by which the desired goal was thought to be attainable. One chronicler, in speaking of the customs in vogue among both Greeks and barbarians in the Augustan age, remarked that while all peoples set aside many days devoted exclusively to religious activities, there was great variety in their ceremonies. Some of the rites were performed with a high display of enthusiasm, while others were celebrated without any marked exhibition of emotion. Sometimes music was extensively employed to give vivacity to the ceremonies, while at other times there was no music at all in connection with the rites. Some cults stressed the notion of the mysterious and performed their most sacred ceremonies in secret, while others were wide open to the public.[17]

In every part of the Roman Empire one found an innumerable array of altars, sanctuaries, and temples, that were visited by people both individually and in large groups, for the celebration of either private or public performances. There was no city or country-side that did not have many sanctuaries. At the more noteworthy shrines people gathered in large numbers on all the great festive occasions. Annually, swarms of pilgrims came from far and near to visit the holy place at Hierapolis explicitly described by Lucian in his treatise on the Syrian goddess. A similar popularity was enjoyed by the Dionysiac religious plays, which in Lucian's day were yearly celebrated in Ionia and Pontus. People from the country round about would leave everything else and sit for whole days watching the ceremonies. Even men of highest rank and responsible positions in society did not refrain from taking part as actors themselves in the performances.[18] The older Greek gods both in their original homes and in the cities to which they had emigrated, were provided with many holidays on which hosts of people were found ready to participate in the sacred rites. Roman, Asiatic, and Egyptian deities enjoyed similar honors not only in their native localities but sometimes also in far distant lands. Long before Christians took up the practice, Gentiles had been in the habit when on a journey of performing devotions at shrines by the way-side. It was the custom for people who were religiously

[17] Strabo, x. 3. 9.
[18] Lucian, *Pantomime*, lxxix.

inclined to halt at a grove or a sacred place to say a prayer, present an offering, and tarry for a season. Even though bent on urgent business, this seemly respect for divinities was not to be forgotten.[19]

In all of the various types of worship, the suppliant was provided with a more or less elaborate ecclesiastical technique. No matter what his status socially or culturally might be, the formalities of the cult enabled him to negotiate with the gods on behalf of any and every interest connected with his life. If he were a general leading an army into battle, or a prince contemplating some mighty enterprise affecting the destiny of empires, or if he were only a menial in the humblest household, he found available in connection with one or another of the existing religions a well-tried and trusted machinery for ascertaining the divine will with reference to all of his needs. Whatever the crisis in life might be, whether it was an affair of public business, a purely temporary and personal concern, or a matter of life and death, no one needed to suffer from ignorance of sacred rites necessary for performing one's duty toward the supernatural powers and for deriving therefrom the guidance and protection desired.

II

Prayer was one of the most common and effective instruments employed by men in their quest for divine assistance. While the philosopher might contend that gods could be trusted of their own accord to bless the pious and punish the wicked, it required only slight practical observation to note that this ideal principle was not always operative in real life. Every one knew

[19] Apuleius, *Florida*, i.

that frequently the good man suffered adversity while the wicked prospered. Evidently man himself must take the initiative in his efforts to obtain the divine favor, and prayer was the readiest instrument at one's disposal for this purpose. Gentiles as well as Christians believed in the propriety of importunate prayer (Luke 11: 5–13). Indeed, neglect of prayer would result not alone in failure to receive such gifts as the gods might otherwise be able to bestow, but it might be cause for offense on the part of the deity. Homer expressed this sentiment in poetic imagery when he called prayers the daughters of Zeus that bring great blessings to the man who shows them due respect. But if they are ruthlessly repelled, they mount to the throne of god and become accusers of man before the deity. Thus the mere neglect of prayer would of itself invite the wrath of heaven.[20]

The Greeks were notably a praying people. The outstanding characteristic in their petitions was a request for help from the gods. In both private and public concerns no important undertaking was launched without first appealing to heaven. Whether people convened in a court of justice, a popular assembly, or a public festivity, the ceremony always opened with prayer. Even the orator contemplating a difficult situation sought divine help to give force and favor to his message. Demosthenes began his famous address on the Crown by declaring that he prayed to every god and goddess for the good will of his hearers and the hope that deity would put it into their minds to yield him an attentive and respectful hearing. Similarly Socrates, before departing from the place where he had been

[20] Homer, *Iliad*, ix. 508.

discoursing with his friends, tarried for a closing prayer addressed to "beloved Pan" and all other deities supposed to frequent the place. The prayer was a means of impressing upon the minds of his hearers the very essence of the teacher's message, which, in the case of Socrates, was a request for "beauty in the inward soul." He prayed for contentment, and harmony between the outward and the inward man: "May I reckon the wise to be the wealthy, and may I have such a quantity of gold as a temperate man and he only can bear and carry." [21]

Prayer was a solemn performance. While Greeks often presented petitions to the gods in a direct and rather informal manner, they early emphasized the importance of a correct ritual. The deity to be addressed was the one popularly believed to have a concern for those particular interests that bore most heavily upon the mind of the individual suppliant. The different Greek gods had their specific spheres of operation, just as men themselves represented different stations and activities in society. It was always important to come to terms with those divinities who were supposed to frequent the territory where one resided. But in the event of a great crisis it might be necessary to journey to some more distant shrine to petition a deity reputed to have under his special care the particular concern involved. In fact, the situation might be so perplexing that it was necessary to consult a seer or an oracle in order to ascertain the name of the deity to whom one might appeal as a specialist in the kind of help of which the suppliant on that particular occasion found himself most deeply in need. But the proper god was always to

[21] Plato, *Phædrus*, 279.

be found, if man persisted with sufficient energy and patience in his quest.

Formal public prayer must often have been a very impressive performance. Thucydides describes such an occasion preceding the departure of the Athenian expedition to Sicily.[22] After all of the ships had been manned and everything for the journey had been put on board, a silence was proclaimed by the sounding of a trumpet. Then followed the service of prayer customarily held before putting out to sea. The ceremony was performed in unison, the sailors on each ship participating in the rites. All were prepared for the moment with the proper bowls of wine and both the seamen and the officers together made their oblations by pouring the wine from gold and silver goblets into the sea. Not only those in the ships but the assembled multitude on the shore, whether they were citizens or any other persons in sympathy with the enterprise, joined in the prayer. The ceremony closed with the singing of a hymn, after which the ships weighed anchor and put out to sea.

Often even the individual made his prayers conform to some standard litany. It was greatly to his advantage to be able to address a deity by the correct title. If cautious and in doubt about the proper terminology one might pray to Zeus and add, "whoever he be, if it please him so to be named, by that title I address him." [23] It was fitting also that special preparation of one's person should be made before approaching the gods in prayer. He who offered his morning libation without having first washed his hands, was not to expect that

[22] vi. 32.
[23] Æschylus, *Agamemnon*, 165.

any heed would be paid to his petition.[24] If the prayer was made at the sanctuary, it was to follow the offering of sacrifice and the pouring of libations. While usually it was uttered in the form of petition, it might also be a thanksgiving. Some prayers were long and others brief. The words might be few, perhaps nothing more than a mere ejaculation, expressing the name of the god, and his characteristic attributes. The emperor Marcus Aurelius, who was far more Greek than Roman in his personal piety, thought that the Athenians had formulated an ideal prayer in the simple petition, "Rain, rain, O beloved Zeus, down upon the fields of the Athenians and upon the plains." [25]

Sometimes no slight fervor manifested itself in connection with prayer, apparently on the assumption that as the petition became more eloquent, the attention of the deity would be more surely attracted. Pagans, like Christians, "lifted up their voice to God," and the more urgent the need, the greater was the vehemence of expression. So it was with the Roman mother, who, on visiting the temple of Venus, asked in a subdued tone that her boys might be possessed of beauty, but in making a similar request for her daughters she prayed in a louder voice.[26] Other petitions were frequently offered in silence, or in low whispers, it being taken for granted that the deities were able to hear even the unexpressed wish of the suppliant. Many a sensitive soul appreciated the importance of genuineness and sincerity as prime essentials for a successful supplication. Beside those who gave the act a magical significance, em-

[24] Hesiod, *Works and Days*, 724 ff.
[25] v. 7.
[26] Juvenal, *Satire*, x. 289 f.

ploying it to compel the god when properly addressed to grant the petition, there were many who said that gods could be neither bribed nor coerced, and that personal rectitude on the part of the suppliant was essential for prevailing prayer. Correctness in ritual was worth something, but purity of life and character were more highly prized by the deity. The man who lived piously might reasonably expect a reward for his virtue, while wicked persons ought not to hope for a favorable response. It was the petition of the righteous man that availed most.

The Romans too placed much store by prayer. It was commonly believed that not only the safety of the public but also the welfare of the individual depended upon fidelity in supplication to the gods. Great stress was laid on proper form. In the early days when the Latin peoples had been largely concerned with the business of agriculture, all the risks of farm life were safeguarded by definitely formulated prayers repeated on stated occasions. When clearing a new piece of land, or planting the seed, or gathering the harvest, or caring for the herds, all procedures were properly insured by carefully formulated petitions. When the Roman people became city dwellers and empire-builders, they still regarded prayer essential for success in their new enterprises. In the course of time they learned more and more to pray in the freer Greek manner, yet they never completely lost the reverence for prescribed formalities that had been so assiduously cultivated by their ancestors.

Evidently in ancient times the Romans had felt, much as did the Hebrews, that it was desirable to conceal the name of the divinity. There seems to have been a prevalent conviction that if a suppliant could call a god by his real name he could force the deity to do man's bidding, yet it was essential that the supernatural helper should be addressed by his proper attribute — his *cognomen* — or else by some obscure title, mutually understood by him and the worshiper. This secrecy was explained on the supposition that every place had a god under whose patronage it prospered and that without a knowledge of the proper formula to be employed in addressing the protecting divinity, it would be impossible to capture his territory. For this reason, the Romans were said to have concealed the name of the god who protected their city, and even the Latin name of the city was kept secret. In conformity with this way of thinking, the Romans prayed to the tutelary divinity of Carthage, that she would abandon her own people and accept the pledged allegiance of the Romans: "Come to Rome, to me and mine, let our temples, sanctuaries and city be more agreeable and dear to you; be propitious to me, to the Roman people, and to my soldiers, so that we may know and perceive it. If you thus act, I promise to dedicate to you temples and spectacles." [27]

While Roman prayers often sounded very much like bargaining with the deities, there was in the language itself, even in ancient times, a note of sober reality, indicating a keen appreciation of the importance attaching to the attitude of the suppliant in the presence of his gods. Several prayers preserved in Cato's treatise on agriculture show a strain of simple but sincere piety in those people who cultivated this type of religious exercise.

[27] Macrobuis, *Saturnalia*, iii. 9; cf. Pliny, *Natural History*, iii. 5 (9). 65; xxviii. 2 (4). 18; Plutarch, *Roman Questions*, lxi.

For example, in connection with the clearing of a grove to make way for crops one offered a propitiatory sacrifice, accompanying the rite by the following prayer:

Whether thou art a god or a goddess to whom this grove is sacred, as is proper, to thee is made the expiatory sacrifice of a pig for the cutting of this sacred grove and for these ceremonies, whether I perform it myself or another does so at my command, that it may be properly performed, in offering this pig as an expiatory sacrifice I make to thee most pious petitions that thou mayest be kindly and favorably disposed toward me, my house, my servants, and my children. Therefore mayest thou be honored by the expiatory sacrifice of this pig.[28]

The Romans conceived the affairs of state as well as the concerns of the individual to be inseparably bound up with the interests of the deities. Formal prayers were said in connection with all phases of public life. These rites were carefully observed in the selection of a king or of other public officials, in the prosecution of wars, in the making of treaties, in the conduct of a public assembly, and in connection with all activities pertaining to the welfare of the state.

A well-known tradition represented that in the choice of Numa as King of Rome, the augurs had prayed thus: "O Father Jupiter, if it is permitted that this Numa Pompilius, whose head I hold, should be King of Rome, I beseech thee to make it evident by unmistakable signs, within those bounds which I have marked." [29] In times of war the resort to prayer was particularly urgent and the rite was performed with great solemnity. In the struggle with the Sabines, Romulus was said to have converted imminent defeat into a glorious victory

[28] Cato, *Agriculture*, 139.
[29] Livy, i. 18.

by a pious appeal to Jupiter. The deity was reminded that the foundations of the city on the Palatine Hill had been laid in accordance with divine instruction. If now he would come once more to the aid of his chosen people, Romulus vowed he would build him a temple as a monument witnessing to posterity that Jupiter had been savior of the Romans. Thus impending disaster was turned into brilliant victory through the aid of heaven. Similarly, a treaty was sealed in the name of Jupiter, who was invoked to strike down the Roman people even as the sacrificial swine was slaughtered, if they should ever prove false to their pledge.[30]

Jupiter was not the only deity addressed. Sometimes the Romans were encouraged to fight by an appeal to their heroic founder, Romulus. Thus the consul, Publius Valerius, closed his oration with the appeal: "O Father Romulus, do thou infuse into thy progeny that determination of thine by which you once recovered from these Sabines the citadel when obtained by gold. Order them to pursue this same path which thou as leader and thy army pursued. Lo I as consul shall be the first to follow thee and thy footsteps as far as a mortal can follow a god." [31] And Scipio, when ready to set sail for the attack upon Carthage, led a prayer for the whole fleet, addressing all the gods and goddesses who presided over sea and land. He begged that they would bring him and his companions home safe and unhurt, "victorious over our vanquished enemies, decorated with spoils, loaded with booty, and triumphant." [32]

[30] Livy, i. 24.
[31] Livy, iii. 17.
[32] Livy, xxix. 27.

In times of peace, the prayer life of the Roman people was no less serious and exacting. Before addressing a public assembly, the magistrates were accustomed to pronounce a solemn form of petition.[33]   In order that legality might be insured for all that was said, strict attention was given to maintain verbal accuracy. Proper formulas for use on various occasions were collected and preserved in the books of the priests. The ceremonies were very carefully guarded, lest a single word should be omitted or pronounced out of its place. The formula to be used by the magistrate was read from a written ritual, while others watched to see that every word was spoken properly, and still others kept guard lest the solemnity of the occasion should be marred by some irregular utterance.[34]   In the course of time these formulas might become unintelligible, even to the priest himself, yet they were carefully preserved and continued to be used as a consecrated litany, which no one might venture to alter.[35]

When mistakes were made in the ritual of prayer, serious consequences were likely to follow. Even the sophisticated Pliny imagined that violations of correct procedure in the past had been attended by terrifying results. Sometimes the gods indicated their displeasure through strange phenomena, manifest in connection with the animal to be sacrificed. On certain occasions the lobe of the liver or the heart had disappeared, or had been doubled while the victim stood before the altar.[36]   Such strange occurrences were thought to invalidate the petition, rendering it utterly ineffective in its

[33] Livy, xxxix. 15.
[34] Pliny, *Natural History*, xxviii. 2 (3); Gellius, xiii. 22.
[35] Quintilian, *Institutes*, i. 6. 40.
[36] Pliny, *Natural History*, xxviii. 2 (3). 11.

appeal to the deities. The only remedy was to repeat the rites correctly. Also there were instances of neglect on the part of an officiating officer who failed to observe the prayers at the right time in connection with certain ceremonies. The omission was thought to be so serious that the Senate referred for advice to the college of pontiffs, who decreed that the whole festival had been invalidated and would need to be repeated. Even the Greek Plutarch seems to have admired the Roman reverence for an exact liturgy. He praised Numa for having instigated rites that demanded the strict attention of the people. So scrupulous were the Romans, he says, that even if one of the horses drawing a chariot at the religious celebration failed to move forward in the usual manner, or if the driver had thoughtlessly taken up the reins with his left hand instead of his right, the whole celebration was performed again from the start. Once the same sacrifice had to be offered thirty times in succession, because of some neglect or mistake or accident that had repeatedly occurred in connection with the service.[37]

It was in agreement with ancient Roman tradition that prayer should occupy a conspicuous place in the religion of imperial times. The Augustan celebration of the *sæculares* in the year 17 B. C. is instructive in this connection.[38] Although the sacrifice was performed according to the "Greek rite," it was still the old Roman formality that marked the words of Augustus's prayer to the Fates:

I entreat and beseech you that you increase the dominion and dignity of the Roman people, the Quirites, in war and

---

[37] Plutarch, *Coriolanus*, xxv. 2.
[38] *Corpus inscriptionum Latinarum*, VI. 32323 (p. 3241).

at home . . . and grant eternal safety, victory and health to the Roman people, the Quirites, and show favor to the Roman people and to the legions of the Roman people, the Quirites, and safeguard the state of the Roman people, the Quirites, that you may be benevolent and propitious toward the Roman people, the Quirites, the college of the Fifteen Men, to me and my house and family, and that you accept of this offering of nine female lambs and nine she-goats properly sacrificed; because of these matters, on account of this female lamb offered without blemish, be and become favorable and propitious to the Roman people, the Quirites, to the college of the Fifteen Men, to me and my house and my family.

While formal Roman prayer continued to be carefully cultivated and guarded by the proper authorities, there was among the people at large an increasing liberty of phrase and variety of content in the prayers of later times. A change had come about through contact with the East, as Greek influence entered this area of interest and more individualistic types of religion from Asia and Egypt made their contribution to the life of the Roman Empire. Cicero, following the example of Socrates and Plato, had made sincerity more important than ritualistic formality. The gods were to be approached with purity of soul. Not that the requirement of ritual purity was to be ignored, but the weightier matter of heart righteousness was of primary importance. Pollutions of the body could be removed by a few ablutions or other cleansing ceremonies of brief duration, but stains on the soul could not be washed out even by long continued rites and by all the rivers in the world.[39] And in Cicero's own most brilliant example of a literary Roman prayer, with which

[39] Cicero, *Laws*, ii. 10. 24.

he closed his prosecution of Verres, he implored the gods to influence the judges in pronouncing condemnation upon the criminal for wickedness, audacity, perfidy, lust, avarice, and cruelty.

Critics of traditional practices in prayer among the Romans were numerous in imperial times. Some persons advised leaving the deities alone to determine for themselves what was expedient for mankind in general and what specific favor was appropriate to each individual. Since man was dearer to the gods than to himself, it would be good taste on the part of a suppliant to pray for a bold and free spirit and freedom from dread of death, leaving it to the deities to grant him what they might think best in other respects. Particularly it should be remembered that the only path to peace lay in the cultivation of virtue; it could not be found through beseeching the deity for special donations of favor. Juvenal deplored the fact, as he stated it in satire, that the most common prayers heard in the temples were petitions to the gods for the increase of man's wealth.[40]

In the experience of many persons during the imperial age, prayer took on a more spiritual significance. A man of Seneca's temper was confident that prayers could not alter the will and purpose of an all-wise God, yet the sincere suppliant was assured of receiving blessings that otherwise would have been withheld.[41] But the rewards were spiritual rather than material. They were an experience of the soul — a heightening of its appreciation of the divine wisdom, a more exalted adoration of the deity, and a nearer approach to godlikeness

[40] *Satire*, i. 23 f; 346 ff.
[41] *Natural Questions*, ii. 36 f.

on the part of the worshiper. Seneca read with approval in Athenodorus, the famous Stoic philosopher of Tarsus, that one should suppress unworthy desires by making only such petitions to the deity as one would be willing to offer in public. To which Seneca adds, "so live with men as if god saw, and so speak with god, as if men heard." [42] God is not so far away that men must raise their hands toward heaven and shout their requests into the ears of an image. Rather, "he is near you, he is with you, he is in you." [43]

III

The ancients trusted not alone in the efficacy of their prayers to secure the favor of the gods. Many other instruments were employed to effect and maintain safe and profitable relations with the deities. Man sought to honor the gods by consecrating to them his finest artistic and esthetic accomplishments in music, architecture, sculpture, and painting. Also, he generously devoted to them a large proportion of such wealth as he possessed. Temples were reared in great abundance and many of these structures were magnificently adorned and richly endowed. Sacrifices and votive offerings were multiplied without limits. Gentile society further sought to safeguard its welfare by establishing and maintaining a definite class of skilled human intermediaries to care professionally for the operations of religion. Many sacred days were set aside during the year, when people could give themselves especially to the discharge of religious duties.

Apparently from a very early date the Greeks had

[42] *Epistles*, i. 10. 5.
[43] *Epistles*, iv. 12 (41). 1.

been accustomed to employ musical devices in their efforts to win the favor of deity. Homer was authority for the belief that one of the chief and most pious duties belonging to mankind was to hymn the praises of the gods in return for the blessings of speech which had been conferred by heaven upon mankind. Music was especially prominent in the rites of Apollo. After describing the celebration of a feast which began with prayer and closed with a solemn drink-offering to the god, Homer adds: "So all day long they worshiped the god with music, singing the beautiful pæan, the sons of the Achaians making music to the far-darter; and his heart was glad to hear." [44] There was something about music which gave to the worshiper himself a sense of nearer approach to the deity. It stimulated an enthusiasm which had the character of a divine inspiration, like that of the ecstatic prophet, and when accompanied by a dance and the playing of instruments, the consequent pleasurable excitation seemed to involve a distinct heightening of religious experience. While moralists might say that men resembled the gods chiefly in doing good, others who were more appreciative of the emotional side of life claimed that man was most godlike when he was happy, and that the highest happiness consisted in rejoicing in festivals and in music.[45]

According to Plato, Greek music had originally been divided into certain kinds sharply distinguished from one another. One type had consisted in prayers, called hymns, offered to the gods. In contrast with these more joyous expressions of feeling, there was another

[44] *Iliad*, i. 470 ff; cf. Plutarch, *Music*, ii.
[45] Strabo, x. 3. 9.

type called lamentations, which apparently were connected with the rites of infernal deities whose death was loudly mourned by the devotees. A third type was the pæan, the choral song or hymn in honor of Apollo's victory over the python, and sung in the celebration of the Pythian games.[46] The fourth class was called the dithyramb, of which Plato thinks the subject was the birth of Dionysus.[47]

The hymns to Apollo were sung to the accompaniment of a lyre. There were also hymns of Orpheus that were chanted in the religious rites. Although they were short and not numerous, yet, in the opinion of Pausanias, for poetical charm they were worthy to rank next to the hymns of Homer, and had received still higher marks of divine favor.[48] Music was employed in the worship of many other gods. Provision was made in the budget of a cult for the support of temple choirs, which was as truly a religious duty as that of providing for the sacrifice. Pantomime and dancing frequently accompanied the processional hymns sung on the way to the temples. It is not improbable that each temple had its hymn book, containing not only words but also definite melodies. In the Apollo cult the hymns were sung to the accompaniment of the harp, while in the rites of Dionysus the flute was used. Other cults combined the use of different instruments, with results not always pleasing to the cultivated ear but quite inspiring for the masses who participated in the rites.

Persons who were offended by the jingle of the popular religious music heard in the processionals and festiv-

[46] Strabo, ix. 3. 10.
[47] Plato, *Laws*, 700.
[48] Pausanias, ix. 30. 5 f.

ities of various cults commented with regret upon the degeneration of musical taste among their contemporaries. Plato says emphatically that he cannot stand the jazz of his day, yet he has a very high appreciation of music in the services of religion. Also the magnificent hymn to Zeus written by Cleanthes, is essentially an individual expression of feeling and probably never was designed to be sung by any congregation. Similarly, the words of Epictetus represent personal rather than community feeling. When he contemplates divine providence and the extent to which his contemporaries seem not to appreciate its favors, he exclaims "because the most of you are blind and insensible, was it not necessary that there should be some one to fill this station and give out for all men the hymn to god? For what else can I, a lame, old man, do, but sing hymns to god? If I were a nightingale, I would act the part of a nightingale, if a swan, the part of a swan. But since I am a reasonable creature, it is my duty to praise god, this is my business. I do it, nor will I ever desert this post, as long as it is vouchsafed me, and I exhort you to join in the same song." [49]

While the Romans were less inclined than were the Greeks to yield themselves to emotional display in religious ceremonies, they did employ at a very early date hymns as a means of communicating with the deity. There were ancient hymns of Mars, no longer intelligible even to the priests in the Augustan age. Also one hears of the hymn and dance in the ceremonies of the ancient priestly gild of the Arval Brothers. [50] But in order to experience to the full the stimulating effect

[49] *Discourses*, i. 16. 3.
[50] *Corpus inscriptionum Latinarum*, i. 28.

of music, accompanied by pantomime and dance and other forms of emotional agitation, the Roman people had to resort to one of the Greek or Oriental cults. Indeed, many of them participated in the wild orgies of Bacchus, the noisy processions of Cybele, and the moving rites of Isis. In such associations they could enjoy the sense of effective approach to god that resulted from the clanging of cymbals, the shaking of the sistra, the fingering of the harp, or the blowing upon the flute.[51] The Romans also adopted the hymn as a form of literature, examples of which are to be found in the pages of Catullus and Horace, but these compositions had essentially no liturgical significance. It was chiefly from the Greeks, and other eastern peoples, that the Romans, even the Roman Christians, learned to hymn their praises and petitions to the deity.

The gods were brought still nearer to man by housing them upon earth among the humbler dwellings of mortals. Like the ancient Hebrews who built a house for their God, lavishing upon it everything that was most precious in their own society, the Gentiles also reared temples to their various gods. These structures were adorned with man's most beautiful handiwork and enriched with his most precious possessions. If supernatural power were to be made fully available for a seeking humanity, it was highly desirable that the deities should be given permanent and appropriate dwelling-places where they might be visited by their devotees. But the sanctity of the divinities would not permit of too great familiarity. The most suitable ground for temples and altars was thought to be a conspicuous spot somewhat removed from the every-

[51] Cf. Lucretius, ii. 618 f; Catullus, lxiii. 8 ff; lxiv. 255 ff.

day activities of men, in order that one might not enter
the sanctuaries with the stain of secular life too fresh
upon one's person. Yet these buildings ought to be open
to the view of every man so that when praying he
could turn his face templeward. Leaving the crowded
area where one had engaged in the commonplace activities of daily living, one performed on the way to the
temples such rites of purification as were necessary for
proper access to the divine presence.[52]

The Greek and the Roman temples were the most
magnificent architectural structures produced in the
ancient world. It was fitting that the abodes of the
deities should be the largest, the most splendidly
adorned, and the most heavily endowed public buildings in the community. Christian preachers found a
host of Gentile gods already magnificently housed and
easily accessible through participation in the more or
less elaborate ceremonies connected with the temple.
To the average citizen of Ephesus, for example, who
happened to be at all aware of the presence of Paul and
his little group of followers meeting in the room which
they rented in the school of Tyrannus (Acts 19: 9), the
new religious movement must have seemed pathetically
insignificant in comparison with the worship of the
great Artemis, whose magnificent cathedral towered
above the other structures in the city and whose foundations covered some two acres of ground. It is little
wonder that the Ephesian populace should have been
ready to shout themselves hoarse in proclaiming "great
is Artemis of the Ephesians" (Acts 19: 28).

Every deity who was believed capable of bestowing
blessings upon mankind was provided with his own

[52] Xenophon, *Memorabilia*, iii. 8. 10; Pausanias, ix. 22. 2.

holy house in every place where he had devotees. In the case of the traditional gods of Greece and Rome, the temples were built and their support was provided by the community or the state, whose business it was to cultivate supernatural resources for insuring the welfare of society. The choicest portions of land were set aside for this purpose, while funds were generously appropriated for the building of the structure, the financing of festivals, the support of the priesthood, the purchase of victims for the sacrifices, the maintenance of the temple choirs, and all other forms of activity thought to be in accord with the wishes of the deity.

The presence of the deity was made more real by an image conspicuously displayed before the eyes of all who ascended the temple steps to look through the open door. The worshipers not only saw the god in visible form, but in the decorations of the building, in its sculpture and its paintings, they read the story of the god's doings and saw many an evidence of his interest in their welfare. In these portrayals by their best artists, the people were provided with pictorial exhibitions of the theology of the rites which in this form had greater reality and meaning for the average person than would ever have been possible had his religious traditions been presented in books systematically formulating the dogma of the cult. Men knew that the deities were kindly and capable, because this assurance was placarded before their eyes. Similarly, Paul endeavored to appeal to eye as well as ear by exhibiting in word-pictures to his Galatian and Corinthian congregations the image of Jesus Christ and him crucified (Gal. 3: 1; I Cor. 2: 2).

The position of the deity in human society was made

still more substantial by the many votive offerings and rich endowments conferred upon the temples. One reads now and then of wealthy individuals who not only built temples at their own expense, but also subsidized their upkeep by grants of land or other emoluments. Herod the Great, although king of Judea, spent large sums of money in building temples in honor of Augustus. Also he rebuilt the temple of Apollo at Cos and endowed the Olympic games in honor of Zeus.[53] In earlier days when Greeks had been more prosperous they had themselves been able to keep their deities in much affluence. The temple which Xenophon dedicated to Artemis with the spoils rescued from the ill-fated expedition of Cyrus, had, in addition to the buildings within the holy precinct, a large amount of contiguous territory that provided a substantial income for the sanctuary.[54]

Frequently a deity owned extensive estates whose income belonged to his temple. His worshipers honored him not alone with votive offerings that were always on display; they also willed him their real estate, or even during their lifetime handed it over to the deity in consideration of a stipend for life. Often one temple owned land in several places. There are many inscriptions that list such properties and specify their incomes. Temple lands were leased and houses rented, and a careful account was kept of the returns. The sacred property consisted of woodlands, of pastures rented to shepherds, of fields cultivated by farmers, of gardens and houses and factories. Certain bodies of water were consecrated to the god, and the fish might not be

[53] Josephus, *War*, i. 4. 11.
[54] Xenophon, *Anabasis*, v. 3.

caught, or else they were the property of the priests. In Delos, for example, Apollo had exclusive rights to the fisheries along the coast, from which he derived no small income. Also two percent of the harbor tolls belonged to him. It was not uncommon for sanctuaries to possess the right of collecting taxes for cult purposes, in which case the taxes were usually farmed out to some competent collector. The propriety of conceding to the deity title to a large share of land or business or other sources of wealth was a well-established idea in the Gentile world long before the Christian doctrine of church property and papal states arose.

Appropriate as were gifts to adorn and enrich the house of the deity, the offering of sacrifice was a fundamental necessity in any attempt to win and maintain the divine favor. For the Gentiles it might truly be said that there was no salvation without the shedding of blood. Purification, expiation, and atonement conditioned all efforts to live on favorable terms with the deity. The correct procedure in the operation of these sacred rites was insured through the maintenance of a properly instructed priesthood. The Christian Justin had no fear that his statement would be denied by any one of his readers when he affirmed that except through his priests the deity received sacrifice from no one.[55] It is true that the Greek offered his sacrifice in a more personal and immediate way than did either the Hebrew or the Roman; nevertheless a priest was necessary for the Greeks in the maintenance of all sacrificial rites.

The customary sacrifices seem to have been thought sufficient under ordinary circumstances to maintain

[55] *Dialogue*, 116.

the deity's favor toward humanity. But on extraordinary occasions and in critical moments many special sacrifices were offered. The greatest gift that could be presented to the deity to expiate man's sin and avert the wrath of heaven was the life of a human being. A few conspicuous examples of human sacrifice were known to tradition. The Carthaginian general Hamilcar, on seeing his army give way while he was conducting the sacrifices, had thrown himself into the fire, evidently in the hope that by making a greater offering to the gods he could turn away their displeasure from him and his people.[56] Apparently among the Romans human sacrifice had once been practised, but long before Christian times legislation had been enacted against the old custom. But on the outskirts of the Roman world there were still evidences of a continuation of this terrible rite.[57] The fact that it was no longer tolerated as a regular procedure in imperial times only added to the prestige of those conspicuous examples passed down in tradition from ancient days. Every one knew about the vicarious self-sacrifice in atonement for the Roman people that was credited to Decius and other noble persons who had, in Cicero's phrase, sacrificed themselves to the immortal gods for the sake of their country.[58] Again when three vestal virgins had been found guilty of violating their vow to chastity, their punishment alone seemed insufficient to expiate so heinous a crime. The whole people needed purification.

It seemed that nothing short of human sacrifice

[56] Herodotus, vii. 167.
[57] Pliny, *Natural History*, xxx. 1 (3); Strabo, xi. 4. 7.
[58] Cicero, *Nature of the Gods*, ii. 3; *Tusculan*, i. 37; *Offices*, iii. 4; Livy, viii. 9.

would avert impending calamity. Two men and two women, two of them Greeks and two Gauls, were buried alive in the Forum in accordance with orders issued by the interpreters of the Sibylline books. Plutarch, accepting this tradition as fact, speculated about it in an interesting way. He was aware that human sacrifice to the gods had long before been discountenanced by the Romans. How, then, could they violate their own laws? Plutarch reasoned that the demand for human victims had been made by demons, to whom the sacrifice was rendered. It had been performed, not as a gift to the great Roman deities, but "in order to appease some alien and foreign demons." [59] In a later day there were Christians who could talk in a similar way about the sacrificial death of Jesus as a price paid to the devil.

An elaborate and highly organized machinery for insuring the successful appeal of humanity to the deities never resulted in the ancient man's forgetting that gods and mortals belonged, respectively, in the realms of the holy and the profane. The temples were sacred places, never to be defiled with impunity. The worshiper might not approach them until he had purified himself both in body and soul. But here, too, he had devised standard means of accomplishing the result. There was in every temple of Apollo a holy water with which the devotee might purge himself before entering the sanctuary. At other times he went down to the sea to perform his cleansing rites. The pious man gave himself very diligently to such ablutions, even though a Diogenes might cynically inform him that he could as successfully wash away blunders

[59] *Roman Questions*, lxxxiii; cf. *Cessation of Oracles*, xiv.

in his grammar as purify his soul by ceremonial means.[60]

Even sinners did not approach the gods in vain. The temple area was an asylum of refuge for the criminal irrespective of the measure of his guilt. There his life was safe, even from the officers of the law. It is true that the police might surround the sacred territory and thus starve the victim to death, but they might not trespass upon the holy ground and bear him away by violence, once he had placed himself under the care of the deity. But the right of asylum bore less clear witness to the mercy of the Gentile gods than to the sanctity of their shrines. The most heinous sin that man could imagine was violation of the sacred precincts. Many a story was told of disaster overtaking some godless warrior or degenerate thief who had entered the house of a god to carry off votive offerings or sacred money. He might for the moment be successful in his wicked design, but ultimately his crime would be punished as surely as that of a Judas who betrayed his master for thirty pieces of silver.

When Christian missionaries first set out upon the task of convincing the Gentiles that the only way of access to the true God was through faith in the hero Jesus, the representatives of the new cause were pitifully lacking in anything like an elaborately organized and officered institution. The spontaneous outburst in a prayer or a prophecy or a psalm, a baptismal rite of initiation performed without reference to any officiating minister or priest, the similarly unconventional observance of a memorial meal celebrating the death of their hero, and their heritage of Scriptural reading and

[60] Diogenes Laërtius, vi. 2. 42; Ovid, *Fasti*, ii. 38 ff.

teaching taken over from Judaism and its synagogue services, were all that Christians had to offer in the way of an institutional machinery for a correct and effective approach to deity. But in time they learned how to construct and employ a much more complicated technique, approaching more nearly the type with which Gentiles were already accustomed to operate.

The expanding church in the course of the centuries presented a much more detailed program for the use of one who desired to become a successful suppliant of the Hebrew God and the Christian Lord Jesus Christ. Christians elaborated and formalized their prayers; they more adequately officered their institution; they set apart priests, clothing them in distinctive garments and assigning them sacred functions; they built structures for housing the deity, adorning them with the full heritage of Gentile art and displaying upon their walls the legends and history of the new cult; and ultimately they filled their churches with statues of their savior and their saints. They set aside holy days and celebrated festivities in elaborate fashion. Before the end of the second century a Christian could boast that the disciples of Christ spent more time in their one great celebration of fifty days between Easter and Pentecost than was consumed by all the heathen festivals in the whole year. This statement was somewhat rhetorical, but Tertullian made it in all sincerity.[61]

In the course of a few centuries Christians were able to convince the entire Mediterranean world that it could find complete access to the divine through the doors of the Christian church. The efficacy of its rites and dogmas was strengthened by the observance

[61] *Crown*, iii.

of an elaborate ritual which captivated the imagination and emotions of mankind. In simple but confident faith the devotee repeated the fundamental assurances of his religion in the adoration of the blood of his savior:

Blood of him who for us was made flesh, born of the holy virgin

—Jesus Christ;

Blood of him who was born from the holy mother of God

—Jesus Christ;

Blood of him who appeared (among men on earth)

—Jesus Christ;

Blood of him who was baptized in the Jordan by the forerunner John

—Jesus Christ, Amen;

Blood of him who offered himself a sacrifice for our sins

—Jesus Christ, Amen.

CHAPTER VI

PROTECTION FOR SOCIETY

REVERENCE paid to the deities was believed to have its abundant rewards. Everything was a concern of the gods. No one could evade their all-seeing gaze and no area of experience lay beyond the range of their operations. Only the Epicurean felt himself immune from their intervention for good or for ill, while the rest of humanity trembled in fear or rejoiced in confidence under the ever present shadow of the divinities. If not with the same degree of assurance, at least with a similar feeling of inevitability, many a Gentile could have exclaimed with the Hebrew Psalmist that it was impossible to escape from deity even though one might mount to the dome of the heavens, descend to the darkest cavern of the lower regions, or take flight on the wings of the morning to the farthest bounds of the ocean.

Inescapable gods constituted both a menace and a security. The ancient man had created the deities out of the raw material of his experience, which had taught him that his environing world could be both hostile and kindly by turns. One who had profited by the relatively well-ordered conditions of the Roman Empire was inclined to believe that on the whole the supernatural powers were well-disposed at least toward all individuals of good standing in society. Prosperity spelled divine protection and its evidences were to be found on every hand. Under the rule of Augustus there rapidly grew up a new sense of safety shared generally by the subjects of Rome from the Pillars of Hercules in the West to the borders of Mesopotamia in the East.

I

The organized Roman state at the beginning of the Christian era was a truly marvelous institution. People of that day were sure that its like had never before been known. They stood in awe of its antiquity, its well-nigh boundless domains and the efficiency of its governmental machinery. As early as the second century B. C., after Rome had destroyed Carthage and conquered Greece, there were studious observers of the political situation who, although not themselves Romans, felt constrained to acknowledge the superior greatness of the new victor in comparison with all world-powers previously known to history. Even the vast Empire of Alexander had been narrow in range and of very brief duration when compared with the rapidly expanding kingdom of the Romans. A century before the establishment of the vast imperial institution founded by Augustus, the Greek historian Polybus [1] had believed that already in his day the Roman arms had conquered practically the whole inhabited world and had instituted an Empire not to be paralleled by any like foundation in the past and destined to remain unrivalled throughout all future time.

In the next century when the Roman domains had been further extended and the republican form of government had given place to the more stable Augustan régime, admiration for imperialism found frequent

[1] i. 2.

expression. Above all, it was thought to be the unique mission of Rome to provide society throughout the whole Mediterranean world protection for life and property, and to supply mankind with an unfailing and effective political administration. While the Romans might not be destined to excel other peoples like the Greeks in sculpture, rhetoric, and philosophy, it was believed to be Rome's mission to give the world the most enduring and beneficent political order that had ever been experienced by mankind. In the words of Vergil:

> Others shall labor the breathing bronze to softer mould, they shall charm the features of life forth from the marble, they shall plead the cause with apter tongue, their wand shall trace the course of heaven, and they shall tell the renascent stars. Rome, be this thy care — these thine arts — to bear dominion over the nations and to impose the law of peace, to spare the humbled, and to war down the proud.

Poets and historians of the Augustan age bore witness to the growing conviction that it was Rome's task to exercise universal dominion and found a kingdom that should never cease. The proper boundaries of the Empire were the limits of the civilized world. Dionysius of Halicarnassus congratulated himself on having for his theme the most magnificent subject that had ever tempted a historian's pen. Those who had written the story of earlier empires dealt with comparatively insignificant matters in comparison with his *Roman Antiquities*. He was convinced that the Roman kingdom was infinitely grander than all its predecessors not only in the extent of its dominions but in the splendor of its achievements and in the length of time which

² *Æneid*, vi. 845 ff.

it had endured. Although he was living in the Augustan age, he believed that he could look back over seven and a half centuries of brilliant history. Rome was now mistress of every accessible country in the inhabited world. She was supreme on every sea, not only to the Pillars of Hercules, but over the navigable ocean beyond. She was declared to be the first political power that had ever set its boundaries upon both the East and the West, and she had experienced such vicissitudes as no other kingdom had been able to survive. "Need I then," Dionysius remarks, "say anything further to prove that I have undertaken to write the history of the most illustrious state and to record the most brilliant achievements of which it is possible to write." [3]

Belief in the eternity of the Roman state was frequently reiterated. Popular tradition affirmed that the temple of Vesta housed an image which had fallen from heaven, and if it was faithfully guarded the Roman commonwealth would endure throughout all future time.[4] Romans spoke of the "Eternal City" which had been founded by Romulus, and of the "eternal fires," kept constantly burning in the vestal shrine which were the pledge of perpetual dominion.[5] Again, when in consequence of an attendant's neglect, the fires had once gone out, they had been miraculously restored by the prayer of the priestess who threw a piece of her linen garment on the extinguished altar where the cloth immediately burst into flame.[6] Rome's title to perpetuity was thought to rest upon a far more

[3] i. 2 f; cf. Vergil, *Æneid*, i. 278 ff; vi. 780 f.
[4] Cicero, *Phillippic*, xi. 10. 24.
[5] Tibullus, *Elegy*, ii. 5. 13; Horace, *Odes*, iii. 5. 11; Livy, iv. 4. 4; xxvi. 27. 14.
[6] Dionysius of Halicarnassus, ii. 68.

stable basis than that of leadership by any general or other high official who might temporarily guide her destiny. It was absurd to imagine that a city built under the auspices and sanctions of the gods and destined for eternity could have her existence conditioned by the frail body of any mortal.[7] She was as enduring as the heavens and the cosmos.

The chief glory of Rome and of her great leader lay in the protection she furnished to society. However much the people might be exploited in the interests of a political institution, both its agents and its subjects could appropriately join in praise of its benefits. They now experienced a quite new sense of national safety. They remembered keenly those previous periods in history when civil wars or an inadequate administration had frequently resulted in suffering and chaos. They were ready with longing and praises for the dawn of a new day. And they visualized the new order, not in terms of a society rejuvenated and reorganized through an assertion of its own inner vital forces, but in the imagery of supernaturalism. It would be a militaristic machine created by heaven that would bring into being the social stability universally craved by the entire population. Tibullus and Vergil shudderingly recalled the degeneracy of an earlier age when under the rule of Jupiter "slaughter and swords were incessant," and they prophesied the coming of a new day — the return of Saturn's rule — when a new king should appear "under whom first the iron age shall cease and the golden age over all the world arise." The same type of ideals was reflected in the popular praise of a ruler when he was addressed as "savior"

[7] Livy, xxviii. 28. 11.

because he conferred the blessings of peace on his subjects. This had been the characteristic justification for imperialism advanced among both Greeks and Romans long before the beginning of the Christian era. Those heroic redeemers whom the Gentiles were accustomed to revere had long ago taken on the character of saviors as a reward for the benefits of civilization which they were supposed to have showered upon mankind.[8]

Alexander the Great had become the model exponent of imperialism in the rôle of humanity's benefactor. His admirers credited him with having been prompted by a desire to civilize wild and barbarous peoples and to establish cultured Greek cities among the rude and unpolished barbarians.[9] Good government, peace, and civilization were said to follow in his train. But those who fled before the victorious Alexander, escaping his forcibly conferred blessings, remained in a state of unrelieved misery. Since he was performing the will of heaven by conducting his civilizing propaganda, bestowing benefits upon mortals, he was thought to be fully justified in using force to accomplish his purposes. The end amply justified the means. Hence those whom he could not win by persuasion he subdued by armies in order that he might fulfil his divinely appointed mission to impart Hellenistic culture to all the world.[10]

Similarly, the Augustan imperialism was widely accepted as the one great hope for Roman society. The world was safe because imperialism was firmly and permanently established. The hope of mankind for

[8] See above pp. 107 ff.
[9] See above p. 111.
[10] Plutarch, *Fortune of Alexander*, i. 4–6.

the future lay in the firmly expected maintenance of this political order throughout all ages to come. Pliny the Elder, notwithstanding his show of opposition to other superstitions, had no difficulty in believing that it was Rome's mission "to unite the scattered empires of the earth, to bestow a polish upon men's manners, to unite the discordant and uncouth dialects of so many different nations by the powerful ties of one common language, to confer the enjoyments of discourse and civilization upon mankind, to become, in short, the mother country of all nations of the earth." [11]

Now and then a Stoic, with his characteristic emphasis on humanitarianism, ventured to criticize popular faith in imperialism's efficacy to redeem society from its ills. Seneca, for example, was particularly severe in his arraignment of the military operations so essential to the maintenance of the Neronian imperialistic ideal. He ridiculed the folly of those human beings who sought to fix tribal boundaries and fought for control of territory. Would ants, he sarcastically asked, if ever they should become endowed with human intelligence, apportion the threshing floor into many provinces? In his opinion, the laudation of Roman imperialism was mainly a cloak to shield pride and greed for gold. In writing of the winds, he remarked that God did not intend them to be used for military advantage by providing schemes for carrying fleets of armed soldiers to every quarter of the world. Such enterprises were a desecration of the sea and the land, in which men were worse than beasts. The latter fought only in retaliation, or from hunger, but men

[11] *Natural History*, iii. 5 (6). 39; xxvii 1. 3.

poured out their own and others' blood simply for greed of gold.[12]

While the Stoic preached the doctrine of human brotherhood, and lauded the blessings of peace to be enjoyed, not through the triumph of military power, but by the exemplification of peaceable attitudes in the lives of individuals, he never devised any really effective program for the accomplishment of his ideals. On the other hand, the imperial organization was busy perfecting itself from the very beginning of the Augustan age and proved so successful in maintaining a state of peace and prosperity superior to that which had been previously known to the Mediterranean world at large that popular faith in the beneficent significance of the Roman political organization became more and more widespread. While it is very true that Augustus and many of his supporters, when preaching the doctrine of Rome's supremacy, eternity, and supreme benefactions, were undoubtedly ready to prey upon a credulous populace, their propaganda could hardly have been successful had not they represented ideas and interests very close to the heart of the populace. Notwithstanding all of the insincerity that one easily detects in the laudatory references to the imperial régime, there was a very deep-seated conviction in ancient society that man's well-being could be safeguarded only by the operations of a powerful political organization. Even though Augustus cautiously refrained from arrogating to himself any appearances of monarchical dignity, there was as yet no thought that mankind could realize protection and safety for itself through the establishment of a strictly democratic government. The assur-

[12] *Natural Questions*, v. 18. 4 ff.

ances of successful politics were assumed to come from without; they were not sought in the inherent potentialities of human society.

The laudatory epithets and inscriptions which hailed emperors as deliverers were quite in accord with the temper of that age. A ruler was called "savior" because he mediated the blessings of peace to his subjects. It was in this spirit that Augustus's birthday was rated equal to the beginning of all creation, since it "gave another aspect to the whole world which would truly have perished utterly, had not Cæsar the common good fortune of all men been born." The mighty prince whose invincible armies brought peace and prosperity to his subjects symbolized in concrete form Rome's guarantee of protection for society. His régime made possible the continued and undisturbed operations of the social order. Agriculture, trade, and commerce, or any other means by which men earned a livelihood, could now be pursued undisturbed by calamities. It seemed quite fitting that Cæsar Augustus should be called savior of mankind, for under his rule "earth and sea have peace, cities flourish well governed, harmonious, and prosperous, the course of all good things has reached the climax, and all mankind has been filled with good hopes for the future and good cheer for the present." [13]

Both Jews and Christians bore similar testimony to the beneficent régime of Augustus. Although they were unwilling to deify the Emperor, they were quite ready to recognize that the new day which he had inaugurated in Roman history was an evidence of heaven's interest in the welfare of mankind. The favor which

[13] *Inscriptions in the British Museum*, No. 894.

Augustus had shown to the Jews in respecting their traditional religious customs, and particularly the Emperor's care to provide a regular sacrifice for himself at the Jewish temple in Jerusalem, seemed to Philo to insure the success and perpetuity of the Roman government. The Empire that made appeal to the Hebrew God would endure without end. Augustus had done well to ordain a continual sacrifice of burnt offerings to be observed "forever and ever, every day from his own revenues, as a first fruit of his own to the most high God, which sacrifices are performed to this very day and will be performed for ever as a proof and specimen of a truly imperial disposition." [14]

Philo thought it quite fitting that a Roman emperor who displayed such piety toward the God of the Hebrews should be praised highly for the benefits which his rule had bestowed upon mankind. Naturally this devout prince was capable of calming storms that had been raging in every quarter of the earth and of healing the social diseases which heretofore had sorely afflicted the residents of the lands about the Mediterranean. Philo believed that at the time of Augustus's rise to power the world had been in a very bad way. Every territory had been filled with unexpected miseries, but the new ruler had delivered all men from their distresses. He gave them not only a temporary release from the bonds of their affliction, but he completely broke, so Philo affirms, all those fetters by which the entire habitable earth had previously been enchained. Augustus having brought all wars to an end, had made the whole world one great arena of peace: "This is he who gave freedom to every city, who set chaos in order,

[14] *To Gaius*, xxiii. 157.

who civilized and made obedient and harmonious nations which before his time were unsociable, hostile,
and brutal." [15]

When Christianity in the second century began to
seek recognition from the Roman state, Christians
praised the feats of Augustus as readily as did Gentiles
and Hellenistic Jews. But Christians offered their distinctive interpretation of the basis upon which emperors
had been the recipient of divine favor. Melito, bishop
of Sardis, when addressing Marcus Aurelius, admitted
that Christianity had been originally a barbarian movement, but called attention particularly to the fact that
the new religion had arisen in the time of Augustus
and thus had become for the Empire an especial blessing of auspicious omen. From that time the power of
Rome had grown in greatness and splendor. Its glory
had continued undimmed throughout two centuries
and would endure for all time, if the government
showed itself favorable toward and appreciative of
Christianity. The new religion and the imperial régime
had arisen contemporaneously and had prospered together. This observation seemed especially significant
to Melito, who added that "a most convincing proof
that our doctrine flourished for the good of an empire
happily begun is this, namely, that there has no evil
happened since Augustus ruled, but on the contrary
all things have been blessed and glorious in accordance
with the prayers of all." [16]

It early became a commonly accepted belief among
Christians that the unification of the Mediterranean
lands under the beneficent rule of Augustus had been

[15] *To Gaius*, xxi. 147; cf. Josephus, *Antiquities*, xvi. 38 ff.
[16] Eusebius, *Church History*, iv. 26. 7 f.

an event divinely ordered with a view to preparing the world for the reception of Christianity. A politically unified world with a universal language seemed to have been prepared by God himself in order that this unity among nations under the rule of one prince might make it easier for the apostles of Jesus to fulfil their master's commission to go and make disciples of the nations (Matt. 28: 19). Wars between rival political powers had to be stopped by God that men might have time to hear the gospel. "How then was it possible," says Origen in his reply to Celsus,[17] "for the gospel doctrine of peace, which does not permit men to take vengeance even upon enemies, to prevail throughout the world, unless at the advent of Jesus a milder spirit had been everywhere introduced into the conduct of affairs." Thus for Christians, as for pagans, the Roman Empire was an establishment of heaven for the benefit of mankind.

II

The Romans did not need to be told by Jews and Christians that heaven had intervened in Roman politics to make possible unaccustomed blessings for humanity. When Philo intimated that the prosperity and peace of the early imperial age had been due to the willingness of Augustus to pay respect to the God of the Hebrews, or when Christian Melito affirmed that this happy state of affairs had been divinely instituted to prepare the way for Christianity's success, these foreign preachers were only reaffirming in different form a principle the truth of which was already widely accepted among the Mediterranean peoples. It was a

[17] xxx.

fundamental belief among the Romans that not only under the Empire, but throughout the whole course of their history, political success had depended upon the favor of the gods. The Roman government was essentially a Kingdom of Heaven, an establishment of the deities, a successful kingdom of this world because a foundation and constant care of the supernatural powers whose help for society was made concretely available by means of political institutions.

It had long been characteristic of ancient society to provide political organizations with religious sanctions. Not infrequently the king included in his responsibilities both sacerdotal and political functions. He was a servant of the deity and a helper of the people in one and the same person. In the case of the Pharaohs, for instance, the prince was so active in the performance of religious rites that one sometimes finds difficulty in distinguishing between the royal and the priestly duties of the ruler. The laws which he promulgated, the wars in which he engaged, and the ceremonies of his court were all fortified by ample divine sanctions. A similar fusion of religion and politics was indicated in the famous legal code issued by the Babylonian Hammurabi as a revelation from the deity. The conquering monarchs of Assyria believed themselves victorious through the favor of their god Ashur. The same reliance upon divine protection characterized smaller nations, like the Moabites, who ascribed their victory over the Hebrews to the favor of their local god Chemosh. The Hebrews of Palestine, in turn, were equally confident that a successful political organization for them would be impossible except as they were ruled by a prince whom God himself had anointed to administer their government. An efficient political administration, competent to give society a full measure of protection, was thought possible only in the form of a divinely established institution.

In the matter of supernatural safeguards for society's well-being, the faith of the Greeks did not fall behind that of their Asiatic and Egyptian neighbors. The Greek city-states trusted in patron deities, and heaven was believed to have displayed its keen interest in the establishment of centers of culture through granting immortality and deification to the reputed heroic founders of many different cities. Oracles were consulted, especially at crucial moments in the course of history, and individuals who were thought to menace faith in the gods were punished as enemies to the state. Famous lawgivers, like Solon and Lycurgus, derived their wisdom from Apollo. There were those who believed that "every law is an invention and gift of the gods."[18] When victorious over the aggressive Persians, the Greeks credited their triumph ultimately to the deities in whom they had placed their trust.[19] Similarly, after the brilliant naval triumph of Salamis the Greek general emphatically affirmed that the victory was to be credited, not alone to the soldiers, but to the favor of the deities.[20] While the Greeks were never successful in welding themselves into a united nation, they were none the less confident that their separate groups, in organizing their governmental machinery for the protection of life and property, were operating not simply as human institutions but as supernaturally protected societies.

[18] Pseudo-Demosthenes, *Against Aristogiton*, i. 15.
[19] Plato, *Laws*, 699.
[20] Herodotus, viii. 109.

In the later history of the Greeks, Alexander the Great was exhibited as a model of piety in his reliance upon the gods. At the beginning of his expedition into Asia he had, according to tradition, taken elaborate pains to insure divine favor for his gigantic enterprise. Before setting out upon his campaign he had erected altars to Athena and Hercules. While crossing the Hellespont he had sacrificed to Poseidon, and the other gods of the sea. Again, on disembarking in Asia he had reared altars to Zeus, Athena, and Hercules. Also he went to Ilium where he performed further religious ceremonies in honor of the Trojan Athena, depositing his own panoply as a votive offering in the temple in exchange for some consecrated relics of the Trojan war which were carried before him into battle. He was said to have retained throughout his career a very deferential attitude toward the deities; he was "strictly observant of his duty to the gods." [21] Whatever may have been the actual facts in the case of Alexander, at least subsequent tradition, which exalted him as a model for later generations, was firm in its conviction that his brilliant political career had been due in large measure to his fidelity in seeking supernatural assistance for his great undertaking. His empire had been essentially a Kingdom of Heaven.

The successors of Alexander were clothed with a like divine authority. The Ptolemies in Egypt and the Seleucid rulers in Syria seemed in the eyes of their subjects to be manifest embodiments of the deities' favor for the existing governments. When their kingdoms came to an end with the Romans' assumption of responsibility for setting in order political affairs in the

[21] Arrian, *Anabasis*, i. 11; vii. 28.

East, Roman generals and emperors were readily endowed by their eastern subjects with divine epithets marking them as ruling by divine right because representatives of God on earth. But this ideal of a divinely ordered state was not unfamiliar to the Roman people even before they had made conquest of the East, where they readily learned to take advantage of the supernatural sanctions which had been so generously bestowed for centuries upon Ptolemies and Seleucids.

It is very true that the oldest form of Roman religion was not primarily political in its emphasis. In the earlier years of their experience the crucial points at which the Romans had felt the need of supernatural powers to guard society had been the door at which an enemy might enter the household, the hearth where the women cooked the food, the store-chamber where supplies were kept, and the boundary stone of the farm under cultivation. But if political interests had not yet extensively invaded the area of religion, it was because the people felt no need of giving especial attention to political affairs, and not because they were predisposed to keep politics separate from religion. In later years when the organization of government became a more crucial problem, interpreters of Roman history were able to look back with much satisfaction upon the primitive period where they found it easy to discover that all of Rome's political antecedents had been fortified by ample supernatural sanctions.

The pious Roman was as firmly convinced as the devout Hebrew that the city of his fathers, and the state which had grown up around this center, were a divine foundation. Livy, who was himself somewhat skeptical of popular tradition, could nevertheless concede that if any people had a right to trace their institutions to a divine source, by making the gods the authors of their governments, certainly the Romans were entitled to that privilege.[22] It was said that Romulus was not only a son of deity, but that he had built Rome at the instance of the gods, whose will had been communicated to him by vultures. Since these birds were accustomed to blood and prey, the occurrence was thought to presage a brilliant career for the new foundation. Also Romulus had given strict attention to the most approved religious rites, thus insuring heaven's favor at the very beginning of Roman history. Romans of the Augustan age believed that in no other newly built city could one have found so many priests and ministers of the deities and so much care for religious procedures as in Rome during this primitive, idealized period of national history.[23]

Of all Rome's ancient heroes, Numa seems to have been thought the supreme model of piety. In his ministrations the greatest assurances of supernatural help had been evident. He, like the Hebrew Saul, was credited with having waited upon the will of heaven before accepting his election to kingship. Not until the augurs had reported unmistakable signs of the divine approval would he accede to the people's request that he become their ruler. Accordingly he passed his whole reign in peace, and demonstrated clearly in his administration of the government that he was unusually favored with wisdom from the gods. Like a veritable Moses to the Romans, he set in order and elaborated the system of religious observances by which his de-

[22] Livy, *Preface*, 7.
[23] Dionysius of Halicarnassus, ii. 18. 21; Florus, i. 1.

scendants could henceforth shape their conduct in a fashion pleasing to the deities.[24]

During the early days when the ancestors of the Romans were gradually forming their government into a city-state, which in time became an aggressive imperialistic power, religion was frequently called upon to buttress the political superstructure. Since their original religious heritages were unequal to the new demands, the Romans frequently imported from the East such new gods as were needed to support their growing imperial ambitions. The popular legends about Rome's formal acceptance of such borrowed rites may often be of doubtful validity but the interpretation put upon those traditions in the imperial age is perfectly apparent. Livy, for example, makes it evident that the notion of admitting a foreign god into the sacred precincts at Rome was taken very seriously and was thought to have fundamental significance for the welfare of the state. While strange rites needed to be kept strictly within bounds, there was a manifest feeling that the Roman government had been able in the past to secure no small measure of benefit through the official adoption of certain foreign religions. In this way a very real supernatural increment had been added to that body of divine guarantees with which the political career of Rome had begun.

The Romans were well aware that their past had not been uniformly prosperous. The career of a state that had begun under the favor of heaven ought, from the ideal point of view, to have been immune from those distresses which had so often overtaken Roman society in the course of centuries of history. At such

[24] Dionysius of Halicarnassus, ii. 60 ff; Livy, i. 20; Plutarch, *Numa*, viii.

times had the gods temporarily failed to perform their duty? Manifestly in periods of threatening disaster their favor had been withdrawn and the Romans, attached as they were to the theory of divine protection for the state, had only one explanation to offer. Disaster had been due to neglect of the deities. Lack of fidelity in the observance of sacred ceremonies was the inevitable forerunner of calamity, while assiduous observance of established rites was a guarantee of prosperity. If Roman society had suffered agonies it was because the government had not always been conducted in accordance with the prescribed rites of ancient religion. A faithful return to the traditional customs was the only sure remedy for present ills.[25]

As the death agonies of the Roman Republic proved to be the birth-pangs ushering in the new Empire, both the disasters connected with the passing of the old order and the happier state of affairs inaugurated by the new were closely associated with the action of supernatural powers. Many a writer remarked upon the decay of religion in the later years of the Republic, a consequence, it was said, of contact with Greece following the destruction of Carthage. Under the influence of Greek skeptical philosophy some men had boldly denied the existence of the gods, or else had affirmed that they took no hand in the management of human affairs. The traditionalists were scandalized by this skepticism. Varro expressed alarm lest the Roman gods should perish from sheer neglect by the people, and Cicero warned his contemporaries that to cast off piety toward the deities would bring chaos to society.[26]

[25] Cicero, *Nature of the Gods*, ii. 3; Livy, xxi. 62; xxii. 1.
[26] Varro, *Antiquities*, (Agahd), p. 141; Cicero, *Nature of the Gods*, i. 2 f.

While Varro and Cicero took a pragmatic view of the value of religion to the Roman state, others saw in the disasters of civil war that attended the fall of the Republic the working of supernatural agencies requiting the Romans for their laxity in religion. Indifference toward the deities was thought to be a deadly menace to the state.

That the fall of the Republic was really according to the will of heaven was most clearly discerned after the event and by those who were most closely connected with the new régime. It is customary to speak of a religious revival inaugurated by Augustus, and to accuse him of proceeding in a sophisticated manner to take personal advantage of popular credulity. But possibly he himself was in considerable measure a real victim of the traditional Roman belief in a god-protected state. Certainly he exhibited a very keen interest in religious affairs as related to the maintenance of the government. Not only does the literature produced under his patronage glow with satisfaction and confidence born of an assurance that the political order is a superhuman creation, but the emperor himself expended a vast amount of energy and capital upon the restoration of priesthoods and temples and the setting in order of the technical machinery for doing business with the supernatural powers. Assuredly he did not wish to be classed among those perfidious persons of the past who were blamed for having brought misfortune upon the Romans through neglect of religion.

Both the disaster and the success of Roman political history were closely linked with the will of supernatural powers. Vergil clothed popular belief in the language of poetry when he wrote that the very sun itself had shown compassion for Rome on the day that Cæsar bled by veiling its shining face in darkness and thus causing a godless age to fear unending night. He recounted a ghastly array of portentous occurrences that had been witnessed in different parts of the kingdom. Terrible voices had been heard in the depths of the silent groves, frightful apparitions had been seen in the early dawn, the beasts of the field had uttered human speech, rivers had been suddenly swallowed up by dreadful cracks in the earth's crust, in the temples images of ivory and bronze wept and perspired, floods had swept away whole forests, had devastated cultivated fields and carried away the cattle in their stalls, wells of water had turned into blood, wolves had appeared in the very heart of the city, sudden electric storms had been very frequent and of great severity, and a fearful comet had shown itself. These terrifying manifestations were prophetic of the climax of agony experienced in the terrible civil strife which brought the Republic to an end. Heaven had thus forecast the fact that "Thessaly and the broad plains of Hæmus should twice be glutted with Roman blood." [27]

The language of Pliny the Elder, as one would expect, was more sober, but it had the same import. When mentioning the comet seen for seven days during the period that Augustus was celebrating games in honor of Venus, he remarked that it was taken by the common people to indicate that the soul of the murdered Cæsar had been admitted to a place among the immortal gods. But Pliny testified that Augustus saw in the phenomenon an indication of heaven's favor for the new régime. While in public he seemed to agree

[27] Vergil, *Georgics*, i. 492; cf. above p. 71 ff.

with popular opinion to the effect that it signified the glorification of the martyred Cæsar, in secret "he rejoiced in this auspicious omen, interpreting it as produced for himself." And even the skeptical Pliny adds, "to confess the truth, it really proved a salutary omen for the whole world at large." [28] Apparently the man in the street, the new ruler himself, and even the most gifted scientist of the next century, each in his own way, coupled the political events attending the establishment of the Empire with the intervention of supernatural forces.

Above all others, Vergil was the prophet of the new day. In his oft-quoted fourth *Eclogue* he boldly forecast the early end of the times of agony and the dawning of a new political order to exhibit more perfectly the kindly will of heaven. Men would then be liberated from their age-long fears, while only a few stains of the old-time sin would survive. Under the rule of a new heaven-sent prince the earth would bring forth her fruits spontaneously, the warring elements in nature would be transformed into agencies of peace, the lion would no longer prey upon the ox, the serpent and the poisonous herbs would be exterminated, and foreign spice plants would grow uncultivated in every field. The ripening grain would no longer be smitten by blight, grapes would hang in abundance on the bramble, and the sturdy oak would drip honey. Such would be the divinely bestowed blessings to attend the inauguration of a new and supernaturally established political order.

Vergil was more fortunate than most prophets in living to see the day when he could believe that his

[28] *Natural History*, ii. 25 (23). 94.

predictions had come true. With the institution of the régime of Augustus the care of the gods for Roman politics seemed amply demonstrated. Now the poet could declare with confidence that in the new Empire one saw the fulfilment of an ancient promise that Ilia should bear to the loins of Mars twin children from whom should arise a state whose fortunes would know no bounds and whose power would never wane.[29] It was this state of mind that made possible among the Romans the growing popularity of that astonishing phenomenon known as emperor-worship. While the deification of eastern princes supplied ample precedents for the practice, it owed its vitality among the Romans chiefly to their custom of seeking political prosperity through an appeal to supernatural powers. In an atmosphere where people had for centuries credited political well-being to divine favor it was not at all difficult to regard the mighty imperial institution as a genuinely superhuman creation and to think of the emperor in whom this authority centered as himself divine.

Not only the people who were governed, but the officials themselves commonly assumed an inseparable connection between religion and politics. Culturally, the rulers were often one with the masses in their devotion to superstitious beliefs. They were quite as anxious as were their subjects to see to it that in the discharge of the duties of their office the favor of heaven was insured and the anger of the gods averted. One must not assume that the average Roman ruler thought the religious ceremonies connected with his administration to be a mere formality devoid of ultimate signifi-

[29] *Æneid*, i. 172 ff.

cance except as they produced a desirable impression on his subjects. That there were officials who were at heart Epicurean skeptics and looked upon the idea of a supernatural guidance for political affairs as mere sham is of course a well-known fact. But in the main people in authority in the state shared fully in the thinking characteristic of that day and acted genuinely on the conviction that the government they represented was a creation and a care of the gods, who by this means were insuring to society a truly divine protection.

III

For Christians also religion was the only sure foundation on which to erect a permanently ideal state. But the earliest Christians had not imagined that a genuine Kingdom of God was to be established after the model of Roman imperialism. The ancestry of their imagery was distinctly Jewish. The kingdoms of this world were all destined to pass away on the day of Christ's return from heaven with his conquering angelic host to overthrow all earthly government and establish an eternal Kingdom of God. In the meantime it was the distinctive task of the disciples of Jesus to gather together a group of the faithful prepared for citizenship in the new régime. They were not to make friends with earthly princes, nor to seek prestige and office in the existing political institutions. Their supreme duty was to preach the gospel of their risen and returning Christ in the presence of an adulterous and sinful generation, from the midst of which they hoped to rescue a select group prepared to receive the Son of Man "when he cometh in the glory of his Father, with the holy angels" (Mark 8: 38).

In the meantime, Christians patiently submitted to the existing forms of government, which their God, according to his own good will, permitted to exercise temporary authority over mankind. It was not their task either to overthrow these unworthy institutions, or to transform them into a more godly type of administration. Since for the time being God permitted heathen powers to maintain the ascendancy in the affairs of this world, it was the Christian's duty to conform to the present ordinances of the deity. The existing laws were to be obeyed, the taxes were to be paid, and Christians were to take great care in avoiding any form of conduct that might be interpreted as resistance to these temporary authorities (Rom. 13: 1 ff; I Peter 2: 13 ff). Resistance on the part of Christians was justified only when earthly rulers made such demands upon them as required disloyalty to their own king, the Lord Jesus Christ, to whom they owed supreme allegiance, but whose kingdom was not of this world (John 18: 36).

With the passing of the years and the further postponement of Jesus' return, the problem of the relation between church and state became a more crucial one for the growing Christian movement. The authorities showed increasingly a disposition to take sides with those who resisted the Christian preachers and in the course of time became active persecutors of the new religion. The growing popularity of emperor-worship in the eastern Mediterranean world, where the Christian propaganda was rapidly spreading, created a further embarrassment. While a Christian was willing to pay his taxes to secular authorities, and to obey all other laws of the heathen state, he could not submit to the popular demand to render divine honor to the emperor. In the presence of the many gods and lords whom the Gentiles yielded their allegiance, the Christian felt impelled stoutly to affirm that for him "there is one God, the Father, of whom are all things, and we unto him, and one Lord Jesus Christ, to whom are all things and we through him" (I Cor. 8: 6). In the last analysis, the kingdoms of this world were in reality instruments of Satan, and the Christian, following the example of Jesus, could not consent to possess himself of all the kingdoms of this world and their glory, since it was his duty to worship and serve the one true God (Matt. 4: 7 ff; Luke 4: 5 ff). Not by conformity to the powers of this world, but by the intervention of God to destroy all heathen rule, were "the kingdoms of the world to become the kingdom of our Lord and of his Christ, whose dominion shall continue forever and ever" (Rev. 11: 15).

The Christian program for the ultimate safety of society by means of a catastrophic destruction of all evil powers and the establishment of a new kingdom through the descent of Jesus from heaven, ultimately underwent a very radical revison. In the course of a few centuries, a complete union between Christianity and the Roman state was effected. It certainly is an astonishing phenomenon to witness the acceptance of this new religion by a government bound up with the heritages and customs of a thousand years of heathenism. But it is no less astonishing that a religious movement, which began with the conviction that "all the kingdoms of the world and the glory of them" were the proper possession of Satan, should ultimately hail with approval so close a union with Roman imperialism as to make it possible for Christianity to become the official religion of the Roman state. But perhaps this evolution of history will seem less surprising if one fully appreciates at the outset that both Christianity and Roman imperialism were in original and fundamental agreement at one important point. They both held to the belief that whatever form of political régime might be instituted for society's protection, it rested ultimately upon a supernatural foundation.

At the outset it was the Roman belief in a divinely protected state that inspired Rome's policy of hostility to the Christian movement. Such persecutions as occurred before the year 250 showed no generally aggressive policy of the government toward the new religion. There were, however, numerous outbreaks of hostility in various localities throughout the Empire as early as the latter part of the first century A. D. The characteristic charge brought against Christians was, in effect, that they were enemies to society. They held secret meetings, they indulged in private religious rites, they refused to participate in local traditional religious activities. When put to the test they would not acknowledge Cæsar as Lord. They declared that the traditional gods of the state were no gods, but merely demons. Now, under a government where religious guarantees were thought to furnish society its most genuine safeties, it is easy to perceive how Christians would incur the hostility of the authorities, who were convinced that the most effective manner in which to safeguard the Roman world was to avoid any course of action on the part of the citizens that might anger the deities, who were believed to have underwritten the prosperity of the government.

It was entirely natural that the controlling purpose of hostile action against Christians by the authorities of the state should aim at correcting the so-called atheism of the new religionists. The Romans never concerned themselves with specific items of Christian teaching, nor did they entertain any unusual measure of hostile feeling toward this new religion merely because it was a foreign cult. Foreign religions were facts with which Roman society had become thoroughly familiar and of which it was generally tolerant. But amid this mixture of religions, Christians soon became conspicuous on account of their unwillingness to worship the traditional gods and to confess the lordship of the reigning emperor. It was this exclusiveness which distinguished the Christians from the adherents of other cults who were unmolested by the authorities. The Christians were called atheists, not because it was thought that they refused to believe in any god, but rather because they did not believe in the established gods. This stand naturally seemed to the Roman authorities to threaten the very foundations of political safety as interpreted by the characteristic psychology of the imperial age.

Following the death of Marcus Aurelius in the year 180, the affairs of the Roman government became constantly more precarious. The incursions of the barbarian tribes grew more menacing and the breakdown of the social order was increasingly in evidence. As these distresses multiplied, the need for restoring the favor of the gods became more imperative. It was the best emperors who faced the situation most seriously, and it was also these same rulers who were the most severe persecutors of Christianity. This situation is an entirely proper one from the point of view of contemporary Roman thinking. Any emperor who sought seriously to stay the forces of disintegration that were already so clearly manifest in the Roman world felt it to be a serious obligation on his part to restore the rites of religion as a corrective, and, in the last analysis, the only sure corrective for the evils of the day. The more numerous Christians became, the greater was the menace to the state from their refusal to revere those supernatural sources of help which were assumed to be the only adequate guarantors of safety for the state.

In their effort to alleviate the distress of the times, the more capable rulers sought not only to restore the worship of the traditional deities, but to supplement their apparently waning power by the introduction of new gods who could be combined with the deities of tradition. Inevitably they turned to the East for these new increments of supernatural power. In the second and third Christian centuries, gods from the Orient were serving far more conspicuously the needs of the Roman government than were the native deities of Italy. In the reforms of Diocletian, for example, which were the most thorough-going that had been instituted since the time of Augustus, it was really the invincible sun-god of Syria to whom the Romans attached themselves in the hope of insuring restoration and permanence to their tottering Empire. After Diocletian's retirement, when he and his former colleagues met for a conference at Carnumtum to devise plans for averting the growing menace of political disintegration, their first act was to restore in that city one of the temples of this Oriental deity. By paying him this new attention they evidently thought they would secure a new increment of divine help for healing the ills of the distressed social order.

Just as Diocletian had been one of the most industrious emperors in attempting to rehabilitate the supernatural protectors of the state, so he had also been one of the severest persecutors of Christianity. His procedure was thoroughly consistent. We can readily imagine that, had Christians been ready to place at the disposal of the state the services of their God, side by side with the worship of other deities, their movement would have been as generously espoused by the emperor as was the worship of the Oriental sun-god. And Diocletian's persecution of Christianity could seem to him successful only in case he had persuaded the members of the Christian movement to transfer their allegiance from the Christian God to those other supernatural powers which seemed to the emperor the mightier and more capable of furnishing society adequate divine protection. And it must also be said that it was not so much the cessation of Christian worship as it was the hope of driving the Christians to the worship of the traditional gods that prompted Diocletian's actions. It had seemed to him that this end could be attained by denying to the Christians the opportunity to worship in their chosen fashion.

The persecution of Diocletian was very soon discovered to be a failure even from the Roman government's own point of view. When the rulers became convinced that any religion had sufficient adherents to constitute a respectable body of worshipers to petition its divinities on behalf of the state, its aid might consistently be sought, provided it supplemented and did not abrogate traditional Roman religion. Hence, for the members of a new religion to worship their own gods side by side with the gods of the state might easily be regarded as a virtue, in that it would contribute to the common welfare a measure of supernatural help, though it might be never so small, represented by the particular deities of the new cults. But the persecutors very soon discovered that Christians, when required to worship the gods of the state, either obeyed only half-heartedly or else positively refused to yield to the imperial demands. Since they were no longer permitted to continue their own form of worship, they might now come to constitute a rather large non-worshiping section of the population. This fact alarmed the observant emperor Galerius, who evidently was a true exponent of characteristic religious psychology of the Roman type. In the course of time he perceived that by the persecution of the Christians the number of channels through which divine power might be drawn down from heaven into the society of the Empire was actually being reduced.

This discovery by Galerius was the signal for a complete reversal of policy in dealing with Christians. He sought to improve the situation by issuing an edict of toleration for Christianity shortly before his death in the year 311. His motive for action is clearly stated in his own words. On perceiving that great numbers of Christians, when prevented from worshiping their own God, did not worship the gods of the state, the emperor decreed that:

We, mindful of our most mild clemency and of the unbroken custom whereby we are accustomed to grant pardon to all men, have thought that in this case also speediest indulgence ought to be granted to them, that the Christians might exist again and might establish their gatherings. Yet, so that they do nothing contrary to good order. Therefore, in accordance with this our indulgence, they ought to pray their god for our good estate, for that of the commonwealth and for their own, that the commonwealth may endure on every side unharmed and that they may be able to live securely in their own homes.[30]

Galerius had acted in accordance with fundamental Roman psychology. He hoped to secure a new increment of supernatural assistance for the Empire through allowing the Christians to worship their own God. The amount of benefit to be thus secured might be relatively small, but nevertheless Christians now constituted a sufficiently large element in society to cause the emperor to regard their cult with respect.

The charge sometimes laid at the door of Galerius by Christian historians that he acted insincerely, or the assertion that he changed his attitude because he felt death to be near at hand, are explanations for which our sources of information offer not the slightest justification. He was a perfectly true exponent to the very last of the traditional religious policy of Roman imperialism. Also Constantine's attitude toward Christianity, when he and Licinius granted a similar toleration two years later, is practically identical with that of Galerius. Constantine was interested in religion because it supported the state through appeal to supernatural power. He said explicitly that it was his aim—

to set in order the conditions of the reverence paid to the divinity, by giving to the Christians and to all others full permission to follow whatever worship any man had chosen whereby whatever divinity there is in heaven may be benevo-

[30] Eusebius, *History*, viii. 17. 6–10.

lent and propitious to us and to all placed under our authority. . . . And these things were done by us, that nothing
be taken away from any honor or form of worship.[31]

The acceptance of Christianity by a Roman emperor
was not essentially different in principle from his adoption of the worship of the Oriental sun-god. His action
was the outcome of a long process of social development.
Gradually the Christian movement had won to itself
larger and larger elements in society. Alarmed at its
so-called atheism, some of the more vigorous rulers had
attempted to whip its adherents into line and prevent
their endangering the state by neglecting the worship
of the national gods. But failing in this attempt, and
discovering that the Christians still survived and the
state suffered no immediate calamity in consequence
of this persistence, the emperor determined to use such
help as Christians were able to give by their prayers
for the state and their pledge of the favors which their
God was able to bestow. The imperial action was
prompted by the long and well-established desire of a
ruler to make his state prosperous and to protect society through appeal to supernatural powers.

When the emperors made overtures, they found
Christians ready to respond. Even as early as the
second century some Christian leaders had discovered
that the real basis of imperial hostility was a fear that
the Christians were dangerous to the state because
their atheism was supposed to threaten its religious
foundations. On learning of this, Christians rapidly
changed from their original attitude of indifference to
politics, or of a tacit hostility, and affirmed more and
more clearly that they were ready to pray for emperors

[31] Lactantius, *Death of the Persecutors*, xlviii.

and to assert that the adherents of this new religion constituted the most valuable element in imperial society because they themselves were in league with the God of gods, the supreme creator and master of the universe. Long before any emperor accepted their promises of help they had been proferring their services to the state through declarations of loyalty on the part of their apologists.

On one point only were Christians unyielding. They refused to worship any deities except those of their own cult, their Lord Jesus Christ and the God whom they had taken over from their Hebrew predecessors. But they unblushingly declared themselves to be the most honest people in the state, the most ready to pay taxes, and the most zealous and effective in their prayers on behalf of the commonwealth.

Ultimately, belief in the eternity and the divine foundations of the Roman state became as essential a belief for the Christian theologians as it had formerly been for the old Roman politicians. The church now became virtually an imperial institution. Christians attained a psychology that enabled them to pronounce the marriage between the Christian religion and Roman politics to be a perfectly legitimate and divinely authenticated union. A transcendentalized imperial system furnished Augustine his model for the true City of God on earth. This outcome was really a much more radical change in the Christians' attitude, as compared with their earlier views, than was the change which the emperors underwent when they admitted Christianity among the recognized religions of the state, or even when they made it the only legitimate religion. When Theodosius, before the close of the fourth century, determined to risk all in the keeping of the Christians' God, he was perpetuating identically the same state of mind that had prompted Augustus, the founder of the Empire, to seek out for his kingdom those supernatural guarantees which were believed in his day by the vast majority of his subjects to be the only adequate sources of protection for a successful government. In adopting Christianity Roman emperors departed less radically from the psychology of their predecessors than did Christians in becoming Roman imperialists.

CHAPTER VII

HELP FOR THE INDIVIDUAL

Gods who protected the Roman state were necessarily more concerned with the welfare of society in general than with the specific needs of the individual. One could not easily imagine that deities entrusted with the guardianship of the Empire's broad domains would have either time or inclination to devote themselves with desired specialization to the needs of every member of its large and varied population. The gods of the state were busy with many great duties. The operations of the government under their care were extensive and complex. Protection had to be insured for armies on far-flung borders, for crops in widely separated areas, for commerce over a broad expanse of sea, and for the prosperity of many large cities. Divinities responsible for world affairs on so vast a scale could hardly be expected to concern themselves with the health of a sick slave in an Egyptian village or with the fate of a wounded gladiator dying in a Roman arena.

It is not surprising that fatalism cast its sinister shadow over a large part of the Roman world. It was only natural that the individual should have felt himself as helpless in his relations with supernatural powers imperialized after the model of the Roman state as he was helpless to procure personal favors from the mighty world-ruling prince residing in the imperial palace. But not all men were ready to surrender their faith in the possibility of divine assistance for even the humblest member of society. If the official gods of the state were no longer capable of serving the common man, then new deities had to be found for this task. As a matter of fact, there never was a period in the history of ancient peoples when gods who served individuals were more diligently sought, or were thought to be more active, than in the imperial age. In the course of time such supernatural help was made abundantly available for every man irrespective of his status in society, notwithstanding the tremendously complicated and varied necessities which the complex conditions of the day imposed.

I

Individuals had the consciousness of their own limitations very forcibly impressed upon them by the conditions of life in the Roman Empire. The unification of that world into one vast social maelstrom made it impossible any longer to trust those safeguards that had formerly satisfied all requirements. In earlier stages of civilization, when groups had been smaller and the range of their activities more narrowly restricted, the well-being of every person seemed adequately safeguarded simply through membership in a local community. The deities who presided over a specific territory were the all-sufficient protectors of every phase of life in that particular region. They insured the fertility of the soil, the perpetuity of the race, the preservation of health, and the success of all activities undertaken by the group, or by individuals in the group, to maintain the prosperity and perpetuity of their civilization. One needed no personal access to the deity, because the life of the individual was thoroughly integrated in the life of the group.

The primitive simplicity of religious thinking characteristic of a local community was no longer possible for the inhabitants of the Roman Empire. The world of both gods and men had become far too cosmopolitan to permit the average person to imagine that all of his interests were sufficiently protected simply by allegiance to the god of his fathers. Many people had been forcibly torn by circumstances from their old moorings, or had been enticed by opportunities for adventure and gain to travel far afield in quest of good fortune. Now in critical moments they found themselves far removed from the old sources of help. In the hour of one's new affliction time and distance, to say nothing of more serious impediments, rendered impracticable any hurried visit to some remote part of the world where one might seek help from the deities who had protected one's ancestors. There was a constantly increasing demand for gods who could help a lone individual in all the varying conditions of life and in any quarter of the world.

The mobility of the population, with its diverse elements blending together at every important center, emphasized the demand for deities whose distinctive function was service to the individual. Peoples of different blood and varying racial heritages mingled together within the confines of a city, a village, the army, and even a single household. Some persons moved about voluntarily and others under the compulsion of necessity. Among persons of leisure, travel for education and pleasure was often extensive. The peace of the Empire, with good roads and a sea free from pirates, enticed many a merchant to seek far distant markets. Industrial and commercial activity became cosmopolitan. Soldiers, recruited from distant parts of the world, found themselves serving now in one quarter of the Empire and now in another. When discharged, they received their allotment of land and took up their residence as citizens in many different places. Slavery also contributed extensively to the fusion of peoples. We have "nations in our household," said Tacitus,[1] and the growing practice of manumission turned loose upon society a vast horde of freedmen who dispersed themselves everywhere over the Roman world in quest of more favorable opportunities for subsistence.

The heterogeneous character of the population demanded a great variety of cults if every person's necessities were to be met. The Greek or the Syrian slave in a Roman family could not be expected to find satisfaction for his distinctive religious needs by worshiping the Roman gods of his master and his mistress. It was essential to his happiness that he should continue to direct his quest for help to the type of divinity he had been accustomed to serve in the land of his birth. Either he might transport his native gods to the place of his exile, or he might abandon all hope of securing religious satisfaction in his new environment. The only other alternative was that he should find in his new home deities who could discharge the same functions that he had been accustomed to associate with the operation of his father's gods. It was necessary that gods migrate with the scattering of their devotees, else many an individual must content himself with a great diminution of religious satisfactions.

[1] *Annals*, xiv. 44.

One's ancestral gods were not always equal to the new demands. The individual frequently confronted crises the like of which he had never met before. In the circumscribed experiences of his native environment supernatural protection had been provided only for such needs as were created by that more limited range of experience. In his new mode of life there were fresh experiences for which he had no precedent and many new problems arose for which he found no answer in his traditions. He was forced to seek new help to supplement the services which had previously been rendered with complete satisfaction by the gods of his fathers. Among his new neighbors he must find fresh sources of supernatural assistance. In association with his companions he might be able to offer them some needed assistance from his heritages, while at the same time he sought from them a knowledge of other gods capable of ministering to his peculiar needs. Thus he might be both a missionary for his ancestral faith and a seeker after an enlarged experience of supernatural assistance to be derived from the faith of his associates.

In this process of give and take among the adherents of different gods in the Roman Empire, religion took on a much more strongly personal character. Cults that offered the individual an opportunity to secure blessing and protection through his own voluntary approach to a deity became most popular. Men coveted contact with supernatural powers whose help could be secured not simply on the basis of membership in a specific race or citizenship in a particular state, but on the strength of one's own deliberate choice of the deity. This meant an assurance of protection realized through participation in initiatory rites open to every individual regardless of race or nation or social status. One approached the gods in a purely personal capacity. Individual initiative was rewarded by membership in a voluntary association of disciples bound to one another and to the deity by the proper performance of sacred ceremonies.

It is no accident that the type of religion commonly called the mysteries gained wide popularity in the Roman Empire. It was in just these cults that the largest opportunity was offered for the cultivation of personal experience, in one's relations with the supernatural powers. To become a devotee of the mighty Isis or of the great mother-goddess Cybele, or even of the ancient Greek Demeter, now depended primarily upon the voluntary procedure of individuals who received in return for this devotion a divine favor unconditioned by any circumstance save the measure of his own fidelity. The worshiper also believed that his personal devotion to the gods was reciprocated by the gods' personal interest in him and his welfare. While good government under protection of the gods of the state might insure for him many blessings, there was still a wide area of his daily experience that remained unprotected. But this was not true of his relations with the gods of the mystery religions. Here he came in contact with deities who were in full sympathy with mankind because they had shared the common experiences of life and death to which every mortal was doomed. Consequently they were especially able to succor humanity in every hour of need.

To this type of religion the great mass of men in the Roman Empire finally turned. The immense gain in the satisfaction and enrichment of personal experience made possible by the mystery religions can scarcely be overstated. The failure of the state cults to meet personal religious needs, which the social conditions of the times had emphasized, was probably the chief reason for the ultimate failure of official Roman religion to maintain itself with any degree of vitality in the later years of the Empire. Even though the Roman government might be thought stable and eternal under the guardianship of the nation's mighty gods, the individual became ever more keenly aware of vicissitudes and crises in his personal experience from which the government offered him no protection. He needed divinities who, though perhaps unable to guide the destinies of a nation, could provide a realistic salvation for an individual, both in the struggles experienced during this life and amid the great uncertainties awaiting him in the world beyond.

In the ardor of his attachment to his new-found deities, the devotee was often ready to claim for them not only power to help the individual, but a universality of operation which in reality rendered the gods of the state practically useless. In the case of Isis, for example, whose worship had originally been connected with a specific sanctuary in Egypt, her disciples in Roman times were convinced that she exercised world-wide powers over all the interests of society. No other god was needed for any of life's exigencies. They declared her to be the source and protectress of civilization, the guardian of mankind, and the eternal mistress of the cosmos. In the liturgy of her cult it was said:

I am Isis, the ruler of every land. . . . I set up and established laws for men, which no one can alter. . . . I separated earth from heaven, I showed the courses of the stars, I set in order the course of sun and moon, I invented traffic by sea, I made strong the right, I brought together woman and man, I appointed for woman the infant in the tenth month. I ordained that parents should be held in affection by children. I decreed vengeance upon those disposed without natural affection toward their parents. I with my brother Osiris made an end of cannibalism. I established religious rites for men. I taught reverence for the images of gods. I founded the temples of the gods. I broke down the rule of tyrants. . . . I made the right to be stronger than gold and silver.[2]

No individual, however unfortunately circumstanced in Roman society, needed to go without the aid that supernatural beings were believed able to afford. Whether it was a question of his physical health, of impoverished emotions, of degenerate character, or of fear for the future welfare of his soul, deities were believed to stand ready to give ample assistance if he personally put forth the necessary effort to place himself into right relations with the higher powers. Certain of these gods specialized in one or another form of help, but so widely had the individual type of religion spread about the world that there was no place where the services of a great variety of such divinities were not available. Moreover, among the Gentiles of that age not the least impropriety was felt in paying respect to many different gods. In fact, the more contacts one could make with the supernatural, the more happily and safely might one expect to live. The notion of a jealous God was a Jewish and Christian concept; it did not belong to the thinking of other peoples in the Roman Empire. If the individual failed to realize to the full a sense of personal protection, it was not because there

[2] Text cited by A. Deissmann, *Licht vom Osten*, 4. Aufl., p. 111.

was not a sufficient number of deities available, but
rather because through some failure of his own he had
not been successful in procuring the divine assistance.

II

The quest for health was one of the most urgent
personal demands made upon the deities by people
living in the Roman Empire. Then as now the healing
of disease was a problem lying very close to the heart
of humanity. Sickness and death were the same hard
facts of universal experience that they are to-day.
Sanitation was bad and medical science had developed
to only a very elementary stage of efficiency. Wasting
pestilences often carried away large numbers of the
population, while less fatal sicknesses were a constant
inconvenience and a source of unending anxiety. The
physical afflictions of humanity were legion. There
were diseases of the mind and of the body, internal and
external, real and imaginary. This situation offered the
divinities an exceptionally fine opportunity to show
their power and to demonstrate their favor for their
worshipers.

It is very true that the Roman world was not totally
given over to the superstitious treatment of disease, as
though it were entirely the deities' affair. The Greek
philosophers had not ignored this very vital area of
human experience. They proposed explanations regarding the cause of disease and suggested methods of
treatment which tended to place the whole matter upon
a purely natural basis. Plato had interested himself in
the subject, and his views were repeated over and over
again by his disciples in later times. He affirmed that
sickness was simply the result of derangement in the

physical body. Perhaps through improper action by the individual, or in consequence of some accident over which one had no control, the constituent elements making up the body of man had been thrown into disorder. In that case the proper and only remedy was to restore if possible the original harmony. Mental disease was also due to the same causes. This was inevitable since discord in the body would inevitably affect the well-being of the soul. Consequently Plato proposed, as the best antidote for sickness, education and a well-ordered life in order that the proper balance might be restored in the elements making up the substance of the body and the constitution of the soul. Accordingly, "mathematicians or any one else who devotes himself to some intellectual pursuit must allow his body to have motion also and practise gymnastics, and he who would train the limbs of the body should impart to them the motions of the soul, and should practise music and all philosophy if he would be called truly fair and truly good." [3]

The medical practitioner seems to have been a well-known figure among the Greeks in Plato's day. The physician's use of "burning, cutting, drugging, starving" served to illustrate an argument to prove that one might well suffer evil in order that good might result.[4] But in general Plato seems to have had a rather poor opinion of Greek doctors. He placed much more confidence in a regimen than in physic. He believed that nature herself was the best of healers and that as a rule physicians were to be shunned, since medicines tended rather to aggravate than to allay disease. His advice

[3] *Timæus*, 88.
[4] *Protagoras*, 354.

was not to destroy nature by purgatives and not to provoke a disagreeable enemy by medical treatment.[5]

Plato's naturalistic views on the cause and cure of disease were perpetuated in different philosophical schools of later times. The Epicureans accounted for all sickness by positing the existence of a particular kind of atom, whose proclivities remind one not a little of the modern germ. Just as there were seeds of many things helpful to our life, so harmful atomic bacilli flew about in the air ever ready to produce disease and death. Where they accumulated in large numbers, they disordered the atmosphere and the air became infected. Thus "pestilences come either from without down through the atmosphere in the shape of clouds and mist, or else they gather themselves up and rise out of the earth when it is soaked with water and has contracted a taint, being beaten upon by unseasonable rains and suns." [6] Under these conditions the only sure way of escape from disease lay in avoiding contact with the infectious germs.

The Stoics viewed disease as an inescapable incident in the natural order of events, but they raised it above the level of mere naturalism and linked it with the will of an over-ruling providence. Now and then Zeus might use sickness as a means of punishing the wicked, but this was not the main purpose of affliction. Indeed, it often happened that the righteous were smitten quite as severely as sinners. It was thought not to have been the primary purpose of the deity to make man subject to disease, but in making a world that would be serviceable and beneficial to mankind, the creator had been

[5] *Timæus*, 89.
[6] Lucretius, vi. 1090 ff.

compelled to allow for the possibility of sickness. Health and disease were necessary complements of one another. In constructing a human body in such fashion that it would serve the purposes of reason and utility, the head, for example, was necessarily fashioned of very small and thin bones. Yet a head thus constructed was easily broken. Similarly, other parts of the body when fashioned for efficiency were always subject to the possibility of derangement. Disease, therefore, being an essential part of the rational order, should be borne with equanimity.

Epictetus advised his hearers not to blame either God or man when one fell sick with a fever. Even the approach of death was to be faced without alarm. "When the physician enters," said Epictetus, "do not dread what he may say, nor be over-rejoiced if he should tell you that you are in a fair way to recover. If he tells you that you are very ill, do not be dejected, for what is it to be very ill except to be near the separation of soul and body." [7] In a similar vein the Stoic emperor Marcus Aurelius declared that when ill one was simply taking orders from the great physician Zeus. Alike in sickness and in health, man experienced nature's good pleasure. Therefore "welcome all that comes, perverse though it may be, for it leads you to the goal, the health of the world order, the welfare and well-being of Zeus. He would not bring this on the individual were it not for the good of the whole." [8] Yet the emperor expressed his gratitude to the gods for occasions when they had shown him in dreams remedies that could be successfully applied to the healing of his sicknesses. [9]

[7] *Discourses*, iii. 10. 2.
[8] v. 8.
[9] i. 17.

Relatively few people in the ancient world were ready to face disease with the philosophical equanimity of a Plato, an Epictetus, or a Marcus Aurelius. The vast majority found it quite out of the question to attain to any such height of serenity and self-control. To them ill-health appeared to be a calamity rather than a normal incident, and they eagerly sought help from every available source. The work of the physician was universally demanded; and when it was possible to suppose that supernatural assurances lay behind him and his work, the thought was especially welcome. But even persons like Pliny the Elder, to whom supernaturalism was distasteful, believed that an efficient physician could by experimentation and observation learn from nature herself methods of treatment and remedies for disease that could be effectively applied to restore the invalid's health.

Although tradition credited the beginnings of the medical practice to a divine founder in the person of the god Asklepios, long before Roman times man had come into full possession of the art. The first person who was supposed to have taken the matter in hand was Hippocrates. In his native land there had been a temple consecrated to Asklepios where invalids when healed had recorded the remedies which, on the advice of the god, they had found efficacious. Legend reported that Hippocrates, after copying these prescriptions, burnt the temple and began to practise medicine on his own account. He attended invalids in their beds instead of requiring them, as had formerly been the custom, to visit some temple. Thus he had become the founder of that branch of medical practice known as "clinics." Pliny remarks that "after this time there was no limit to the profits derived from the practice of medicine." [10] From Greece the medical practitioner early migrated to Rome. A certain Archagathus was said to have visited Rome in the year 218 B. C. At first he was received favorably by the authorities and called *vulnerarius* (healer of wounds). But on becoming better acquainted with his methods, the Romans named him *carnifex* (executioner). Nevertheless representatives of the medical profession, most of them Greeks by training if not by birth, were much in demand among the Romans in the imperial age.

If we use the word in a very liberal sense, we may say that there were two distinct "schools" of medicine known at Rome in the time of Pliny. The first may be called the practical school. Its adherents were rigid traditionalists. Their primary interest was to determine what remedies had proved efficacious when tested by the actual experience of the past. They gathered from every possible source recipes for the treatment of every kind of malady. Strongly as Pliny approved of their method, it seems to one to-day utterly ridiculous. Pliny made many a tedious collection of their worthless nostrums. He advised, for example, the following treatment for headache: "A good remedy," he says, "are the heads taken from the snails which are found without shells in an imperfect state. In these heads is found a hard stony substance about as large as a common pebble. On being extracted from the snail, it is attached to the patient, the smaller snails being pounded and applied to the forehead." This was only one of a dozen or more absurd prescriptions which the reader was seriously advised

[10] *Natural History*, xxix. 1 (2).

to try, in case the first recommendation did not prove effective.[11]

Other physicians pursued methods that seem to-day much more sensible. Pliny classed them as belonging to the "hypothetical" school. Pliny said, criticizing Asclepiades who was credited with founding this school, that instead of employing the simple remedies of former times—such, for example, as Pliny's prescription for the cure of headache—he had reduced the medical art solely to an estimation of primary causes, thus making it only a conjectural art. There were, according to Asclepiades, five great principles for treatment of all diseases, namely (1) diet, (2) use and non-use of wine, (3) friction, (4) exercise on foot, (5) exercise in carriage or on horseback. Pliny went on to say that the simplicity of these treatments insured their popularity and won for their author wealth and fame. But Pliny lamented that true medical skill was being thus displaced by mere words, it being found more agreeable to sit in school and listen to the talk of a professor than to go hunting new remedies in the desert, searching for this plant or for that in all the various seasons of the year in quest of new medicines for human ills.[12]

Among Jews and Christians the profession of physician was not always popular. The Chronicler remarked with evident disapproval that King Asa when sick did not seek health from Jehovah, but went to the physician, with the result that the king soon "slept with his fathers" (II Chron. 16: 12 f). But the writer of Ecclesiasticus, doubtless influenced somewhat by Greek culture, advised that the physician be held in honor as

[11] *Natural History*, xxix. 6 (36).
[12] *Natural History*, xxvi. 3 (7 f).

one whom God had approved. Moreover the Lord had created medicines out of the earth, and a prudent man would not treat them with disdain. It is very true that when sick one ought first to make things right with God, "pray unto the Lord, and he shall heal thee, put away wrong-doing and order thy hand aright, and cleanse thy heart from all manner of sin," and after that bring in the physician, for "verily the Lord hath created him" (38: 1–15).

In later times the medical profession found greater favor in Jewish circles, but the early Christians concerned themselves little if at all with medicine as a natural art. While Luke was remembered as "the beloved physician," whose companionship had been affectionately esteemed by Paul (Col. 4: 14; Philemon 24; II Tim. 4: 11), the apostle had plainly indicated that for Christians the healing of disease was distinctly an affair of religion (I Cor. 12: 28; II Cor. 12: 8 f). Christian tradition represented Jesus himself in the rôle of a great physician during his earthly career. When a woman who suffered "many things of many physicians" barely touched the hem of Jesus' garment, her disease was immediately healed. During his public career he had gone about among the people curing all manner of sickness; and after his death the same therapeutic energy, emanating from him in his risen glory and mediated through the activity of his disciples, was declared by Christians to be the only hope for the ills of humanity.

Jews and Christians were not the only nor the first persons in the Mediterranean world to advocate the therapeutic value of religion. By the beginning of the Christian era the Gentiles were thoroughly habituated to the custom of seeking both the cause of disease and its cure in the realm of the supernatural. It was a widespread belief among all the peoples of the Mediterranean world that sickness was not a normal incident in life but was a calamity resulting from the intervention of extraneous forces. Hesiod's story was known to all the Greeks. There had been no diseases among men in their primitive ideal state until that unhappy day when Pandora lifted the lid from the fatal box. Since that day unwelcome diseases haunt mankind. They move silently through the air, Zeus having deprived them of a voice, and fill the world with woes.[13] Often sickness was believed to be due to the anger of a divinity, who thus avenged himself on humanity. It was not uncommon for the superstitious Gentile to regard his bodily infirmity or the death of a relative as "plagues from god and assaults of the demon." Even the propriety of seeking remedial measures under such circumstances was sometimes questioned. Might not a patient who summoned a doctor appear to be fighting against the deity? Plutarch deplored the benighted condition of those who were so deluded as to push away the physician, while they exclaimed in despair, "Let me alone to suffer my punishment, impious accursed as I am, hateful to gods and demons." [14] Among the Romans there was a prevailing belief that the gods, when disobeyed, punished men with bodily afflictions.[15]

That sickness was punishment for offense against the deity was also a common Jewish notion. Adam and Eve because of their sins were supposed to have brought

---

[13] *Works and Days*, 90 ff.
[14] Plutarch, *Superstition*, vii (168C).
[15] For example, Livy, ii. 36; ix. 29; xxv. 26; Tacitus, *History*, iv. 84.

down the curse of pain on mortals. Jehovah's displeasure with the Egyptians had been the cause of the terrible plagues with which they had been afflicted, but God had promised to the pious Hebrews that he would "heal all their diseases" (Exodus 15: 26). This same belief extended to the Jews of the Dispersion. Philo said that one who neglected the sacred laws should be afflicted by diseases of the body which separately afflict and devour each limb and each part, and which also rack and torture one all over with fever and chills and wasting consumption and terrible rashes and scrofulous diseases and spasmodic convulsions of the eyes and putrefying sores and abscesses — to mention only a few items in Philo's list of punishments to be expected by the wicked.[16]

Christians followed the example of their Jewish and Gentile contemporaries in taking sickness to be a mark of divine displeasure. Before commanding a lame man to walk Jesus had first announced the forgiveness of the victim's sins, and on another occasion he had admonished one whom he had healed to "sin no more lest a worse thing befall thee" (Mark 2: 5–12; John 5: 14). Also Paul saw in the sickness and death of certain members of the Corinthian community the chastening of the Lord for their improper observance of the Eucharist (I Cor. 11: 30–32). But the notion of divine retribution was quite too narrow a basis on which to account for all sickness among Christians. Sometimes admittedly good people were themselves ill, and it followed that one must ascribe sickness to the activity of arbitrary evil powers who, whenever the opportunity offered, laid hold alike upon the wicked and the right-

[16] *Curses*, v.

eous. Paul believed that his own personal infirmity was an affliction from Satan, although God permitted it for Paul's own good (II Cor. 12:7).

When individuals believed themselves to be the helpless prey of demonic agencies, who everywhere sought to afflict men with diseases and to lay them low in death, the only genuinely effective remedies had to be found in the area of the supernatural. It was this pervasive psychology in the ancient world that insured the magician, whose activities have already been mentioned, his great popularity. He was the one who knew how to call to the assistance of an afflicted humanity the counteracting demonic powers able to drive off the spirits that had caused men's diseases. In the last resort it was the gods themselves upon whom the ancient man felt compelled to rely for deliverance from the ills to which his flesh was heir.

Both Greek and Roman traditions were rich in memories of occasions when deities had served as physicians among men. When the inhabitants of a Greek city were dying of pestilence, it was Dionysus who came "with healing steps over the slopes of Parnassus." [17] The people of Phocis cherished a shrine of Apollo whose oracles were thought to be a source of healing wisdom for all sick persons who sought help from the deity. [18] Tradition narrated also that the mother-goddess Demeter on her first visit to Eleusis had found Triptolemus at the point of death but by touching the mouth of the boy with her own had restored him to life. [19] Other divinities like Hercules and Rhea were called upon to

---

[17] Sophocles, *Antigone*, 1142.
[18] Pausanias, x. 33. 5.
[19] Ovid, *Fasti*, iv. 537 ff.

"drive away disastrous maladies and dispel dire diseases to earth's remotest bounds." [20]

Among the multitudes of divine healers who served Greeks, Apollo and his son Asklepios stood out most conspicuously. Above all else it was this service that had entitled Asklepios to his place among the heroic redeemers of mankind.[21]   His reputation for health-giving ministrations rested on abundant tradition. He had been divinely bred to heal the manifold diseases of mankind. While on earth he had cured all who came to him. Whether one was afflicted with ulcers, or suffered from wounds, or was a victim of summer's heat or winter's cold, an appeal to Asklepios was never in vain. Some invalids he treated with charms, others were given soothing potions, to others he applied plasters made from herbs, and on others he performed amputations. But, tempted by the promise of gold, once he had exerted his mighty skill beyond proper limits and had restored a dead man to life.[22] This act had brought the earthly career of Asklepios to a close, but in his new rôle as a demi-god, he continued to help all those who sought healing at his shrine.

In Roman times invalids from all parts of the world flocked to the most famous sanctuary of Asklepios at Epidaurus in Greece, where healing was generously dispensed to hosts of suppliants. The lame, the blind, the paralytic, in fact persons suffering from all kinds of maladies, found at this shrine healing for all of their afflictions. Those who had been cured left behind ample testimony to the power of the god. If one

[20] *Orphic Hymns*, xii. 14 ff; xiv. 12 ff.
[21] See above p. 119 f.
[22] Pindar, *Pythian*, iii. 45 ff.

were too ill, or so unfortunately circumstanced that
he could not make the journey to Epidaurus, he was
not necessarily shut off from the help of the deity.
Some friend might carry his petition, which would
be answered either by a vision to the sick man in his
own home, or by a return message of information
that would guide him to the recovery of his health.
Also the god might be found at lesser shrines in
various places about the Mediterranean long before
Christian times.

The Romans were as confident as the Greeks had
been that the health of mankind was a care of the gods.
When a pestilence afflicted the community, the pious
Roman doubled his devotion to the deities. Among
the many occasions when such help was sought, Livy
reports a particularly striking incident. In the city of
Rome itself a deadly pestilence had broken out. The
disease spread so rapidly that the Senate ordered the
people to make special supplication to the gods. Whole
families, including the children, joined in the ceremonies
of petition, imploring the protection of heaven for the
threatened city. One might see "prostrate maidens in
every quarter, sweeping the temple with their hair and
beseeching a remission of the divine displeasure and
extermination of the pestilence." Livy adds that conditions immediately improved, but he is in doubt as to
whether the favorable outcome was to be credited to
the religious devotion of the people, or to an improve-
ment in the state of the weather.[23] Whatever may
have been Livy's doubts, certainly the populace accepted the legend without question.

Early in their history the Romans learned that their

[23] Livy, iii. 7.

native gods were unequal to the task of protecting the health of even the city of Rome. As the population increased and the needs of the growing Empire became more extensive, the Romans borrowed gods from the East to meet the new demand. By the beginning of the Augustan age both Apollo and Asklepios had become official protectors of the Roman health. In his famous *Sæcular Hymn* Horace confirmed the Roman trust in Apollo, not only to drive away sickness from an individual whose frame might be racked by pain, but to insure for Rome in the future a happier day when the community would no longer experience devastating pestilences. For his kindly services as guardian of the public health he was honored with a temple and became as truly a possession of the Romans as he had previously been of the Greeks.[24] *Salutaris* and *medicinalis* were his fitting epithets in inscriptions.[25]

Asklepios early came to Rome to add his divine assistance to the preservation of Roman health. He too was reputed to have come to the assistance of Romans in an hour of dire distress. A pestilence was raging and the skill of the Roman physicians had been of no avail to stay the contagion. In desperation the authorities ordered that the Sibylline books be consulted, and they advised that Asklepios should be brought from Epidaurus to Rome. As soon as the necessary arrangements for the formal introduction of this god of health could be made, his cult was officially introduced into the city. In the form in which the story passed down in Roman tradition, his coming was a tremendously momentous event in the history of the

[24] Livy, iv. 25. 3.
[25] *Corpus inscriptionum latinarum*, vi. 639.

Roman people.[26]   Now they had a new divine guardian
of public health, who served not only the community
at large but also every individual who sought his
assistance.   The deity was as much concerned with
healing the humblest suppliant as with warding off
pestilence from the Empire.   A certain Valerius Aprus,
whose only dignity seems to have been that of a "blind
soldier," could confidently attest his gratitude to the
god who had restored his sight by instructing him to
anoint his eyes for three days with a salve made from
a white cock's blood mixed with honey.[27]   Even a sick
slave who had been left to die on the island in the Tiber
where the temple of Asklepios stood, enjoyed complete
freedom from his old master when the deity had restored the slave to health.[28]

Healing gods from Asia and Egypt also migrated
extensively about the Mediterranean.   Sick persons
had a wide choice among the divine physicians to whom
they might appeal for restoration of health.   Local
divinities, like Sandan of Tarsus, still retained their
reputation for curative power.   Although in far-distant
Sardinia, the man from Syria could enjoy the healing
ministrations of the Phœnician Eshmun, as is attested
by the dedication of a bronze altar by a certain Cleon
in gratitude to the god who had "heard his voice and
healed him." [29]   The Phrygian mother of the gods
could be hopefully petitioned by sick persons in Greece
as early as the time of Pindar.[30]   When Alexander the
Great was ill in Babylon, the temple of Serapis, or of

[26] Livy, x. 47; Ovid, *Metamorphoses*, xv. 622 ff.
[27] *Corpus inscriptionum græcarum*, No. 5980. 15 ff.
[28] Suetonius, *Claudius*, xxv.
[29] *Corpus inscriptionum semiticarum*, I. 143.
[30] *Pythian*, iii. 77 ff.

his Babylonian counterpart, was thought to be the final court of appeal on the question of the prince's restoration to health.[31]   In the next century the cult of Serapis spread extensively about the eastern Mediterranean, where he was conspicuously a deity prone to afflict with sickness those who disobeyed his commands and to insure for his faithful devotees "the health of the body." [32]   From his new home in Egypt the healing fame of Serapis penetrated to the limits of the Roman Empire, and on account of his activities as a divine physician he was often called Æsculapius by the Romans.[33]

The Egyptian Isis enjoyed a similar reputation. Her curative powers were attested by numerous representations in her temples to be found everywhere about the Mediterranean in the Augustan age. She was declared to have been the discoverer of medicines and therefore to have especial delight in healing diseases. It was claimed that persons who had been pronounced incurable by the physicians had been restored to perfect health on appealing to the goddess.[34]   Other suppliants sought the aid of more transcendental divinities, like the seven gods guarding the world's axis and holding power over the lightning and the earthquake. They too were trusted to bestow "good health and soundness of body, strength of hearing and sight." [35]

When Christian missionaries entered the Gentile world preaching the healing power of their risen and

---

[31] Arrian, *Anabasis*, vii. 26.

[32] G. Vitelli, *Publicazione della societa italiana per la ricerca dei papiri greci e latini in Egitto.   Papiri greci e latini*, IV. Nu. 435.

[33] Tacitus, *History*, iv. 84.

[34] Diodorus, i. 2. 25.

[35] A. Dieterich, *Eine Mithrasliturgie*, 2. Aufl., p. 14.

heaven-exalted Lord Jesus, they found audiences well
prepared to hear their message. It was incumbent on
Christians to make the most of this opportunity. They
were confident that the power of the risen Jesus was
superior to that of any demon, or mightier god, of
Gentile fame. They bore testimony to the power of
Christ, not only through their own courage and enthusiasm as healers of disease in his name, but by recalling
the story of his earthly career as a mighty wonderworker before whom all demonic powers that tortured
and afflicted men had trembled and fled. Christians
were confident that Jesus had been even more effective
in his ministrations to the sick than ever could have
been the case with any Dionysus or Demeter or Apollo
or Asklepios or Isis or Serapis. Jesus had not only
excelled all others in restoring health to the sick, but
he had surpassed all rivals in his power to restore the
dead to life. Christians had no need for a natural
science of medicine because they were confident that
supernatural help had been made abundantly available for them through the mediation of their Great
Physician.

III

An enduring government and a healthy body secured
by the favor of heaven were accounted great blessings
in ancient times. Yet many persons were keenly conscious of still another form of good quite beyond the
reach of the average individual without divine assistance. The well-being of his spirit seemed of greater
moment than the strength of his body or the stability
of politics. Neither the permanence of the social
order nor the continuance of physical health could

insure the eternal welfare of his spirit when at last the inevitable hour arrived for the separation of his soul from the body and its earthly associations. It behooved him, therefore, while still in the body, to seek help for the health of his soul.

The mental life of the ordinary individual, who made up the rank and file of the population, was one of much anxiety. The world was full of terrors, seen and unseen. The dangers, invisible though they might be, that threatened the human spirit were dreaded even more than were such calamities as earthquakes, pestilence, or like misfortunes more easily perceived by the physical eye. The inner life of feeling, with its interplay of emotions, seemed quite as real as more external phenomena, if not in fact the greatest reality with which one had to reckon. Dangers threatening the well-being of the spirit were only the more dreaded because less easily perceived by the eye of sense, or because they emanated from supernatural powers whose evil will could not easily be thwarted. When this problem became an individual affair, as it was for large numbers of people throughout the Roman world in the imperial age, then the gravest concern in one's life was how to secure for one's spirit an adequate divine protection and strength by which the immortal part of man could successfully evade or resist its enemies.

The soul had many foes. Gentile belief in the existence of demons has already been sufficiently described.[36] While good demons helped men, there were vast hordes of evil spirits that might work irreparable harm to an individual unskilled in the art of self-protection. Wicked demons had an unenviable repu-

[36] See above pp. 96 ff.

tation. Their own lot being a very unfortunate one, they sought to even the balances against them by multiplying the misfortunes of humanity. Sometimes these demons were assumed to be superhuman beings who had fallen from their high estate and who were now suffering punishment for their sins. Empedocles had said that they were the objects of celestial wrath whom heaven cast into the sea and whom the sea in turn spit out upon earth. The winds of earth carried them to the sun and the sun hurled them back again to earth. No part of the universe would harbor them. Thus they suffered chastisement to the end that ultimately they might be purified and admitted once more to their normal position among good demons.[37]

Evil demons had an insatiable appetite for the human soul.[38] They could cause it many inconveniences while still in the flesh, but could not work their will upon it to the full until after its departure from the body when its state of existence became more like theirs. This hunger of the demons for disembodied spirits was said to have inspired the ancient custom of human sacrifice, and to have been the cause of pestilence and devastating diseases which from time to time had carried away vast numbers of people. It seemed proper also to make demons responsible for those cosmic convulsions when the forces of good and evil had contended together for the control of the universe.[39] Although the demons had at that time been defeated, they were still capable of causing a great deal of trouble for the soul of the individual both during his earthly pilgrim-

[37] Plutarch, *Isis and Osiris*, xxvi (361C).
[38] Plutarch, *Cessation of Oracles*, xiv (417D).
[39] Plutarch, *Cessation of Oracles*, xxi (421D).

age and especially after the decease of the body. There seems to have been a sinister feeling abroad that the demons had the first right to the soul, which in its natural state was a normal object upon which these evil powers preyed. Consequently, the great human struggle at the present moment was to ally one's self to the counteracting forces of good, so that the soul might receive assurance of new strength and new life in preparation for the world to come.

Man lived also under the menace of the cosmos. He was nervously conscious of his own helplessness in the presence of the inexorable operations of the world about him. There was a heartlessness in its treatment that often made him exceedingly uncomfortable. He could easily have said that nature was "red with fang and claw." How could he escape from the clutches of this world-power that seemed now to be grinding him to dust and whose eternal might would continue its heedless bruising of his spirit after the soul's departure from the body? The world itself was a supernatural thing, whether one thought it dominated by the stars, or under the compulsion of necessity, or ruled by the irresponsible goddess of fortune. Juvenal spoke for only a minority of his contemporaries when he remarked that "the only pathway to a life of peace is by way of virtue. If one has understanding, thou, Fortune, hast no divinity; it is we who make of thee a goddess and place thee in heaven." [40] Most men feared the baneful goddess and despaired of their power to escape her buffetings until they had obtained assurances of protection by some superior divinity. They craved the experience of a Lucius who, when received into the cult of Isis,

[40] x. 363 ff.

could say of Fortune, "let her go now and rage with all her fury and let her seek some other object for her cruelty; for direful calamity has no power over those whose lives the majesty of our goddess [Isis] has claimed for her own service." [41]

Again, there were many persons who thought the physical body itself an enemy of the spirit. Plato's famous saying that the body is the prison-house of the soul was never forgotten. This essentially Orphic teaching, that soul and body belonged to different spheres of existence, gave to man the uneasy feeling that his spirit was entombed in an evil body bent on chastizing the spirit and dragging it down to closer union with matter. If the individual remained unaided by any power outside of himself in this unequal struggle between the imprisoned spirit and the evil body, death would not bring liberty to his soul but would leave it in a condition so tarnished and impure that it might be forced again and again to return to a bodily habitation. Although the soul itself was originally divine by nature, there could be no effective deliverance from its present life without new help from a divine source.

The deities now of chief interest to man were those who could inspire a feeling of salvation realizable in the emotional experience of the individual. Safety from evil demons and freedom from their machinations, whether in this world or in the world to come, could be attained only through the consciousness of union with some more powerful kindly divinity pledged to protect needy humanity. One turned to such a god as the only hope of deliverance from the indifferent or unkindly cosmic powers representing the vast organism

[41] Apuleius, *Metamorphoses*, xi. 15.

that men to-day call the course of nature. The ancient man craved fellowship with a divine friend whose all-seeing eye and supernatural power could liberate the helpless individual from this heartless nexus of events. And if he were to realize any sense of victory over the impulses of the flesh, he felt it could be done only through the incoming of fresh divine energy to supplement the native force of his spirit in the unequal struggle.

The human spirit's quest for an experience of salvation did not remain unanswered. Long before Christianity had arisen there were many Gentile religions inviting those who felt the need of divine assistance for the inward man. The rites of the various mystery religions offered an especially good opportunity for the attainment of a new emotional experience readily interpreted as an effective acquisition of fresh divine power. The stimulation of the senses by music and processionals, the play upon the feelings attending various acts in connection with the rites of initiation, the pledge to secrecy solemnly imposed upon all of the candidates, and the wild orgies connected with many of these rites, all served to produce the desired emotional agitation. The necessity of presenting one's self voluntarily for membership, as well as the purifications and other preparatory rites to which one had to submit, only heightened the effect. Everything that was done happened to one as an individual, and this strong emphasis upon the personal relations between the devotee and his god gave precisely the sense of divine interest which alone could produce in needy humanity feelings of solace and satisfaction.

The ancient mysteries of Demeter had been famous

for their contribution to the happiness of mankind both in this world and in the world to come. Pindar had said that those persons who had beheld the scenes exhibited in the Eleusinian mysteries descended into Hades without anxiety, for they had learned in the sacred rites "both the end of life and its divinely decreed [new] beginning." [42] Sophocles had borne similar testimony to the significance of the ceremonies. He remarked that those mortals were thrice happy who possessed this secret wisdom. On reaching Hades "they alone had a joyous existence, while all others suffered evil things." [43] The Bacchic initiates also were confident that "to us alone is there a sun and joyous light" in the lower world.[44] These sentiments continued to find expression far down into later times. Throughout the Roman imperial age many mystery cults were making similar promises. The devotee of Isis was assured that, if he kept faith with the divinity, under her protection his life on earth would be blessed and glorious. When the alloted span of his earthly career came to an end he would descend to Hades unafraid, there to dwell in Elysian bliss and to behold the goddess shining in the subterranean firmament and illuminating the dense Acherontic night.[45]

As late as the beginning of the fourth century A. D. Gentile religions were still claiming power to mediate a full salvation for the soul both here and hereafter. Christian preachers themselves bore witness to the fact, although they declared it absurd for members of the

[42] Cited by Clement of Alexandria, *Stromata*, iii. 17.

[43] Plutarch, *On Hearing Poems*, iv (21F); cf. Plato, *Phædo*, 69; Isocrates, *Panegyric*, xxviii; *Peace*, xxxiv.

[44] Aristophanes, *Frogs*, 455 ff.

[45] Apuleius, *Metamorphoses*, xi. 6.

heathen mysteries to affirm that they "are born of god and are not subject to the laws of fate, and that if they strictly regulate their life his palace stands open to them." It was foolish, continued the Christian apologist Arnobius, for the heathen to believe that "by offering the blood of certain animals to certain divinities they can be made divine and freed from the laws of death. These are empty allurements that kindle vain hopes; no one except Almighty God is able to save souls." [46] But there were still many devout adherents of the pagan mysteries who preferred to trust the gods of their fathers and who found in the experience of initiation a rich religious satisfaction. Such was the confidence of the man who prayed to Serapis: "Guard me from my destiny decreed by the stars, withdraw me from my cruel fate, allot me good things in my generation, enlarge my life, O Lord, with all goodness, for I am thy slave and suppliant, and I praise thy true and holy name, O glorious Lord, ruler of the world, master of fate, foster parent, judge [divider], Serapis." [47]

Initiation into the mysteries was likened to the experience of death itself. It filled one with terror but issued in triumph. The joy which persons felt on completing the process of initiation could fairly be compared to the joy in store for the soul when finally it would depart from the body and be purified for entrance into the state of immortal bliss. [48] One might say that in the confidence experienced by the devotee he already passed from death into life through the rites of initiation, thereby anticipating the joys of future bliss.

[46] Arnobius, *Against the Heathen*, ii. 62.
[47] Leiden Papyrus, J 395 (W), xiv. 36 ff, cited by A. Dieterich, *Abraxas*, p. 178.
[48] Plutarch, *Face in the Moon*, xxviii (943D).

The two types of experience were closely parallel. Again, it is Plutarch who, in vivid language, draws the comparison:

When death overtakes one the experience is like that of initiation into the great mysteries. For this reason the word "to die" [*teleutan*] and the word "to be initiated" [*teleisthai*] correspond. At first come wanderings and wearisome mazes, until the consummation, a strange and interminable passing through darkness; then before the end many terrors, shudderings, sweatings, and amazements. After this a wondrous light bursts forth, revealing the welcome of pure meadows and open plains, songs and dances and holy apparitions wherein he who is now all perfect and initiated obtains freedom and relief.[49]

Apuleius's description of the feelings of Lucius when initiated into the mysteries of Isis is no mere literary invention. Apuleius repeats in its main features a long current tradition, now characteristic of various cults:

I drew near to the confines of death, I trod the threshold of Proserpina, I returned therefrom being borne through all the elements, at midnight I saw the sun shining with a brilliant light and I approached the presence of the gods beneath and the gods of heaven and stood near, and worshiped them. Behold, I have related to you things which though heard by you must necessarily remain unknown.[50]

Further details of the initiatory experience might not be divulged, but the emotions awakened by the ceremonies could easily be appreciated, even though an outsider might not be permitted to enter with the candidate into the holy of holies. Well might one celebrate as his natal day that joyous hour when his initiation had been accomplished. Henceforth he was the

---

[49] *Concerning the Soul, Fragment* vi. 2 (edition of Bernardakis, vii. p. 23).
[50] Apuleius, *Metamorphoses*, xi. 23.

possessor of a new life into which he had been born through participation in the rites of the mysteries. He could not soon forget his *natalem sacrorum*.

Each of the mystery cults, of which there was a great variety in early Christian times, was conspicuous for the performance of ceremonies tending to excite the emotions. Some of the rites are crudely primitive and revolting to modern sensibilities. For example, the Bacchic ceremonies were accompanied by the most extravagant displays of frenzy. The devotee, having eaten raw the flesh of the victim and imbibed its warm blood, danced in wild delight frenzied by the divinity that now filled his human frame. The worshiper was possessed by the god, was "maddened by the deity." The rites of Cybele and Attis were similarly orgiastic. In other cults the display of emotion was less extravagant. But whatever the degree of excitement attained and by whatever means, the satisfactions experienced were always of the same type. The individual received from the god a new strength, a new hope for the future, and a new courage with which to face the common tasks of life. The temptation to indulge the passions for their own sake was early recognized and severely condemned. If it were not to Dionysus but only for sensual satisfaction that one danced in the procession and sang the phallic song, then it were an utterly shameful affair. Heraclitus prophesied punishment [51] and fire after death for those who celebrated the Bacchic ceremonies in this unholy manner. Sincerity was essential to efficacy even in the highly orgiastic rites of Dionysus.

Thoughtful people saw behind the transforming experience of initiation more than a mere display of physical

[51] *Fragment* 14 f (Diels).

feeling. It is very true that the mysteries perpetuated certain observances offensive to the finer tastes of cultured people in Roman times. Plutarch could not believe — and he could cite the ancient Xenocrates in support of his skepticism — that any god, or good demon, took pleasure in the buffoonery practised in the Eleusinian processions, when people made wry faces and perpetrated coarse jests, or resorted to blows and abusive and obscene language. He explained that these absurd performances were resorted to as a means of warding off evil demons, who were especially pleased by such conduct. If they were not given this satisfaction they might work great harm. The boisterous doings were thus a kind of exorcism, "propitious and soothing acts for the purpose of turning away wicked spirits," in order that the more sacred rites to follow might not be contaminated.[52] But when the demons had been driven off and the candidates came to the most solemn part of the ceremony they conducted themselves in a very different manner. Now the clamor and rudeness of the initial ceremonies gave place to "profound silence and religious fear." [53] A reverential quiet pervaded the place while the initiates waited to hear the secret discourse, the "holy word," from the lips of the priest, whose utterances were received with awe and gratitude.

For men like Plutarch, disposed to reflect on the deeper meaning of the mysteries, the rites seem to have had a distinctly transcendental significance. They were thought to be symbolic of experiences of the deity that were full of meaning for mankind. The ene-

[52] Plutarch, *Isis and Osiris*, xxvi (361B); *Cessation of Oracles*, xiv (417C).
[53] Plutarch, *Progress on Virtue*, x (81E).

mies of the mystery gods had been wicked demons, like Typhon who slew Osiris, or the Titans who tore Dionysus limb from limb. On the contrary, the supernatural powers who had authorized the mysteries were the good demons who had triumphed over their demonic foes and through their victory insured salvation for their devotees.[54] Pursuing this line of thinking, it was easy for the members of the mystery cults to believe that they were under the protection of divinities who had successfully engaged in a mighty cosmic struggle with the forces of evil. Having come off triumphant, they could give their followers the full assurance of safety from all dangers both present and future. Typical of this sentiment are the words which the priest addressed to the new members of the Phrygian mysteries who had just witnessed the holy pantomime portraying the experiences of the deity: "Be of good courage, devotees of the god who has been saved, for you too shall have salvation from troubles."[55]

The mysteries also gave a sense of deliverance from imprisonment in the physical body. The purgations preceding initiation, the fasts and ascetic practices connected with the rites, were all aids in the mortification of the flesh; while the emotional uplift experienced in the consummation of the initiation ceremonies gave the spirit a new sense of its own superior strength. The imprisoned soul had now been given new wings by the grace of the deity whose very presence was felt within the individual. It was not so much through the meritorious character of one's own deeds that high privilege had been attained. Freedom from the power of the

---

[54] Plutarch, *Cessation of Oracles*, xxi (421D); *Isis and Osiris*, xxvii (361D).
[55] Firmicus Maternus, *Error of the Profane Religions*, xxii.

physical nature had been possible only as one obtained
in religion a new divine increment of being to supplement the life of the spirit. Men spoke of being born
again, born unto eternity.[56]

The Greeks were thoroughly familiar with religions
capable of providing the soul a release from its bodily
imprisonment. Even while in the flesh it was possible
to experience a regeneration by which the burden of
mortality was removed and a sense of transformation
into divinity realized. We do not know how Empedocles had attained the state of mind that enabled him
to declare himself an immortal god and no longer a
mortal man, but we may safely assume that his confidence had a religious basis. The Orphic tablets clearly
reflect the notion of divine regeneration realized through
participation in sacred rites. Like Dionysus himself who
attained to immortality, the blessed and happy initiate
"put off mortality and became divine." He duplicated
the experience of the divinity's suffering, the memory of
which was perpetuated in the ritualistic formula, "Hail
thou who hast suffered the suffering; this thou hast never
suffered before; thou art become god from man." [57]

This primitive Orphic imagery was perpetuated
through the succeeding centuries and affiliated with
kindred notions in other cults, until it pervaded the
whole Gentile world in early Christian times. The
member of the Eleusinian church was described as one
"begotten of the deities" Demeter and Persephone [58]
and the Christian Tertullian[59] commented on the fact
that the devotees of these gods professed to effect regen-

---

[56] *Corpus inscriptionum latinarum*, VI. 736. 510.
[57] O. Kern, *Orphicorum Fragmenta*, p. 108, No. 32 f; cf. No. 32c.
[58] Pseudo-Plato, *Axiochus*, xx. 371D.
[59] *On Baptism*, v.

eration by means of their rites. The worshiper of Osiris was encouraged by a similar hope; he too became an Osiris through participation in the rites of the cult, even as the ecstatic bacchanals became incarnate Bacchuses. The suppliant prayed to the Mithraic sun-god for the attainment of immortality as a present experience: "Transform me, now oppressed by my lower nature, into an immortal generation. . . . in order that I may become regenerate in mind, that I may be consecrated and the Holy Spirit may give me breath." [60] One sought as a magical charm a consciousness of identity with an all-powerful deity as a means of insuring protection from all evil powers in heaven, on earth or in the lower world:

Enter my mind and my heart every moment of my life and fulfil all the desires of my soul. For thou art I and I am thou; whatever I say must come to pass; for I bear thy name as a charm in my heart and all the power of Styx shall not overcome me. No spirit, no demon, shall resist me, nor any other plague from the evil spirits of Hades, because of thy name, upon which I call and hear in my soul.[61]

IV

Christianity aimed to meet every spiritual quest of the Gentile world. There was no form of personal religious need for which the Christian preachers, in the course of time, did not find an answer in their own faith. They had no sympathy with Epicurean naturalism, and hardly less with Stoic self-sufficiency. On the contrary, they were of like mind with the more superstitious heathen who sought help for his individual necessities

[60] Cited by A. Dieterich, *Eine Mithrasliturgie*, 2. Aufl., p. 4.
[61] Leiden Papyrus, J 395 (W) xviii. 1-5, cited by A. Dieterich, *Abraxas*, p. 196.

in the sphere of the supernatural. But Christians greatly simplified the suppliant's program by alleging that there was only one source from which all valid assistance was to be derived. They declared that faith in Christ gave one full access to the supreme divine power adequate for all the varied needs of every person within the total population of the Roman Empire. Whether one sought protection from the machinations of evil spirits, deliverance from bondage to cosmic powers, or release of the spirit from its bodily imprisonment, Christianity stood ready to declare that membership in its communion would insure a satisfactory experience of salvation.

It is indeed surprising that the new religion, which had arisen in a Jewish setting where the prevailing types of personal religious quest seem to have been of a somewhat different character, so rapidly adjusted itself to the new environment. But its early rejection by the Jews of the Dispersion and the decision that the Gentile would not need to identify himself with the Jewish race in order to share fully in the benefits of the new cult, opened the way for further growth along the lines of a purely personal and voluntary type of religion answering to the emphatic demands of the contemporary social situation. This state of development in Christianity had been reached, at least in the circles where Paul and his helpers labored, by the year fifty. Thereafter the whole Gentile world was an open field for the new movement, itself so plastic and uncrystallized institutionally that it was free to develop a new structure suitable to the needs of its expanding life. In this respect it had a great advantage over all its older rivals.

From the very outset Christianity was primarily a religion offering supernatural help to the individual.

It professed to protect him from all sorts of immediate dangers ever threatening one who thought himself living in a demon-infested world. As interpreted by Paul, its outlook was also cosmic. In imagery similar to that used by Plutarch in explaining the meaning of the pagan mysteries, Paul declared that Jesus through his death had in reality effected a triumph over the demonic "rulers of this age" (I Cor. 2:6-8), a victory involving great blessings for mankind. As the most significant moment in the mysteries was an exhibition of the deity's suffering and triumph, so Paul centered his preaching on a portrayal of the crucifixion of Jesus (Gal. 3:1; I Cor. 2:2) and promised the believer both deliverance from the "present evil age" and an assurance of victory over all the powers of Hades (Gal. 1:4; I Cor. 15:54 f). The import of such language cannot have failed to arrest the attention of many a Gentile the moment these words fell upon his ears. So far as the popularity of Paul's preaching was concerned, Paul made a wise decision on reaching Corinth where he determined not to make any further efforts to convey his message to Gentiles in the style of a philosophical argument such as he had attempted in Athens. The populace wanted to hear about saviors who through their own heroic careers had opened up new ways of help for needy individuals. They were prepared to be impressed by a vivid portrayal of "Jesus Christ and him crucified" (I Cor. 2:2).

The Gentile enjoyed an immediate experience of the divine power in the moving ceremonies of the mystery cult. The god filled him even in the present. A piece of the deity, as it were, entered into the believer, giving him new courage for the present and bright hopes for

the future. For Paul also this notion was fundamental.
Every Christian was a new being, a supernaturalized
man, in whom Christ had taken up his abode. In
Romans 8: 9–11, the thesis was forcefully stated:

If any man hath not the Spirit of Christ he is not a Christian. And if Christ is in you, the body is dead because of sin;
but the Spirit is life because of righteousness. But if the
Spirit of him that raised up Jesus from the dead dwelleth in
you, he that raised up Christ Jesus from the dead shall
quicken also your mortal bodies through his Spirit that
dwelleth in you.

Here Paul put in a nutshell the basal idea of all
mystery religions. An immediate experience of union
with a divine hero who had triumphed over death
insured for the believer a similar victory.

The Gentile was less interested than Paul the Jew in
having the "mortal body" redeemed, but no salvation
would have seemed worthy of the Gentile's attention
that did not yield a vivid sense of union between his
own soul and the deity. Previous to the experience he
had been a lonely and helpless mortal, but now he had
become a new man. He had received into himself a
divine increment of being that gave fresh strength to
his immortal soul. He had no such difficulties as moderns sometimes feel in taking literally certain phrases
in the writings of early Christians. He could readily
understand their meaning when the preachers of the
new religion spoke of the necessity of becoming a "new
creation," of being "born again," or of having "Christ
in you the hope of glory" (Gal. 5: 15; II Cor. 5: 17;
John 3: 3; Col. 1: 27). Experience in the rites of the
mysteries had taught Gentiles to take the imagery of
union with the deity in very realistic fashion, and they

could support their interpretation by reference to an abundant display of emotion in connection with their religious ceremonies.

Christians, too, had assisting rites, which at first were relatively simple, but in time became as elaborate as those of a Demeter, an Isis, or any other mystery god. Paul spoke of the initiatory ceremony of baptism by which all believers had "put on Christ" and had been "made to drink of one Spirit" (Gal. 3: 26 ff; I Cor. 12: 13). And the connection between initiation into the mysteries and the experiences of death was not wanting even in Christianity. All "who were baptized into Christ Jesus were baptized into his death" and arose from the cleansing waters to a newness of life anticipatory of the blessed immortality which Christ had won for himself and would bestow on his followers (Rom. 6: 1–14). From the moment of their initiation those who entered Christianity lived on a high emotional level. In their assemblies, by the rites of their worship and their sacred meal, their experiences of contact with the divine were frequently renewed. They continued to possess and to be possessed by "the Spirit." It was only a different way of stating the same thing when the Christian was said to be filled with the "Holy Spirit," with the "Spirit of God," with the "Spirit of Christ," or with "Christ." These variant phrases designated the one divine increment experienced as a new possession of every believer who had received initiation into the Christian society and whose emotions were kept holy and vigorous by participation in the repeated ceremonies of the cult.

The Christian experience carried with it also a sense of deliverance from the material body. The natural man was in a hopeless condition; the spiritual man only was saved. But even though harboring the Spirit, the body continued to be a menace to the well-being of the soul. The flesh was a drag upon the spirit of man, even the Christian man. Paul was always conscious of the "law of sin which is in my members" from which Jesus Christ alone could give ultimate deliverance (Rom. 7: 23). The "doings of the body" constantly jeopardized the life of the Spirit, and could be effectively suppressed only by resort to divine help made available through the indwelling Spirit of God. The safety of the Christian lay in heeding the admonition, "Walk by the Spirit and ye shall not fulfil the lust of the flesh" (Rom. 8: 12 ff; Gal. 5: 16 ff).

The soul of the Christian was not only imprisoned in a sinful body from which it sought release, but was also entangled in an evil universe where its welfare was menaced by wicked spirits holding primal authority over this present corrupt age of darkness (Eph. 6: 12). Christ was extolled as the deliverer of the cosmos from all these demonic powers; he was triumphant in every part of the spirit-world. Since his release from Hades and his exaltation to heaven, the angels above, everything on earth, and all spirits of the lower world had been forced to confess the supremacy of his name (Phil. 2: 9 f). He was far above "all rule and authority and power and dominion and every name that is named" for this age and for all future time. All things were now in subjection to him (Eph. 1: 20–22). He had met "the principalities and the powers" in deadly conflict and had despoiled them of their authority (Col. 2: 10–15). No sinister astral divinities, however cruelly they turned the wheel of fate, held any power over the destiny of the soul that had experienced a union with Christ.

CHAPTER VIII

THE DESTINY OF THE SOUL

EVERY one in the ancient world believed man to be composed of at least two constituent parts, the body and the soul. There could be no question regarding the fate of the body. Even though kindly divinities might temporarily alleviate physical ills to save one from an untimely end, death was inevitable. The body was destined for final disintegration. Whether deposited in a grave and left to decay, or burned to ashes on a funeral pyre, ultimately it became inanimate dust. From this stern fact of universal experience there was no escape.

A happier destiny was in store for the soul. Because of its more ethereal nature it was able to survive the decease of the body, from which it had departed at the moment of death. How long it would retain consciousness, where its future dwelling might be, and what experiences awaited it in its new abode, were questions that made a strong appeal to the imagination. They had long been a serious concern of Greeks, Romans, Egyptians, Jews, and other peoples making up the cosmopolitan population of the Roman Empire. Various opinions were current. Many persons found greatest satisfaction in a resort to popular notions, inherited from their ancestors, or borrowed from the traditions of their new associates in the syncretistic society of the time. Others attempted a reinterpretation of tradition in the light of new intellectual interests, and a few ventured upon a program of radical skepticism.

I

In a notable treatise Aristotle critically summarized the opinions of earlier Greek philosophers regarding the nature, essence, and attributes of the entity commonly called soul. He quite ignored popular religious notions and concluded that even the views of the philosophers — the Pythagoreans, Empedocles, Democrates, Anaxagoras, Plato, and all the rest — were untenable. What gave him chief offense was the disposition of his predecessors to make the soul too independent of the body. He drew a sharp distinction between soul (*psyche*) and mind (*nous*), and identified the former with the vital principle possessed by both man and animals. He affirmed that "nothing which has perception is without soul." [1]

In formulating his positive definition of soul, Aristotle's point of departure was a distinction between matter and form, subject and attribute, each being viewed as a substantial fact. Matter exists, form exists, and the two exist together. Matter represents potentiality, while form gives it attributes and the capacity for actuality — ability to fulfil the end of existence, so to speak. Similarly, body and soul have to one another the relation of matter and form, the soul giving function, attribute, or self-realization to a body which has in it the potentiality of life, that is, to a body possessing organs. To take an analogy, if the eye were an animal, eyesight would be its soul, in default of which it would

[1] Aristotle, *Concerning the Soul*, i. 5. 27.

no longer be a living eye. While body and soul were each allowed a real existence, just as the wax and the imprint both exist, a disembodied soul was inconceivable. Hence the soul was not immortal.[2]

Fortunately for the average man's peace of mind, the Aristotelian psychology had no popular champion in the Roman Empire. But there were active preachers of skepticism, disciples of Epicurus, who proclaimed with evangelistic zeal the mortality of the soul. Epicurus had been a thorough-going materialist, yet he had believed that every man possessed a soul. This constituent part of the human personality was assumed to be composed of very fine and delicate particles of matter, infusing and giving life to the coarser material of the visible body. But the atoms of which the soul was composed were thought to be so fiery, ethereal, and vaporous in character that they no longer held together when released from the body. After death the soul of the individual immediately perished, its atoms being reabsorbed into the great mass of primeval matter whence they had originally come. While this atomic substance endured eternally, the individual soul lost its identity at the moment of death, when its particles were dispersed even more rapidly than the atoms of the body.

There has been frequent occasion to observe the missionary zeal with which Epicureans attacked the popular religious notions of the time. Similarly, their teaching regarding the soul was inspired by a desire to deliver man from the fears which beset him in this life as he meditated on what might await him in the world beyond the grave. By proving that the soul perished immedi-

[2] ii. 1. 9.

ately upon leaving the body, the Epicurean thought he was conferring a great blessing upon the human race. All fear of death would be abolished by removing the dread of future punishment. Stories learned by the Romans from the Greeks, who had described dreadful tortures inflicted upon unhappy mortals in the world below, were denied and ridiculed by Lucretius. He would have his Roman audience realize that no man need fear any such punishments as were recounted in the Greek fables. It was only a diseased imagination that had created the picture of a Tantalus eternally tortured by the menace of a huge stone suspended above his head. Nor was there any Tityus with a carcass sprawled over nine acres on which birds of prey constantly feasted. Sisyphus, vainly endeavoring to roll a stone to the top of a hill, was also a pure fiction. Moreover, Cerberus and the Furies, the wheel of Ixion, and Tartarus of the flaming throat were things "which nowhere are, nor sooth to say can be." [3]

In the next century Pliny the Elder also vigorously denied the immortality of the soul. He insisted that all of man, soul and body alike, passed into oblivion at death, even as he had been without existence before birth. There was no more sensation left in either the body or the soul after the breath of life had ceased. It was only vanity and self-deception on the part of man that inspired him to project himself into the future. Thus he had been deluded into believing that his soul would be immortal, or he had adopted the doctrine of transmigration of souls, or again had pictured for himself a life among the shades below, where departed spirits would receive worship from people who still

[3] Lucretius, iii. 978 ff.

lived upon the earth. Pliny advised men to compare themselves with the animals, whose mode of breathing was in no way different, and to remember that many other animals enjoyed a longer span of life than that of man, yet no one ever predicted immortality for these creatures. He impatiently exclaimed: "What downright madness it is to suppose that life is to recommence after death. . . . This pleasing delusion and this credulity quite cancel that chief good of human nature, death, and, as it were, double the miseries of him who is about to die by anxiety as to what is to happen to him thereafter." Man's more sensible procedure would be to remember that previous to his earthly existence he had been utterly unconscious and the same blissful oblivion awaited him after his life upon earth came to an end.[4]

The happy oblivion to follow death was a theme often treated in more popular Roman literature. Seneca, although never a thorough-going Epicurean, gave picturesque expression to this skeptical doctrine. There is no longer any conscious existence of the soul after its departure from the body. It is like smoke vanishing in the air, or like a cloud driven before a violent north wind. It evaporates into nothingness. Those who desire future happiness may as well abandon their hopes at the doors of death, and those who cherish fears may lightly set them aside. It is a waste of time to indulge in curiosity regarding where one shall rest in the hereafter. The dead dwell in the same place where those abide who have no existence before birth. Body and soul alike share in this fate. All pictures of a lower world, with its relentless ruler and the watchdog Cer-

[4] Pliny, *Natural History*, vii. 55 (56).

berus guarding the approach to Hades, are vain talk and empty words with no more reality behind them than the terrifying phantoms experienced in a ghostly nightmare.[5]

Many Roman epitaphs are famous for their jaunty treatment of the future life. It is true that such inscriptions may sometimes record the witticisms of survivors rather than the serious views of the departed, but apparently it was felt to be entirely appropriate to make the deceased declare that he had passed into the never-ending sleep of non-existence. His life on earth had been a brief interlude between two eternities of absolute nothingness. One favorite epitaph ran thus: "I was not, I was, I am not, I care not." The living were admonished to cultivate the carefree life and enjoy sensation while sensation was still possible. Sentiments like the biblical "Eat, drink and be merry, for to-morrow we die" recur time and again. Undoubtedly Epicurean materialism was thought by some persons a veritable gospel worthy to be practised during one's lifetime and to be paraded upon one's tombstone after death.

Stoic philosophy had hardly more to offer in the way of personal hope for the future than had Epicureanism. Stoicism taught the immortality of the soul, but allowed the individual little or no opportunity to enjoy future blessings in his own right. Every man's soul was, as it were, a piece of the great world-soul, or rational force, pervading the universe. This divine fire was resident in the body from the moment of birth and imparted the power of reason to the living man. With death the soul left the body to be reabsorbed into the primal

[5] *Troades*, 392 ff.

ethereal substance from which it had come. Like a drop of water returning to the sea, the spirit of man passed out into the vast ocean of soul stuff. Buoyed up by this faith in the divine constitution and destiny of the soul, the Stoic had no fear of death. All souls were divine by nature and all returned home to God. There was no room in this program for either punishment or reward on any such extensive scale as was provided in the popular mythology of the Greeks and the Romans. The Stoic speaker in Cicero's dialogue on the *Nature of the Gods* remarks, "Where can we find any old woman so silly as to believe the ancient stories of the horrors of the world below?" [6] It might have been the influence of Stoicism quite as much as of Epicureanism that prompted Seneca to commend the blessed oblivion experienced by one after death, just as he also could declare that "the tales which make the world below terrible to us are merely poetic fiction, for death restores us to the peaceful rest in which we lay before we were born." [7]

Orthodox Stoic teaching was never able to come to terms with the popular beliefs about the future life. Even those Stoics who allowed for a period of conscious personal immortality after death could not promise any hope beyond the great world conflagration to issue in the dissolution of all forms of being and a return of the world-substance to its primitive fiery state. At most personal immortality could be of only limited duration. A great catastrophe awaited the whole world when all nature would perish, the stars would be dashed together, and all the lights of the universe

[6] ii. 2. 5.
[7] *Dialogues*, vi. 19. 4.

which now shone at regular intervals in their appor-
tioned parts of the heavens would then blaze up in one
common conflagration. The elements of the earth
would all be dissolved or entirely destroyed in order that
all might be created anew in innocence, with no remnant
of the old order left to tutor men in vice. "A single
day," says Seneca, "will see the burial of all mankind.
All that the long forbearance of fortune had produced,
all that has been reared to eminence, all that is famous
and all that is beautiful, great nations, all will descend
into the one abyss and will be overthrown in a single
hour." [8] Stoicism really had no message for the man
who felt that his present life was safe only when he
was under the special care of divinities and that his
welfare for the future depended upon a continuance of
supernatural favor in the world to come.

Disciples of Plato were in a better position to satisfy
the current demand for evidences of the soul's immortality. Under the influence of Orphic belief in
the transmigration of souls, Plato had contended for
the preëxistence of the individual soul and its continuation after death. Resorting to mythological
imagery, he had pictured the soul in the likeness of a
charioteer whose car was drawn by two winged horses,
the spirit and the appetites. When perfect and fully
winged the soul soared upwards, while the imperfect
soul lost her pinions and finally fell to earth. [9] The
manner in which it ordered its career while in the flesh
determined its future destiny. At death it returned to
the other world out of which it had come to receive its

[8] *Dialogues*, vi. 26; *Natural Questions*, iii. 29; Cicero, *Nature of the Gods*,
ii. 46; cf. Pliny, *Natural History*, ii. 107 (111).
[9] *Phædrus*, 246.

rewards for the deeds done on earth according as they had been evil or good. In the course of time the soul was compelled to resume its existence on earth. Only the few who had reached the climax of perfection or vice remained permanently in heaven or hell. The great majority returned to earth for another trial, in order that they might have the opportunity to redeem themselves by correct living. After passing through the necessary reincarnations and the intermediary periods of retribution, they attained to a life of eternal blessedness. For example, the soul that had dwelt three times in a philosopher was thereupon released from the necessity of further embodiment.[10]

Plato's arguments for belief in immortality continued to be repeated by successive generations of disciples all through the period of the Roman Empire, but pure Platonism offered scarcely more popular satisfaction than did Stoic or Epicurean teaching. As a matter of fact, the Platonic view might make the individual far more uncomfortable. Even though the soul did survive the body, the outlook for the ordinary man was still rather hopeless. His future well-being lay in his own hands and was not the care of any supervising divinities. On the hypothesis of Plato, the soul determined its own destiny. If it lost its wings through a bad choice, it had to win them again by severe self-discipline. The vulgar herd, as the philosopher was accustomed to designate men unschooled in the wisdom of the day, preferred to trust tradition as perpetuated in the contemporary religions and to accept without criticism the teachings of the cults.

Even philosophers like Cicero among the Romans

[10] For example, *Gorgias*, 525 f; *Phædo*, 113 f.

and the Greek Plutarch conceded the possibility of finding reliable teaching on the immortality of the soul in the popular beliefs of the common man. The opinions of antiquity had weight with Cicero on the ground that the ancients stood nearer to the origins of faith and therefore might intuitively have discerned the truth more clearly than it had been perceived even by philosophers in later times. Moreover, the religious customs of antiquity, based upon a belief in the perpetuity of the soul, had been guarded by men of the greatest genius who would hardly have shown such care for these things had they not been firmly persuaded that death did not end all. The philosopher might also learn something from the mysteries, particularly those of Demeter, whose great lesson was that of immortality. The ancients had been at some disadvantage in not possessing a knowledge of philosophy, consequently they had only such reasons for their belief as could be supplied by natural in contrast with philosophical wisdom. Hence the deductions which they drew were often false, while the conviction itself was to be trusted.[11]

There is one point at which Cicero insistently rejected popular opinion. He could not accept current imagery regarding the lower world. He believed that the idea of shades below was entirely fictitious. The fact that bodies used to be buried seemed to him the source of the notion that the dead continued their existence underground; and later, when cremation became general, the imagination had recreated the body as the dwelling place of the soul among the shades. To all of this Cicero took vigorous exception, holding that the

[11] *Tusculan,* i. 12–17.

philosopher would free himself from sensuous images and think of the immortal spirit as wholly incorporeal, its ultimate home being in the heavens; "its origin is not to be found upon the earth, for there is nothing in the soul of a mixed or concrete nature. . . . It is heavenly and divine and on that account must necessarily be eternal." [12]

II

The philosophers' speculations about immortality did not greatly concern the common people in the Roman Empire. Even many of the educated favored a form of belief indefensible on the strict grounds of reason and logic. Epicurean doubt might often be reiterated, but its advocates were more vociferous than numerous. Stoic apathy satisfied only the hardy minded who when brought face to face with death found it increasingly possible to adopt Platonic and Orphic notions. Relative to the total population of the Roman world at the beginning of the present era, the number of persons who did not hold some form of belief in immortality was small. The ridicule of the satirists and the zeal of the skeptics were not directed at imaginary opinions. [13] The popular foibles on which these writers traded had to be real in order to be profitable. The great mass of the population still held to traditional belief in the continued existence of the soul after its departure from the body.

The Greeks from very ancient times had been much interested in the destiny of the soul. The survival of the individual after death was believed to have been proved by many an experience of the living, who in

[12] *Tusculan*, i. 27.
[13] Juvenal, ii. 149 ff; xiii. 49 ff; Lucian, *On Mourning*, ii ff.

dreams had been visited by the spirits of the departed. Achilles's well-known vision of the deceased Patroclus is typical.[14]   The hero dwelt beneath the earth in a quiet, shadowy, uneventful place, provided his friends had done their duty by the deceased in properly placing the body to rest with fitting funeral rites.

Many a story was told of a restless spirit's return to earth when the deceased had not been properly buried, and consequently had not been furnished with the necessary counterpart to the body in the world of the shades.   Often too it felt a lack of clothing or other adornment, which should have been burned on the funeral pyre in order to provide it with a suitable wardrobe for its new abode.   Once Periander, the tyrant of Corinth, sought advice from the spirit of his deceased wife, but she refused to help him until she was supplied with some new clothes fit to wear in the stylish society of the ghosts.   When there was a great festival at Corinth, where all the ladies were attired in their best, Periander ordered them to remove their garments which he forthwith burned in his wife's honor, this being the prescribed means of sending finery to the lower world.   After this, it is said, he made a second appeal to his wife who answered him according to his wishes.[15]   At another time it might be only the lack of a single slipper that would occasion the re-appearance of a ghost upon earth.   But when a wife appeared in a vision to her husband, telling him where the slipper was to be found, he immediately burned it and thus laid the ghost.[16]   The ancient Greeks knew

[14] See above, p. 52.
[15] Herodotus, v. 92.
[16] Lucian, *Liar*, xxvii.

that their dead friends still lived, separated from the scenes of their former existence by a thin partition between this world and the lower regions. In support of this belief numerous instances could be cited of occasions when the deceased had returned to show themselves to their friends, to make known their wants, or to comfort the bereaved.

Among the Romans there was the same primitive belief that the ghosts of the dead abode underground and that their continued existence had often been proved by apparitions. They demanded attention from the living, and when this was not forthcoming they might seriously menace the well-being of those still on earth. Much attention was given to ceremonies especially observed in order to satisfy these restless spirits of the lower world. In performing burial rites the pious Roman offered "as sacrifices for the dead, bowls foaming with warm milk, and goblets of the sacred blood, and gave the soul repose in the grave and with a loud shout addressed him a last farewell." [17] That the departed were in need of food was recognized by the Romans as well as by the Greeks. [18] It was in accordance with this ancient belief that the pious mother of Augustine, devout Christian that she was, used to deposit cakes and bread and wine at the shrines of the martyrs. [19]

For Romans as for Greeks, the proof of the soul's immortality seemed to be abundantly attested by apparitions. These were thought to have been of very frequent occurrence in the past and to be always

[17] *Æneid*, iii. 66 ff.
[18] Catullus, lix; Homer, *Odyssey*, xi. 23 ff.
[19] Augustine, *Confessions*, vi. 2.

possible in present experience.[20] This belief survived in folklore and was not infrequently cited in literature. The possibility of the soul's coming forth from its tomb, or from the lower regions, to visit the scenes of its former activities was a constant menace to the Roman's peace of mind. There were several days in the year when he conducted religious rites designed particularly to satisfy the desires and needs of the deceased. The February festival of *Parentalia* in honor of one's dead relations, followed by the feast of All Souls (*Feralia*), needed to be observed with great diligence, otherwise angry spirits would wreak vengeance upon the living. Again, the *Lemuria* in the month of May were aimed especially to conciliate and appease ghosts. It was a husband's fear of unfriendly visits from his deceased wife that inspired the inscription: "O dearest, spare thy husband I implore thee, spare him, that for many years longer he may continue to bring thee sacrifices and garlands and fill the lamp with fragrant oil."

Experience with haunted places had similar evidential value. Even men of education, like Pliny the Younger, were much impressed by the story of the haunted house at Athens where the philosopher Athenodorus had spent an uncomfortable night.[21] Ghosts often made places uninhabitable for mortals, especially when the spirit was that of one who had been violently killed or not buried with proper ceremony. At the time of Caligula's death his body had been taken privately to the Lamian Gardens, where it was hastily and only partially burned and remained carelessly covered over with earth. Thereafter the keepers of

[20] See above pp. 53 ff.
[21] See above p. 54.

the Gardens were frequently disturbed by apparitions and not a single night passed without some terrible alarm in the house where Caligula had been slain. But finally the house was destroyed by fire, and the sisters of Caligula on returning from banishment completed his obsequies. Thus his ghost seems ultimately to have been laid in peace.[22] Plutarch's Roman readers would fully sympathize with the belief still current at Chæronea that people in the neighborhood of the bath where Damon had met a violent death sometimes still saw specters and heard alarming sounds.[23]

At other times apparitions were welcomed as a means by which the departed conveyed to friends left behind an assurance of future life. Propertius in one of his elegies recounts a vision granted to him by the deceased Cynthia soon after her funeral. The appeal which such literary productions made to readers lay in the common longing for visions and a generally accepted conviction that they were possible. Propertius described the appearance of Cynthia as she hovered over his couch at night. He remarked upon the fact that she had the same hair and the same eyes upon which he had looked when she was laid out for burial. He noted that her dress was scorched and clung to her side and that the fire had destroyed the gem she generally wore on her finger. Although she had come from the lower world, the waters of the river of forgetfulness had washed her lips and consequently she did not relate her experiences in the nether regions. She lived once more after the manner of her former earthly self, breathed as in life and spoke, but her fingers

[22] Suetonius, *Caligula*, lix.
[23] Plutarch, *Cimon*, i.

rattled like those of a corpse. While this imagery is undoubtedly a highly poetical creation of the author, it is nevertheless true to popular belief in the survival of the human spirit, about which the poet himself might have been skeptical. But he professes to have been convinced by the experience when he writes: "There are then such things as spirits, death does not end all, but the lurid shade overcomes and escapes the funeral pyre." [24]

The gravestones of the Romans, while often exhibiting skepticism regarding the future life, much more abundantly attest belief in the perpetuity of the soul. In early Roman as in ancient Greek imagery, the dead though still surviving are almost entirely lacking in individuality and abide in shadowy and unattractive dwellings beneath the ground. When burial was customary, the tomb itself seems to have been regarded as the dwelling place of the spirit. The vault was called an eternal home where the spirit reposed and where friends of the departed came to pray that the earth might rest lightly upon the deceased. Attendance upon the tomb was a matter of great importance, and there were occasional expressions of hope on the part of the living that in the time to come they too would be permitted to dwell once more with their departed friends. But it is perfectly apparent that the Roman underworld previous to the incoming of Greek imagery, had not been those happy Isles of the Blest which Hesiod and Pindar had portrayed for the encouragement of the Greeks.[25]

[24] *Elegies*, v. 7. 1.
[25] Hesiod, *Works and Days*, 160 ff; Pindar, *Olympian*, ii. 109 f; cf. *Fragment* 129 (Schroeder).

Duty to one's dead kinsmen is perhaps the chief burden of Roman epitaphs even during the imperial age. The ancient Roman feeling of obligation to ancestors thus perpetuated itself in later times. One who discharged faithfully his duty to the ghost of his ancestors, was pronounced blessed, while he who refused such service was declared accursed. The feeling of obligation to the dead was very strong and deep seated. The tomb continued to be a sanctuary where provision was made for the needs of the deceased. Food and drink were provided for the departed, implements which had been used during one's lifetime on earth were dedicated to the spirit, the playthings of children were buried with them, and the lady of society was allowed to keep her cosmetics for further use in the abode of the shades. A bereaved father burned around the funeral pyre of his son the boy's most prized possessions — his dogs, ponies, nightingales, parrots, blackbirds, and other playthings that had given him pleasure when alive.[26] The custom of gathering at the tomb of the dead, where a chamber was provided for members of the family or clan to convene on stated occasions, was a custom also perpetuated by Christians, as is amply attested by the chapels in the Catacombs.

When Christians addressed prayers to their beloved dead, or displayed other worshipful attitudes, they were true to old Roman sentiments. Even Cicero had yielded to the impulse of his ancestral inheritance, when on the death of his daughter Tullia he asked Atticus to attend to the building of a sanctuary in her memory. It was not an ordinary tomb (*sepulcrum*)

[26] Pliny, *Letters*, iv. 2.

that Cicero desired, but a shrine like that dedicated to a deity. He knew that the skeptical Atticus would be somewhat surprised at this seeming reversion of the scholar to a primitive Roman religious feeling, yet Cicero insisted: "I am anxious to avoid any likeness to a tomb, not so much on account of the penalty of the law, as in order to attain as nearly as possible to an apotheosis." And he further indicated that he was not locating the monument in the villa, but in the open country where it could be seen by all, with a view to the greater reverence in which it would be held by posterity. Cicero believed not only that his deceased daughter still lived but also that she survived in the form of a divinity.[27]

III

Among both Greeks and Romans the earliest form of thinking about the future life placed relatively slight stress on the notion of individuality. Also in early days the idea of a blessed immortality for worthy souls and punishment for the wicked was not conspicuous. It was the group life rather than the career of the individual that was uppermost in thinking, and the lower world rather than the sky was still the common abode of all deceased persons. These primitive notions never disappeared among the populace, although in later times they were extensively supplemented by new conceptions better suited to the type of social experience characteristic of the imperial age. By the beginning of the Christian era three new notions had clearly emerged. The vague imagery of mass immortality had given place to the more vivid portrayal

[27] Cicero, *Atticus*, xii. 36.

of a future for the individual soul. There was also a livelier interest in rewards and punishments, and a growing disposition to transfer the abode of the blessed from the underworld to the realm of the stars, while the lower regions were reserved for evildoers.

The new importance of the individual in Roman society showed itself quite as clearly in contemporary thinking about immortality as in other fields of religious interest. When greater stress was laid on personal relations between the worshiper and the deity, there soon developed a keener sense of individual responsibility for the future welfare of the soul. The personal relations between man and God, true of life in the present, were thought to carry over into the world beyond, and stimulated interest in future rewards and punishments. Since it was the mystery religions that met most widely the individual needs of the common people in the Roman Empire, these cults were chiefly responsible for the rise of new ideas regarding the future life. Among the Greeks the mysteries of Demeter, the Bacchic rites, and Orphism had indeed at a comparatively early date made their influence felt in this general direction. In Roman times their teachings circulated more widely about the Mediterranean, and were augmented by other mystery cults, like those of Attis and Adonis and Osiris and Mithra, in which the notion of immortality occupied a prominent place.

The hope of future bliss nourished by the mystery religions was not of the philosophic type. There was here no disposition to prove immortality by argument. Belief was based upon revelation rather than reason. The ecstasy experienced in the rites was proof of the soul's ability to enjoy communion with the deity. Furthermore, since the gods revered in these mysteries had themselves died and triumphed over the grave, the soul of the devotee when joined to the god by the efficacy of initiation ceremonies expected to share in the deity's triumph. Similarly, those persons who remained outside the cult would miss the blessings which the future held in store for believers and would be doomed to an eternal life of misery. One's present status before the divinity would endure beyond death. Those who already enjoyed the assurance of salvation would be happy in the world to come, while those who neglected the possibility of securing this divine favor in the present had no hope of being able to correct their error in the land beyond the grave.

As a matter of fact, the Greek mystery religions had made a significant contribution toward the formation of Plato's doctrine of immortality. He was often critical toward their practices and as a philosopher he rejected many of their beliefs. He advanced philosophical arguments to prove the immortality of the soul, while the devotees of the mysteries relied upon emotion and faith, phrased in terms of revelation. Yet Plato was ready to concede that the founders of these religions "had a real meaning and were not mere triflers, when they intimated in a figure long ago that he who passed unsanctified and uninitiated to the world below will live in a slough, but that he who arrives there after initiation and purification will dwell with the gods." [28] Thus far Plato could agree with popular faith, but he would now substitute for the rites of the mysteries an acquaintance with the wisdom of the philosophers. To

[28] *Phædo*, 69.

the injunction "be initiated" in order to be saved, he would add "be initiated into philosophy." Thus, and only thus, could one be sure of a blessed hereafter. Plato made this point clear when he affirmed the preëxistent soul's responsibility for selecting its new mode of life on earth. It was granted, so to speak, an opportunity to work out its own salvation with fear and trembling by choosing reincarnation in the body of a philosopher. But the mass of mankind preferred to trust the rites of a mystery cult.

Also among the Romans, even as early as the time of Cicero, the mysteries were reputed to be especially valuable for their teachings about immortality.[29] All through the early imperial age their significance in this respect increased. Throughout the first and second centuries of the Christian era they were the chief tutors in immortality for the rank and file of men in the Roman world. Long before Christianity appeared upon the scene many an advocate of these religions had been able to say to his hearers that trust in the divinities whom he preached would insure for one a blessed hereafter, and that these hero-gods had really "brought life and immortality to light" through the gospel of the mysteries. When one felt life drawing to a close, or in an hour of sore bereavement, even the better educated person sought comfort from this source. When endeavoring to console his wife for the death of their young daughter, this was Plutarch's last resort. To the arguments for immortality which he had received from other sources, he added also reference to the mysteries of Dionysus. Ultimately he trusted the religious symbols displayed in those sacred

[29] *Tusculan*, i. 13. 29; *Laws*, ii. 14. 36.

rites to convince the bereaved mother that not only the god himself, but also the child of his devotees survived in the world to come.[30]

More specific information in regard to the status of the individual after death was also available. In Greece the expectation of rewards and punishments had received much stimulus from Orphic and Pythagorean teaching. Orphism, as every one knows, had laid great emphasis upon the contrast between soul and body, the latter being inherently evil while the former was by nature divine. On account of sin committed in a previous state the soul was imprisoned in the body both for the sake of punishment and to provide an opportunity for discipline. Also in the lower world after death the soul experienced further catharsis. Subsequently, when it came to dwell again upon earth in another body, receiving once more the benefits to be derived from religious rites, it advanced to a still higher stage of progress in overcoming the downward drag of the physical nature. By this process, continued until the guilt of the soul had been fully removed, it repaired at last to its divine home to enjoy eternal blessedness. This type of teaching, associated with the Dionysiac mysteries and promulgated in its philosophical form by the Pythagoreans, had largely influenced Plato.

Later Pythagorean views are represented in the teaching of Apollonius of Tyana. After he died his disciples continued to be much interested in the question of the soul's immortality. One day a member of the group skeptically remarked, "I have done nothing now for over nine months but pray to Apollonius that

[30] *Consolation to his Wife.* x (611D); cf. I Cor. 7: 14.

he would reveal to me the truth about the soul; but he is so utterly dead that he will not appear to me with any response to my entreaty, nor give me any reason to consider him immortal." But five days later the same young man, having fallen asleep, while some of his companions were reading, suddenly leaped up and shouted, "I believe thee!" Turning to his companions he exclaimed, "Do you not see Apollonius the sage, how that he is present with us and is listening to our discussion and is reciting wondrous verses about the soul?" But they, being inadequate mediums, were not sensitive to the vision and the youth himself delivered to them the message of their deceased teacher: "The soul is immortal and no possession of thine own but of Providence. After the body is wasted away, the soul, like a swift horse, freed from its traces leaps lightly forward and mingles itself with the light air, loathing the spell of harsh and painful servitude which it had endured." [31] According to the Pythagorean ideal, the soul after its long period of discipline in the body escaped from its fetters and passed beyond into a new godlike existence entirely freed from all limitations of the body.

The possibility of blessedness carried with it also the menace of punishment. Under the influence of Orphic imagery the contrast between the destiny that awaited good and evil souls, respectively, became greatly accentuated during the imperial age. Art as well as mythology served to depict the future state of punishment. One of the characters in Plautus's *Captives* [32] remarked that he had frequently seen pic-

[31] Philostratus, *Life of Apollonius*, viii. 31.
[32] v. 4. 916 ff.

tures of the torments inflicted in the lower world, but he believed that nothing could ever happen there equal to his experiences in the stone quarries. Pausanias [33] also described a famous painting by Polygnotus in the club-room at Delphi, where the artist visualized the tortures of Hades with the explicit purpose of encouraging men to be pious. Every one is, of course, familiar with the vast amount of mythological scenery rich in suggestions of the soul's immortality that is available to-day in museums of Greek and Roman antiquities. Sometimes happiness, sometimes wretchedness, is symbolized in these representations. Frequently they have for their theme some god's or hero's triumph over death, thus implying a similar destiny for mortals, who, if unsuccessful in their struggle, must surely face an unhappy fate.

In the case of the Greeks it is evident that from the fifth century B. c. on, retribution for souls in the future had been a thoroughly familiar notion. It early spread to Rome, and had become the common property of all people in the Empire by the beginning of the Christian era. There were a few skeptical Epicureans, but the great majority of the population accepted unquestioningly the doctrine of immortality with accompanying rewards and punishments. Among the educated there was a wide disposition to reject popular opinion with reference to the place of torment. But even this form of skepticism was by no means general. Most people held firmly to a belief in immortality with rich rewards for the righteous and eternal torments for the wicked.

In earlier phases of thinking both the good and bad

[33] x. 28.

had been assigned their respective abodes in the lower world, but in the imperial age there was an increasing tendency to adopt astral notions which had come in from the East. Now it was possible to transfer the dwellings of the dead, and particularly of the righteous, to heaven. The soul was said to partake originally of the nature of the stars and hence its final home was the ethereal regions. Persons inclined toward fatalism even imagined that the destiny of the soul was ruled by the stars, and that the entire earthly career of a new-born child could be read beforehand by one wise enough to discern the signs of the heavens. But whatever might be thought about the power of the stars over the living individual, one readily believed that after death the fiery ethereal spirit returned to its home in the upper regions. It now seemed fitting to transfer the abodes of the righteous dead to heaven, leaving the whole of the nether regions to the wicked. Moreover, astral thinking had little interest in a place of torment, and such provisions were made for the purification of souls on their way from earth to heaven that the infernal regions were no longer greatly needed. This is not to say that the place of torment vanished from the imaginations of the great mass of the people. One ought rather to say that those educated persons who had taken offense at the crude imagery of ancient Greek and Roman eschatology now found a way of escape other than that of the Epicurean skepticism. They could, as moderns are wont to do, abandon the notion of hell and retain the imagery of heaven. But the uncultured felt no such drive toward modernism.

In the case of an illustrious individual the ascension of the soul to heaven was a magnificent phenomenon.

Of Julius Cæsar, for example, it was said that his departed spirit assumed the form of a comet visible for seven days after his decease. [34] Likewise the soul of the great Pompey, even though his body had gone down to ignominious defeat with the fall of the Republic, "could not rest in the glowing embers, nor could a few ashes contain that mighty shade. He sprang forth from the fires and leaving the body beneath, which the flames had as yet but half devoured, rose to the vault of heaven." He soared aloft to those regions where heavenly bodies are at home, and where dwell spirits that are most akin to divinity, "whose burning virtue kept them pure in life and brought them to the everlasting spheres." [35]

The souls of more ordinary mortals experienced a purification as they passed through the lower spheres to the regions on high. Plutarch in his interesting treatise on the face in the moon [36] details the process by which the soul attained to astral purity. Following Aristotle's analysis, Plutarch holds man to be composed of three parts: body (soma), soul (psyche), and mind (nous). At death the body is left behind and returns to earth from which it came. The combined souls and minds mingle in the air for a time, suspended between the earth and the moon. The wicked are tortured in this intermediate space, but the virtuous finally gain a foothold on the moon. In the course of time the mind is liberated from the soul by a second death. The soul, left behind upon the moon out of whose substance it was originally formed, goes back to the moon as body

[34] See above p. 73.
[35] Lucan, *Pharsalia*, ix. 1 ff.
[36] Chapters xxvii–xxx.

does to earth, while the mind, which is the truly immortal part, passes on to its native home in the sun.

This new theology, which transported both Hades and the Elysian Fields to the regions of the heavens, and made intellect superior to both soul and body, never in reality displaced the older way of thinking. Greek and Roman literature continued to abound in descriptions of the nether regions where the wicked were punished in a place of torment and the righteous received their happy reward. Wide credence was given to a great variety of stories recounting visits of men to the lower world, where they had obtained detailed knowledge of the doings in those regions and had returned to encourage and admonish their contemporaries. In the Homeric poems, known either indirectly or at first hand by all peoples in the Roman Empire, Odysseus was the typical visitor to Hades. [37] There he had seen the judge Minos, sitting on his throne and delivering sentence upon the spirits who descended to the House of Hades. Tityus, lying upon his back, was being constantly devoured by vultures, in punishment for a terrible deed of violence perpetrated while he was yet upon earth; Tantalus stood in water that came up to his chin, but was never able to quench his thirst; Sisyphus, straining every nerve to roll the monstrous stone to the brow of the hill, was perpetually frustrated in his efforts. Hercules, on the other hand, was seen in his happy abode banqueting among the deathless gods.

Plato's story about the experiences of a certain Er, although perhaps not intended by the author to be taken literally, nevertheless expressed popular convic-

[37] *Odyssey*, xi. 566–631.

tion concerning the possibilities of obtaining information about the state of the dead. During a twelve-day absence from his body, Er had visited the halls of judgment in the lower world where the righteous were directed toward the road leading to the happy state, while sinners were commanded to descend to the lower regions. Er also was permitted to see souls returning to earth, some of them coming from heaven and others from hell, to receive a new incarnation. Listening to the conversation of these returning ghosts, he gathered a good deal of information that naturally was of much interest to mortals. As a matter of course, the knowledge acquired by him supported the Orphic-Platonic teaching about the transmigration of souls, but it was particularly valuable for the light it shed on the tortures suffered by the wicked in the place of torment. Yet after these souls had received adequate punishment, they were permitted to return to earth once more. Only the worst of criminals and the worst of tyrants were denied this privilege. Er's vision served a very practical purpose in warning men to hold fast "to the heavenly way and follow after justice and virtue always, considering that the soul is immortal and able to endure every sort of good and every sort of evil." [38]

Vergil treated the same theme for the Romans in a description of the visit made by Æneas to the lower regions. The place of torment was here described much more vividly than in Homer. Various classes of sinners were distinguished, the punishment appropriate to each being explicitly described. The lesson to be learned by men was that they should do justice and pay honor

[38] Plato, *Republic*, 614 ff.

to the gods. So frightful was the scene of torment that it quite defied adequate description. The guide of Æneas could only exclaim in desperation, "not though a hundred tongues were mine, a hundred mouths and a voice of iron, could I number all those forms of crime or rehearse the tale of vengeance." [39] The dwelling place of the blest offered an agreeable contrast. This region was one of pure delight, where men who had lived worthily in the past now enjoyed their well-earned reward. The happy company was composed of those "who battled and bled for their fatherland; they who were priests and holy while life knew them still; they who were loyal bards and sang meetly for Phœbus's ear, or ennobled life by arts discovered; with all whose service to their kin won them remembrance among men." [40]

Accounts of visits made to the lower world, where one beheld the torments imposed upon the wicked and the rewards granted to the righteous, continued to be a favorite theme throughout the imperial age. Visions of sinners in distress served to warn the living of the fate awaiting them unless life were regulated according to worthy standards of righteousness. A striking example was that of Thespesius of Soli, a very wicked youth who was granted a three days' release from the body to pay a visit to the lower world. Here he acquired a knowledge of the future that inspired him after his return to alter completely his previous manner of life. He came back thoroughly convinced not only that the wicked were afflicted in this life, but that in the world to come they would be subjected to hideous

[39] *Æneid*, vi. 625 ff.
[40] *Æneid*, vi. 660 ff.

tortures. He described some of the sights that he had been permitted to behold in the place of punishment. Even his own father was among the victims. There were welts on his soul, and gashes and scars, imposed because he had once poisoned several of his guests in order to confiscate their property. He had never divulged this secret, but it had been easily discovered in the lower world by the marks which the crime had left upon his naked soul. There was no escape from one's sins, because the ghost itself bore the scars. A great variety in forms of punishment corresponded to different sorts of crimes. Demons were employed extensively in the work of torture. Sometimes they immersed the soul in a lake of boiling gold and then, pulling it out, threw it suddenly into another lake of frigid lead. Next they dragged it over rough masses of iron. This program was repeated over and over again while the victims howled in agony, as they remembered what they had already endured, and cringed in terror before what awaited them at the hands of their relentless tormentors.[41]

The satirical Lucian treated this favorite theme in a lighter vein, but he was well aware that in dealing with the subject he easily found himself on common ground with his audiences.[42] Century after century it continued to be a popular belief that the soul was immortal, and that through the reported visions of seers and the repeated stories of literature men knew the fate awaiting the wicked and the blessings in store for the righteous. There was a direct line of succession in such

[41] Plutarch, *Whom God is Slow to Punish*, xxii ff.
[42] *Dialogues of the Dead*, xxx; *Menippus*, xiv ff; *True History*, xxxi; *Liar*, xxiv f.

imagery right down through the ancient world from Homer, Pindar, Plato, Vergil, Plutarch, and Lucian to Dante and Milton.

IV

When the Christian preachers began their missionary activities among the Gentiles, they were compelled to face the already widely discussed problem of the soul's destiny. But Christians were fully prepared to meet the issue. Belief in the immortality of the soul was an essential conviction of Christians from the very outset. But at first they were inheritors of Jewish views upon this subject, a fact that necessitated some important readjustments in their thinking as the new religion passed from Palestine into the Gentile world.

In earlier Hebrew imagery comparatively little attention had been given to the destiny of the individual soul. But by the beginning of Christian times Jews had very definitely adopted belief in the immortality of the individual, with suitable rewards and punishments awaiting him in the future life. Yet Jewish thinking differed from Greek and Roman in one important respect. The Jews insisted on the necessity of a bodily resurrection before the soul would be able to attain to its final beatific state. The ultimate determination of the soul's destiny awaited the coming of a Day of Judgment, when the body would be raised and reinhabited by the spirit. The individual, thus once more complete, would be assigned to an appropriate place in a new order of existence. The righteous would enter a paradise of delight, while the wicked would be assigned to a place of torment.

The earliest Christian preachers endeavored to convert Gentiles to the Jewish way of thinking. Christians asserted that the end of the world, accompanied by a final judgment, was to be expected at an early date. This event would be inaugurated by the return of Jesus. His coming was momentarily expected; the day of the Lord was at hand. He would appear suddenly as a thief in the night. But this vivid expectation of a catastrophic end, to be attended by a resurrection of the dead, remained year after year unfulfilled. Moreover, the resurrection of the physical body had never been an integral part of the Gentile belief in immortality. Christians, therefore, were soon confronted by the necessity of making some readjustments in their thinking regarding the destiny of the soul. Had they remained true to their original type of imagery they could not have pictured any very vivid realization of either rewards or punishments after death until the resurrection had been accomplished and Jesus had returned to inaugurate the Day of Judgment. While Christians were slow to admit that resurrection and judgment were unimportant, they did find it possible to project both of these items a long way forward into the future; while, in the meantime, they adopted also the more distinctively Gentile belief that the departed spirit freed from the body realized immediately after death the blessings deserved by the righteous and the torments in store for unrepentant sinners.

Christians troubled themselves little if at all with problems distinctive of the philosopher. They did not even feel it necessary to posit a preëxistence for the soul in order to hold, in Platonic fashion, that belief in its immortality could be logically justified. Their conviction, like that of the Gentile populace, rested on a tradition guaranteed by supernatural authority. Visions of departed friends who had returned from the lower regions, or the sights that had been witnessed by favored seers when permitted to gaze upon the places where the dead dwelt, were chiefly relied upon for information about the future state. The Corinthians were well prepared to give heed to Paul's argument in proof of the immortality of the spirit when he cited Jesus' own reappearances after death in support of this belief. For Paul these phenomena were evidence also of a bodily resurrection, but the Corinthians, being Gentiles, not unnaturally found considerable difficulty in following Paul's reasoning on this point. A Greek could ask many embarrassing questions about what sort of a body one might expect to acquire in the event of a resurrection. To many a Gentile it would in reality have seemed a calamity to force the soul once more to be shut up in the prison-house of a physical body.

The value of individual religious experience in shaping the future destiny of the human spirit now received in Christianity an emphasis distinctly Gentile in its character. Those persons who had been accustomed to believe that through union with the deity they could even in this life anticipate the beatific state of the soul after death, were informed that a similar type of experience was possible through entrance into the Christian society, where one realized at the very moment of initiation a consciousness of union with the triumphant Christ. The disciple henceforth felt assured that his title to immortality rested, not upon any inherent necessity in the nature of the soul itself, nor upon his personal efforts to live a life intrinsically worthy of happy rewards, but upon the power and favor of the deity in whom he had placed his trust, and of whom he was a faithful devotee. In Christianity, as in the cult of Dionysus or Demeter or Isis, an assurance of immortality was an integral part of present religious experience. Because the savior lived on in glory his followers also would find abundant entrance into the abodes of the blessed (John 14: 19).

When Christians undertook to portray the respective states of the wicked and the righteous after death, they were not at the outset very well equipped with imagery for this purpose. Their eyes had been fixed upon a coming Day of Judgment after which rewards and blessings would be meted out in proper fashion. The state of the departed dead previous to the Day of Judgment had not been given great attention. But with the shift of Christian thinking necessitated by the spread of the new religion to the Gentile world, more attention had to be given to the state of the soul immediately after death. Christians no longer consigned departed spirits to the Hebrew Sheol there to await impatiently the inauguration of the Day of Judgment. Rather, abandoning their Jewish antecedents and adopting Gentile patterns of thought, they now visualized the possibility of the saints' immediate entry into Paradise, while sinners went directly to their place of eternal punishment.

When portraying the tortures due the wicked, Christians had two sources of inspiration upon which to draw. In their Jewish heritage they found vivid pictures of the afflictions to be imposed on unrepentant sinners after the great judgment. On the other hand, their Gentile environment supplied them with a similar array of tortures prepared in Hades for the unrighteous.

At this point Orphic imagery was particularly suggestive. Christians were able to appropriate a considerable amount of this lower world paraphernalia. Such documents as the Apocalypse of Peter show rich borrowings from earlier Gentile speculations. This apocalypse pictures the disciples asking Jesus to show them the state of their righteous brethren after death in order that Christian preachers may use this knowledge for the encouragement of their hearers. The request is granted. The disciples are given not only a vision of the delightful abodes of the blessed, but a more detailed view of the frightful tortures of the wicked portrayed in a fashion already familiar to us from descriptions found in Homer, Vergil, and Plutarch. Punishments are allotted in accordance with specific crimes and the horrors of the scene are typically Orphic.

In describing the delights of heaven, Christians at first had employed the Jewish imagery of an ideally purified life in Palestine. Their task in this respect was rendered comparatively simple through the appropriation of distinctively Jewish pictures of the rewards due the righteous after the Day of Judgment. But with the spread of the gospel to Gentile lands new elements gradually entered into the Christian picture. Very soon features appear that are clearly derived from popular Greek and Roman thinking. Both in literature and in art early Christianity drew freely upon the newly available heritages furnished by its Gentile converts. The beatific scenery of the Elysian Fields was reproduced in Christian settings. Christians lent their support especially to the already prevailing tendency to transfer the abodes of the blest from the lower regions to the starry heavens. The Christian paradise was not beneath the earth but in the sky, whither the heathen paradise had already been carried by Gentile theologians like Seneca and Plutarch.

So far as Christianity's capacity to provide suitable rewards and punishments for individual souls was concerned, it no longer greatly mattered whether the return of Christ to awaken the dead and set up the Day of Judgment was to occur to-morrow or centuries hence. This originally Jewish imagery continued to hold a conspicuous place in the dogma of the church, but it was supplemented by a vivid portrayal of the dead saints' immediate participation in future bliss, while deceased sinners went at once to their place of torment. The mansions in the sky, which Jewish thinking had reserved for God, the holy angels, and a few heroic human figures like Moses, Enoch, Elijah, and Christ, were now opened in Gentile fashion to all righteous souls. The Hebrew Sheol no longer housed the ancient worthies. With more than Herculean power or Orphic persuasion, Christ, by his descent to Hades, had rescued those spirits in prison (I Peter 3: 19; 4: 6). Henceforth the murky darkness of Sheol was lighted up by the lurid glare of eternal fires of torment. Jewish imagery, depicting afflictions to be visited upon sinners after judgment, and Gentile pictures of present agonies experienced by sinners in the lower world, were blended into one ghastly array of fiendish tortures awaiting every soul that passed the gates of death without an experience of the redeeming power of Christ.

CHAPTER IX

THE FATE OF THE MIND

MEN of culture in antiquity were much given to admiration of the intellect for its contributions to civilization. Whatever the gods might do to help mankind, the human mind itself was thought capable of bestowing great benefits on mortals. In their praise of philosophy Epicureans, Stoics, Platonists, and Pythagoreans all found common ground.

Lucretius could imagine nothing more pleasant than to view life from "lofty and serene positions well fortified by the learning of the wise." Worldly possessions, kingly glory, and noble birth were insignificant in comparison with the blessings of philosophy and its power to dispel darkness from the human soul.[1] Stoics looked to philosophy for the guidance that made men wise and good.[2] A Stoic emperor, distracted by the duties of office and reflecting upon the uncertainties of life, remarked that "everything having to do with the body is unstable as a river; everything having to do with the soul is a dream and a vapor; life is a battle and a stranger's pilgrimage; posthumous fame is oblivion. What, then, can give one guidance? One thing, and only one, philosophy."[3] In the opinion of Seneca, a virtuous life and an enlightened mind were philosophy's distinctive gifts. She was far superior to all

[1] Lucretius, ii. 7 ff.
[2] Epictetus, *Discourses*, i. 15; ii. 11.
[3] Marcus Aurelius, ii. 17.

300

other learned arts, in that it was her peculiar task to guide men in matters of conduct and to teach them the nature and power of heaven.[4]

Cicero's language had been more extravagant. He declared philosophy to be the parent of all the arts, a gift and invention of the deities. It was she who had first instructed mankind in the worship of the gods, and had taught justice, modesty, and culture of soul. On one occasion he apostrophizes her thus:

O philosophy, thou guide of life, thou discoverer of virtue and expeller of vices, what had not only I myself, but the whole life of man been without you! To you it is that we owe the origin of cities; you it was who called together the dispersed race of men into social life; you united them together, first, by placing them near one another, then by marriages, and lastly by the communication of speech and languages. You have been the inventress of laws; you have been our teacher in morals and discipline; to you we fly for refuge; from you we implore assistance; and as I formerly submitted to you in a great degree, so now I surrender up myself entirely to you. For one day spent well and agreeably to your precepts is preferable to an eternity of error.[5]

A satirist might sneer at the disagreements among the philosophers and declare them incompetent to solve the problems of life,[6] but all through the period of Christianity's gradual rise to prominence in the Roman Empire philosophy held a conspicuous place in the affections and respect of cultured persons. It was thought to be the only adequate remedy for the aberrations and diseases of the human mind, and to constitute the principal item in all education. Under the guidance of

[4] *Epistles,* lxxxix. 6; *Natural Questions, Prologue,* 1.
[5] *Tusculan,* v. 2.
[6] For example, Lucian, *Menippus,* iv f.

philosophy the child learned to worship the gods, to honor parents, to reverence elders, to respect the laws, to obey rulers, to love friends, and when grown, to respect wives, to be affectionate toward children, to be considerate of servants, to bear prosperity with restraint and adversity with poise, to enjoy pleasures without becoming dissolute, and to be angry without indulging in violence.[7]   In this atmosphere it is not surprising that Christians were ready to claim philosophers like Socrates and Seneca as their confrères, or that Christianity should have called itself the truly divine philosophy.   The new religionists could ill afford to despise so honorable a discipline or ignore the vast superstructure of cultural attainments which it was assumed to support.

I

On Gentile soil the early Christian missionaries found themselves in the presence of a highly developed civilization, where religion had already called into its service a wide range of cultural achievements.   Homer and a long line of successors among Greek and Latin poets had frequently hymned the praises of the traditional gods.   The Parthenon at Athens and the Pantheon at Rome were representative products of that skill with which successive generations of heathen builders had dedicated themselves and their possessions to the gods of their faith.   Every city was richly adorned with monuments of religious art.   For centuries poets and architects, sculptors and painters, and men of lesser genius, had brought the richest offerings of their culture to the shrines of the gods.

[7] Plutarch, *On Educating Children*, x(7E).

There was a relatively large reading public within the Roman Empire at the beginning of the Christian era. Although the printer's art was as yet unknown, publishers did a successful business in copying manuscripts by hand and placing them on sale in the various Mediterranean cities. While classics like Homer and Vergil were always in demand, good books by more recent authors found a ready market. Perhaps the literary judgments of men at Rome in the early days of the Empire were less keen than they had been at Athens in the age of Pericles; nevertheless Roman society in its own way had a very high appreciation of literature. Men liked good writing in prose and verse, and they had been taught by long established custom to expect more or less lengthy treatments of religious themes in both the new and the old books that came to their hands. The religions of the Roman Empire were happy in calling into their service a poet like Vergil or a novelist like Apuleius.

Antiquity was rich also in esthetic satisfactions for the eye. To the present day the fragmentary remains of an ancient temple, or the torso of a Greek divinity, elicits the admiration of every lover of art. But to one living in Athens, Rome, Alexandria, or Ephesus in the first century of the present era, these objects were a part of the normal environment. Also the daily living of the average citizen was relieved of its monotony by many a pageant on festival days, or even by more ordinary ceremonies celebrated in connection with worship at one or another shrine. The imposing ritual, the gorgeous robes of the priests, the gaiety of the festal procession, all were an impressive sight for the people of the day. It might be the occasion of the Adonis feast at Alexandria, when people dressed in their best assembled at the temple to hear some famous soprano render a new song which Theocritus had written in honor of the god. Or at Athens one might join the procession to Eleusis to participate in the pageantry of a Demeter initiation. Perhaps at Rome it was a wild band of devotees celebrating the rites of the Phrygian goddess Cybele that occupied the center of the picture. Everywhere religion had learned to avail itself of the esthetic values attaching to gorgeous robes, an elaborate ritual, and other displays provocative of emotion through an artistic appeal to the eye.

Roman culture presented also an appeal to the ear. The beauty of the spoken word was even more widely in demand than was the charm of the written page. During the first four centuries of the present era the sophist held an eminent place in the cultural life of the Mediterranean world. He was a universally admired public entertainer, a master performer in rhetorical declamation, who might reside permanently in the city of his choice, or might move about from place to place delivering his inexhaustible torrent of words on every variety of theme. The public admired him for his readiness of speech, for the breadth of his allusions, and for what was commonly believed to be the encyclopedic character of his knowledge. Although his themes were not necessarily religious, probably he rarely delivered a lecture in which he did not draw more or less largely for his inspirations upon traditional religious notions.

It was the sophist who accustomed the people of the Roman world to demand the services of men mighty in words. A contemporary satirist, who followed the same trade, describes the advice given to one who would be a successful public speaker:

When your audience has chosen a subject for you go straight at it and say without hesitation whatever words come to your tongue, never minding about the first point coming first and the second, second. The great thing is to go straight on and not have any pauses. If you have to talk at Athens about adultery, bring in the customs of the Hindus and the Persians. Above all, have passages about Marathon and Cynegirus, that is indispensable. And Athos must always be turned into sea and the Hellespont into dry land, and the sun must be darkened by the clouds of Median arrows . . . and Salamis and Artemisium and Platæa and so forth must come in pretty frequently; and above all, those little Attic words I told you about — *hatta* and *depouthen* — must blossom on the surface of your speech and be sprinkled about freely, whether they are wanted or not, for they are pretty words, even when they do not mean anything.[8]

Pagan society was not lacking, however, in preachers of a more serious temper. They too made their appeal to the ear in more tasteful but no less forceful words. There is an austere Puritanism, yet a very real charm, in the discourse of the ancient Cynic-Stoic missionary. He declared himself to be a messenger from Zeus, sent to men to instruct them about good and evil. It was his mission to warn them of the wrong way and to lead them back on the right path. He spurned the rhetorician for seeking praise from his audience, and affirmed that unless the discourse of the preacher made his hearers seriously minded with reference to the problems of existence and conduct, both the message and the speaker himself were void of vitality. He used to say to his audiences, "if you have time to praise me I speak

[8] Lucian, *Rhetorician*, xviii, as cited by E. Hatch, *The Influence of Greek Ideas and Usages upon the Christian Church*, pp. 95 f.

to no purpose." To attend his lecture was likened to a visit to a surgery:

You are not to go out of it with pleasure but with pain. For you come there not in health, but one of you has a dislocated shoulder, another an abscess, a third a fistula, a fourth a headache. And am I to sit uttering pretty, trifling thoughts and little exclamations, that when you have praised me you may each of you go away with the same dislocated shoulder, the same aching head, and the same fistula and the same abscess that you brought? [9]

Cultivation of the mind occupied a large place in Roman life. Among people of culture great importance was attached to the education of the child. There were many elementary schools in which boys received instruction, and the municipalities supported public schools of higher grade that in a way corresponded to the modern high school and college. There were also great universities, like those of Athens, Tarsus, and Alexandria. Then, too, there was the private school of the philosophical teacher who attracted pupils to his lecture hall where year after year he inducted them into the secrets of his particular way of thinking. These educators were Epicureans, Stoics, Platonists, or men learned in the tenets of different schools, for whom, as Epictetus says, young men left their parents, their friends, their relatives, and their estates.

The supreme achievement of the ancient mind is to be seen in this philosophical quest. By careful observation of phenomena and rigidly logical deductions, successive generations of Greek and Roman thinkers had endeavored to comprehend the true nature of the world in which they lived and to solve various specu-

[9] Epictetus, *Discourses*, iii. 23. 29 f.

lative problems that inevitably suggested themselves
to the inquiring mind. The operations of the disciplined
intellect were brought to bear on questions regarding
the nature of both God and man, and every educated
person sought to systematize his knowledge according
to the manner of thinking prevalent in one or another
of the different philosophical schools. While all philosophers did not agree in their answers to the various
questions that one might propound, there was general
agreement among people of culture that all problems
should be answered in the philosophical way. Knowledge was to be acquired and justified by the activities
of the mind, and conclusions were to be deduced in
accordance with men's intelligence and reason. Intellectualism was conceded to be the crowning achievement of the cultural quest among the Greeks and the
Romans.

II

The Christian movement at the outset was singularly
free from the leaven of Græco-Roman culture. Even
when the movement passed beyond Palestine to find
a new home on Gentile soil, as illustrated in the Christian churches of Paul's founding, it retained its non-
cultural character. Indeed, its representatives were
aware of this fact, and sometimes they made it an
occasion for boasting. The lack of human wisdom in
early Christianity was thought to make all the more
evident its divine origin and power. The first Christians
coveted none of the cultural achievements of their pagan
neighbors.

Primitive Christians owned no buildings devoted to
the services of religion, and apparently felt no need for

such equipment. They might assemble at any place found convenient, either out-of-doors, or at the home of one of their members, or in a public hall hired for the purpose when the community became sufficiently prosperous to justify the necessary expenditure. But the building of a church edifice that should be a monument of beauty was no part of their original inclination. To employ for religious purposes ornamentation in painting and sculpture would have seemed to them improper, if not revolting. But within a few decades they learned to draw crude pictures on the walls of their catacombs, to build churches that rivaled in beauty the pagan temples, and to adorn these structures with a great wealth of symbolism in carving, painting, and sculpture. For the Jewish members of the early Christian group, and we may believe that even for Paul himself, to paint or carve an image of Christ would have seemed the height of sacrilege. But early in the fourth century Eusebius found it gratifying to believe that an image of Jesus wrought in bronze had been set up by one of the women he had healed during the time of his stay on earth. Thus his memory was thought to have been happily preserved by the help of heathen art.

In respect to literature it might seem that Christianity at the start was better prepared to meet Gentile culture on its own ground. The sacred Scriptures of the Hebrews, already translated into the Greek language of the Mediterranean world for use among the Jews of the Dispersion, were held to be also a properly Christian book. But how crude it seemed to a Gentile who had even moderate literary tastes! And in fairness to Christianity it ought at once to be said that its advocates claimed for the book no eminent literary merits. Any such claim would have been regarded by them as resort to a very inferior standard of judgment. Rather, they stressed its authority as revelation. They called upon its readers to admire its antiquity, and they admonished them to heed its message. For Christians it was a divine, not a human, document, and consequently was not to be measured by currently accepted literary standards. But before many years had elapsed Christian authors appeared, who strove to emulate the example of the great literary men of the Greek and Roman world. While deploring the mythological content of the ancient pagan literature, its stylistic qualities were highly esteemed and sometimes successfully copied by Christian writers.

In the very early days of its missionary endeavor Christianity had no substitute to offer Gentiles for the rich pageantry characteristic of many pagan cults. One has only to observe the conduct of those worshiping Christian assemblies described in the twelfth and fourteenth chapters of Paul's first letter to the Corinthians to appreciate the relative poverty of the early Christian ritual. The society had no ministering officials garbed in priestly robes, no impressive formalities of worship, and no elaborate litany. Prophets spoke as the Spirit moved them, but there was little place for the delivery of a formal sermon. Some of the hymns, and perhaps even the music, were composed on the spot, and the whole performance was conspicuously lacking in those cultural appointments that adorned worship in connection with many of the heathen cults. But in the course of time Christians learned the art of enriching their public ceremonies. They chose formal leaders and robed them impressively. They devised an elaborate ritual and a carefully ordered litany. Ultimately, they also acquired an impressive Christian pageantry which captivated the imagination even of the Gentiles.

The first Christian preachers made no pretension at skill in rhetoric. Even among Jews they had been accounted unschooled Galileans, conspicuous for their crudity of speech. Although Paul was an educated Jew, he virtually confessed to failure in his only recorded attempt to vie with the rhetorician on the latter's own ground. Apparently Paul had believed that his sermon on Mars Hill at Athens had been rather futile. When he moved on to Corinth he doubted whether he had ability to preach his gospel persuasively to Greeks. But he made the venture and won disciples, not by his skill in rhetoric, but by his earnest portrayal of Christ as savior. The Corinthians had been impressed by Paul's earnestness, although fully aware of his lack of polish in speech. When the more eloquent Apollos appeared on the scene, they greeted him with applause and had no further desire to listen to the more prosaic Paul.

The apostle Paul's fine disdain for the sophist's art was not to remain a permanent Christian attitude. As time passed Christianity increasingly drew to itself men who had been trained in the rhetorical schools. These new converts placed their mastery of words at the service of the new religion. Christian preaching in the fourth century, as represented in the sermons of Chrysostom, Ambrose, or Augustine, displayed in no small degree the polish of a sophist's discourse. But Christian preaching, in taking on elegance of form, did not completely lose the serious character which it had had in the earlier age. Paul, in the simplicity of his devotion

to deity and in his strenuous moral idealism, had much
more in common with contemporary Stoic missionaries
than he had with the professional rhetorical lecturer.
Later Christian preachers never completely abandoned
this heritage of seriousness, but they learned to clothe
it with a skilful diction that had been acquired in the
course of their training in the rhetorical schools. Yet it
is true that they did not always withstand the temptation, so persistently pressing upon a professional orator,
to give more attention to the form than to the content
of his discourse, and to manipulate language for the
purpose of pleasing hearers rather than with a view to
improving their character. Even Christian preachers
were not always unwilling to receive applause from their
hearers, and they could hardly say, with the old Stoics,
that if their auditors had leisure to praise them then
their message had been uttered in vain.

The systematic education of children had not engaged
the serious attention of the early Christian preachers.
Their expectation of an early end for the present world
made any mechanical equipment for the preservation
of culture over many years to come an unnecessary
undertaking. Paul had advised the Corinthian Christians to reduce the cares of family life to a minimum.
When parents raised questions regarding the future of
their children, the Apostle dismissed the matter rather
summarily by stating that the Christianity of one
parent was sufficient to insure the salvation of the
child (I Cor. 7: 14). The value of an educational system for training up the youth found no place in the
Christianity of Paul. Even the notion of recruiting the
membership of the church in future years from among
children who had been reared under its instructions,

seems never to have occurred to him. He declared that the time is shortened and the fashion of this world is passing away. Men were not to be saved by the operation of a cultural technique of their own devising. The Kingdom of God was imminent. Suddenly it would descend from above to replace the present evil order of society in truly supernatural fashion.

Among the second generation of Christians, educational ideals began to take shape. Experience soon taught the importance of training the children for membership in the new religion. The church also learned the desirability of giving to converts from heathenism preliminary instruction about Christianity before admitting them to full membership in the new religion. Within less than a century after Paul's death, Christianity had in its midst teachers who conducted private schools and delivered lectures to pupils after the manner of the philosophic lecturer familiar to the Roman world of that day. By the end of the second century an institution that might be called the first Christian college was established at Alexandria, already a noteworthy center of heathen educational activity. The influence of the Christian schools at Cæserea and Antioch under Origen and Lucian is too well-known to call for comment. Before the close of the fourth century Christians had interested themselves so extensively in education that it was not unusual to find them even in the public schools of the Empire teaching the Greek and Latin classics, a privilege which the emperor Julian denied them when he sought to rehabilitate paganism.

Paul had remarked that the quest for wisdom was characteristic of the Greeks, but he deplored the futility of their search. The "foolishness" of Christian preaching was to be preferred above all the wisdom of the Greek philosophers. To him it seemed strictly in accord with the divine plan that the Corinthian church should not be composed of those who were wise after the flesh. God, it must be believed, had chosen the simple-minded people in order that he might ultimately exalt them to a place of honor in his kingdom, while all worldly wisdom would be brought to naught. But here again Paul's judgment upon contemporary Gentile culture is much severer than that which his successors were to exercise. In the next century one hears loyal Christian preachers proclaiming their appreciation of Greek philosophy. In many cases they themselves had been trained in the philosophical schools before they had adopted Christianity. The cultural values which had been thus acquired could not be hastily cast aside. These converts continued to be philosophers and found what seemed to them genuine Christian inspiration in the study of ancient Greek worthies. Greek philosophy was believed to have been Christian wisdom, even though it had appeared on earth before Jesus had been born. God had allowed his truth to foreshadow itself to the Greeks through activities of the Logos before this became incarnate in the earthly Jesus. Accordingly, educated Christian men freely appropriated the technique of Greek philosophy as a properly Christian instrument.

Truly the grain of mustard seed, to which Jesus had once likened the Kingdom of God, had grown to be a gigantic plant whose spreading branches sheltered birds of widely varied plumage. A great wealth of cultural features, originally characteristic of Græco-Roman society, now found welcome lodgment within the new religion. Christianity in the fourth and fifth centuries had become not only the chief repository of pagan culture, but claimed this inheritance as its own peculiar possession. Its rivals were no longer permitted to rear and adorn architectural monuments to the memory of their ancient gods. The old temples fell into decay, or were transformed into grand Christian churches. Christ and the apostles displaced the gods of Olympus in the devotion of sculptors and painters. The production of literature and the cultivation of rhetoric found their only encouragement within ecclesiastical circles. Education also became exclusively a Christian enterprise, and no philosopher could gain a hearing outside the pale of the church.

III

Christianity inherited from the past a two-fold educational ideal, one Semitic in origin and the other essentially Greek. On its Jewish side Christianity owed a large debt to the educational program of the synagogue. Among the Hebrews learning was the care of religion. The church sponsored and fostered the school, and provided educators with both the materials for study and the ideals to be attained. The prophet and the priest came before the sage; and, when the wise man spoke, his message was not primarily a product of his personal intellectual effort but was the utterance of wisdom given to him from above. Revelation and sacred tradition furnished him specific answers to all the important questions that the inquiring mind might ask, if left free to make its own uncensored interrogations regarding the world and mankind. The answers had been rendered in early days by poets of artistic feeling, by prophets of high emotional energy, by priests devoted to the interests of their cult, and without the aid of the philosopher.

Under these circumstances the function of the mind in religion was easily defined. The teacher and the thinker were servants of the established institution. It supplied the incentives for their activity and guaranteed the validity of the ideas and ideals which they represented. Sacred tradition was the mistress of knowledge. And since this tradition was preserved in an infallible book, there was neither necessity nor justification for attempting to tap other sources of wisdom. If one had any curiosity about the beginnings of things, this was to be satisfied by repeating the stories that had been told around the camp-fires in days of old. Now that these stories had become a part of Scripture, they were no longer thought to be the works of pious imagination but were accepted by the later generation as the very utterances of God. If it were a problem of conduct that engaged the attention, a sacred authority was also available. And thus it was over the whole field of intellectual and educational activity. An educated person was essentially the purveyor of scriptural wisdom; religious tradition assumed proprietorship over all cultural interests.

Among the Greeks, intellectualism had a different genesis and was nourished in a different atmosphere. There religion did not at the outset assume the responsibility for education. Schools and universities were secular institutions, and the individual thinker recognized no allegiance to any authority beyond his own mental compulsion. Even ethical instruction was left mainly in the hands of the educationalist; it was not chiefly the concern of either priest or prophet. Yet one must not imagine that religious and intellectual interests among the Greeks existed in complete isolation from one another. Quite the contrary was the fact. Not only did current religion assign the Greek philosopher his chief problems, but often it assumed the right to censor his conclusions. Yet he did not recognize himself as its servant, nor was he the conspicuous spokesman for any existing religious institution. In this setting the intellectual quest of the Greek was of a quite different type from that of the Jew.

The Greek philosopher spoke as an individual and based his utterances on his personal observation of things as he saw them. His conclusions represented the results of his own mental agitation rather than the reiteration of authoritative words derived from an ancient revelation. Over against custom and tradition he set intellectual acumen and logical integrity. He sought to read the secrets of the world by observing the things about him in nature, and when his mind ranged beyond nature into metaphysical realms, his own mental processes provided the norm for constructing the order of the world beyond. In principle he recognized no question not open to further investigation and no territory too sacred for the operations of his prying gaze. Probably one ought also to add that in this process of intellectual inquiry the Greek philosopher had no desire to desecrate sanctities or overthrow idols. The very search for truth through mental activity was itself the most sacred enterprise upon which he thought he could enter. He would know anew and better, by direct processes of investigation, the truth that had been too dimly and imperfectly perceived by his predecessors.

Religion was so pervasive an interest in Greek society that the philosopher, whatever may have been his original purpose, early found himself on the defensive. This tension was only heightened when he applied his curiosity to the problems of religion. While to-day we may regard the religious beliefs of the ancient Greeks as a body of absurd mythology, for the men of Athens in Socrates' day the myths were just as really valid theology as the pronouncements of the Council of Nicæa were for orthodox Christians of the fourth century. More than one philosopher was to learn that the attempt to intellectualize traditional religion led out upon an exceedingly thorny pathway. Current beliefs were jealous of their rights, and they could always claim to possess the validity of tradition and to represent majority opinion. In their own way the Greeks were as loyal to their religious traditions as were the Jews to theirs.

Had the intellectual ideals of the older Greek thinkers prevailed, an extensive rephrasing of current religious notions would have been necessary. In accordance with his new technique of scholarship, the philosopher sought to redefine the character of the traditional gods, at the same time making his definition accord with the results of his critical observations and mental deductions. As the cosmos became unified in his mind, the multitude of popular deities was reduced to a single person or power. Miracles disappeared from nature, whose processes now took on an orderly and more permanent character. Fear also was cast out from religion, and the conduct of men toward God and toward their fellows became the subject of careful study and logical definition. In short, for the philosopher research and rationality were made to supplant traditional myths and sacred customs. But this strenuous effort of the intellect ultimately broke down even among the Greeks. Before their cultural heritage was passed on to Christianity a more conciliatory policy of handling the problem of religion and learning in relation to one another had been generally adopted.

The odds in favor of religious tradition were tremendous. In very ancient times religion had called into its service the vivid Greek imagination and had capitalized a wealth of esthetic impulses. Literature and art and pageantry spoke a sacred language. Artists and poets had painted pictures of gods in the colors of fancy that made a wide popular appeal. Out of the storehouse of imagination they had brought forth answers to questions about the origin of the deities, the creation of the world and of man, and the activities of the gods in connection with the beginnings and history of human society. Long before the rise of philosophy the ceremonies of the cults and the riotous play of mythological imagery had become impregnably intrenched in the habits and affections of the Greek people. Ultimately, the philosopher assumed discretion to be the better part of valor and decided to abandon direct attack upon the established traditions. Instead, he sought to effect an honorable compromise.

The method of procedure varied from time to time, but the outcome was always the same. Intellect ultimately yielded to tradition. The most influential schools of philosophy in the Roman Empire, particularly the Stoics and the neo-Platonists, gradually succumbed to this popular demand. By means of allegorical interpretations they found a way to transform without seeming to reject traditional beliefs, and they even devised a technique which made it possible for them to resort to revelation rather than to the normal operations of the mind as a means of attaining to the highest type of knowledge. While the Stoic could not take literally the stories about the gods reported in Homer and Hesiod, he soon learned how to peer behind the external form of the myth in his search for a more acceptable meaning. For the man of culture there was only one divine energy pervading and controlling the universe, yet even the scholar might use the terminology of popular polytheism since he understood that its gods were merely convenient names for different manifestations of the one divine essence.

In the course of time the whole content of popular mythology was effectively allegorized. If the untutored man took the legends literally he was not to be denied their use, but an effort was made to instruct him in the true meaning of the various stories. If, for example, it seemed incongruous to believe that a supernatural being like Hephestus should be permanently lame, or if the story of Zeus in a moment of rage hurling Hephestus down from heaven was thought unworthy of a deity, Stoic teachers stood ready to extract noble truths out of this mythological imagery. The incident had not actually occurred, but the story had been told to teach a spiritual lesson. Hephestus's precipitous plunge from heaven signified figuratively that men had been divinely blessed by the rays of the sun falling upon the earth and by the use of fire obtained from lightning, while the lameness of the god kept before one's mind the truth that all earthly fire is inferior to its more brilliant heavenly source. Thus all the familiar labels of tradition could be retained. Intellectual effort spent itself in devising new allegorical meanings to light up the old phrases. The old skins were filled with new wine, although doubtless the exponents of the method would have stoutly affirmed that they were merely restating old truth in new language.

The neo-Platonists went even beyond the Stoics in yielding to tradition and revelation at the expense of rigorous mental effort. For Plotinus, the founder of the school, the attainment of ultimate reality came as the climax of an emotion. The goal was not to be reached simply by strenuous intellectual discipline. Highest knowledge lay outside the area of the mind's activity; it was in essence a new revelation of the un-knowable. Mystical experience was now far more important for philosophers than was the empirical quest for knowable facts in the world of nature, and the organization of knowledge in accordance with a rigid logic. The popular religious cults, with their stimula-ing rites, offered an easy means of inducing the revela-tory emotions that men craved. The later advocates of neo-Platonism were little more than diligent apolo-gists for traditional pagan cults. Intellectual effort expended itself in mystical yearning and in the alle-gorical interpretation of ancient mythology. It was now thought to be the supreme duty of the philosopher not to question the validity of the myths, but to affirm their divine character. Creative mental effort had thus been virtually eliminated from the sphere of religion. The dominance of faith over knowledge remained un-challenged.

IV

Ultimately among Gentiles, as among Jews, intellectualism was completely subordinated to the dogmas and institutions of religion. Established tradition claimed to be the final authority regarding what man should think about the great problems of life and the cosmos. It was inevitable that Christianity should inherit this prevailing custom of subordinating intellectual search to accepted opinions. One might recognize two sorts of wisdom, the one natural and the other supernatural, but it was always the latter that dominated. Paul expressed the Christian ideal held by him in no uncertain language. Since the world through its wisdom knew not God, it had been decreed that the world should be saved by a revelation which the philosophers of Paul's day might call foolishness. But even the foolishness of God was wiser than the wisdom of men. The Christian preacher affirmed that he dealt with the higher wisdom, not of this world, but God's wisdom in a mystery that had been hidden in former times but was now revealed in the new Christian religion.

We have already observed that the Christian movement in its earliest phase had relatively little concern with education. But this situation soon changed. The values attaching to the Old and New Testament Scriptures made Christianity eminently the religion of a book, and the possession of a book implied a body of instruction to be imparted. Thus education early became a necessity to the Christian cause. But at first its didactic activities followed the pattern provided by Judaism. Christian learning was biblical, and it did not aim at the acquisition of new knowledge by means of independent mental effort. Its subject-matter was necessarily religious tradition, that is, a body of sacred wisdom, rather than what might be called natural knowledge. And it was the function of learning first and last to serve the interests of an established faith received on the authority of tradition.

In the early Christianity there was still another educational agency more specifically Greek in its origin. This was the individual Christian philosopher, who set up his school in Rome or Alexandria or some other cultural center and carried on his work of instruction quite independently of the local ecclesiastical organization. While he made large use of the Bible as a source of proof-texts to support his teaching, he also felt at liberty to cite freely from the pagan poets and philosophers. He had no intention of deviating from the commonly accepted Christian faith or of denying the validity of its traditions. But sometimes he did, after the manner of the Greek philosopher, exercise no slight independence of thought in his interpretation of tradition. One might say that he had established independently of the organized church a secular school, in which, however, the instruction was primarily religious. Yet in his new institution there were latent possibilities of independent research which even he himself did not at the time fully appreciate. His was a college or a university under no religious supervision except such as he and his fellow-instructors might themselves provide.

By the year 200 A. D. signs were not lacking to indicate that possibly Christianity would furnish the suggestion and opportunity for free intellectual research which Judaism had never stimulated and which paganism had vainly tried to effect. Certainly it is true that

Christianity in the third and fourth centuries could count among its representatives some of the keenest minds in the Mediterranean world. An Origen in the East and an Augustine in the West could safely have been trusted to adorn culture at any period in its history. Yet, within Christianity as truly as within Judaism and paganism, intellectual initiative was always faced by the fact that religion possessed its well established sacred tradition. With the exception of Judaism, this was even more conspicuously true of Christianity than of any other religion in the ancient world. While the books of Homer were virtually a Bible for the Greeks they were never so definitely canonized as were the books of the Old and New Testaments in the Christian church. The stories which the Christian Bible contained about how the world had been created by the deity, how he had ordered the course of human history, and how he had established the new religion, were even more inviolable for a Christian society than were the similar stories among the Greeks for the society in which their ancient philosophers had attempted to introduce the sobering influences of the human mind into the fanciful imagery of current mythology.

It was inevitable that the earliest efforts of intellectualism within Christianity should have been expended in an apologetic task. The Christian mind did not seek to blaze out new ways to truth, but devoted its powers to the defense of old ways. It was not assumed that true wisdom could be derived from a critical observation of the cosmos, or from the severest syllogism that human skill could devise. On the contrary, wisdom was to be found by consulting a historic and ancient body of written revelation. Knowledge of God was possible only through a knowledge of the sacred book. Hence the highest consecration of one's intellectual powers consisted in devoting them when necessary to a defense of the validity and finality of the Christian revelation. Nevertheless, Christians were not slow to recognize the demands made upon them by their immediate cultural environment. Students of the Bible, like Stoic interpreters of Homer, strove to modernize their religious traditions by the use of allegory. For the literal meaning of Scripture they substituted figurative interpretations suited to the conditions and thinking of a later age. Christian scholars like Origen and Augustine lavished a wealth of mental energy on this allegorical task.

In still another respect the intellectual quest was compelled to walk very circumspectly within its Christian home. Christianity esteemed itself not only a historic revelation; very early in its career it declared itself to be a divine institution. Now, intellectualism is essentially individualistic in its genius and can thrive only where perfect liberty is accorded the scholar to pursue his research and deduce his conclusions without institutional interference. The young college-trained presbyter, Arius, on returning to Alexandria in the year 318 A. D., ought to have known better than to pit his opinion against that of a powerful ecclesiastical official. Arius was helpless before the authority of the bishop. But what hope was there for the full development of intellectual vigor within Christianity when an ecclesiastic, without distinctly academic interests, had power to silence a devout and well-trained man of the younger generation who had, as it were, recently emerged with honors from the leading Christian university of the day? Christianity's rapidly increasing institutionalism was

incompatible with the cultivation of a free and vigorous
intellectualism. Already in the fourth century the free
Christian college, such as was being conducted by
Origen at Cæsarea and Lucian at Antioch, was doomed
to give way to another type of educational institution
that would be strictly under the control of the church.

Furthermore, Christianity always remained a thorough-going supernaturalism. The present world of nature and normal human experience were consistently
slighted, if not indeed thoroughly despised. It was
necessarily thought improper to assume that any valuable knowledge of the true God was to be discovered by
acquaintance with a world that was supposed to be
infested with and dominated by wicked demons. At
best the thoughts of the natural man could be but vain
efforts of the imagination. The opinions of the ancient
philosophers, even when admired by Christian scholars,
had to be redeemed from the curse of the natural world.
One said that this Greek wisdom had in reality been a
Christian revelation faintly disclosed by the divine
Logos operating outside of Hebrew territory, or else
it had been pilfered from the Old Testament by the
demons who had taught it to the Greeks in order later to
embarrass the Christian missionaries. All true wisdom,
it was assumed, had to be of supernatural origin.

The Greek spirit had begun to lose its more strenuous
intellectual urge before Christianity appeared on the
scene, but the process was now accelerated. Pagan
philosophers turned to Christianity in considerable
numbers. The new religion had the most attractive
equipment then available for insuring satisfaction when
one sought to supplement the acquisitions of the mind
by an appeal to authoritative tradition. No pagan cult

had any heritage that could rival the Christian Bible as a source of ancient revelation, and no heathen deity was served by an institution equal in power to that of the Christian church for mediating divine help to needy mortals. Equipped with these safeguards Christianity could freely receive into full fellowship any Greek philosopher who knocked at its doors. But it was the letter rather than the spirit of the older Greek intellectualism that Christianity thus acquired.

Unquestionably such philosophy as was appropriated by the church rendered the new cause great service. It could not be without beneficial effect upon the representatives of Christianity to strive to think the thoughts and copy the mental processes that had characterized a Heraclitus, a Socrates, a Plato, or even an Epictetus or a Plotinus. To keep such company was a great mental stimulus, provided a Christian maintained his interest in defending the validity of his religious tradition, adhered to the creeds and practices of his established institution, and never questioned the propriety of seeking ultimate wisdom in the realm of the supernatural. If he transgressed any of these bounds immediately he became a heretic and an outcast. Of the mind's scientific quest, by which new and valid wisdom is acquired through observation of nature or the reading of immediate experience, the Christian philosopher who remained orthodox could have no genuine appreciation. That spirit of scientific research which had gradually developed among the Greeks until it ultimately produced an Aristotle, failed to find a home in the Christian intellectualism of the ancient church, just as it had failed to dominate the later pagan philosophy of the imperial age.

Christian scholars no longer followed Paul, who had declared all worldly wisdom to be worthless, yet they universally assumed that any knowledge acquired outside of the Bible and the church was valid only in so far as it accorded strictly with revelation. Tertullian's famous dictum, *credo quia absurdum*, represented an extravagance of faith to which his contemporaries and successors did not usually aspire. They preferred to think their beliefs far from absurd, and to be capable of a thoroughly rational justification. Yet the ultimate test of propriety in belief was revelation, with which it was the fate of the human mind to be in eternal accord. Augustine and his followers stated the characteristic Christian attitude more adequately than did Tertullian. As Augustine expressed it, "we believe in order that we may know, we do not know in order that we may believe. Faith, then, is to believe what you do not see, while truth is to see what you have already believed." Or, again, in the words of Anselm: "I do not seek to understand in order that I may believe, but I believe in order that I may understand. For this, too, I believe, that unless I first believe, I shall not understand." But in order to make Christian belief intelligible Anselm was convinced that it ought to be justified by the operations of the human mind. A real sense of duty prompted him to write his treatise, *Cur deus homo*. He held one to be guilty of negligence who did not, after he had become established in the faith, strive to understand what he had believed. But the theologians of the church never lost sight of their inherited conviction that faith should precede and transcend knowledge, and that no knowledge was valid which did not accord with traditional beliefs. As Thomas Aquinas remarked, there are mysteries of faith which are above reason, yet the natural mind is itself the servant of faith. Thus, one was to recognize both "the light of natural reason" and "the light of divine revelation," but was always to subordinate the former to the latter. The supernatural mind was still thought to rule supreme over the mind of man.

INDEX

INDEX

Aaron, 42
Abaddon, 44
Abihu, 42
Abimelech, 42
Abraham, 7, 11, 41, 103, 139
Abstractions, deification of, 114
Achilles, 52, 109 f., 132
Acts, supernaturalism in, 26
Adam, 237
Adonis, blood of, 125; death of, 124; grave of, 124; resurrection of, 124
Æneas, 52, 129; visit to Hades, 52 f., 291
Æsculapius, *see* Asklepios
Agabus, 88
Agamemnon, 110
Alexander the Great, apparitions of, 60; benefactions of, 191; civilizing work of, 111; deification of, 112; divine parentage of, 135; reliance on deity, 200
Allegory, Christian, 324; Gentile, 318 f.; Stoic, 15, 319
Altars, location of, 176
Ananias, 27; vision of, 37
Ancestors, worship of, 45
Angels, abode of, 5, 22; apparitions of, 38 f.; Jewish belief in, 4, 11; Philo's doctrine of, 104
Anselm, 327
Anthropomorphism, polemic against, 58
Antioch, 3
Aphrodite, 124
Apion, a necromancer, 103
Apocalypse, of Peter, 209
Apollo, 109, 120, 123, 173, 180, 199; apparitions of, 63; father of Asklepios, 135; father of Augustus, 137; father of Plato, 138; healer,

239; Holy Water of, 182; hymns to, 174; temple of, 63
Apollonius of Tyana, 63, 132, 285; divine parentage of, 138; raising of dead by, 133
Apollos, rhetorical skill of, 310
Apostles, appearances of Jesus to, 35
Apotheosis, of Tullia, 281
Apparitions, *see* Appearances
Apparitions, Christian belief in, 35 ff.; Epicurean denial of, 48; Gentile belief in, 48; Jewish belief in, 41 ff.; of Alexander the Great, 60; of angels, 38 f.; of Apollo, 63; of Castor, 63; of Elijah, 39; of God, 41 ff., 59; of Moses, 39; of Patroclus, 52; of Pollux, 63; of Proteus, 63; of Romulus, 61; Pliny the Younger's view of, 51; Plutarch's view of, 50; possibility of, 34; proof of immortality by, 276; purpose of, 55; Roman belief in, 53
Appearances, *see* Apparitions
Appearances, of Jesus, 56; of Jesus to disciples, 35 f.; of Jesus to Peter, 47
Appian, 115
Apuleius, 101, 253, 303
Aratus, 15
Archagathus, 234
Aristotle, 13, 156, 326; view of soul, 265
Arius, 324
Arnobius, 252
Artemis, of Ephesus, 177
Arval Brothers, 175
Ascalaphus, 120
Ascension, Augustus's, 117; Cæsar's, 117, 289; Mithra's, 128; of

331

Cosmopolitanism, in Roman Empire, 223

Cosmos, a menace to man, 248; deliverance from, 263

Culture, Christian attitude toward, 207 ff.

Cybele, 126, 154, 226; in Rome, 150; processions of, 176; rites of, 254

Cynthia, 278

Damon, 278

Daniel, 9

Dante, 294

David, 9, 46, 139

Dead, abode of, 276; food for, 276; status of, 285

Death, Stoic view of, 270

Deborah, 87

Decalogue, 8

Decius, prayer of, 77; self-sacrifice of, 181

Deification, among Romans, 113; of abstractions, 18, 114; of Alexander the Great, 112; of Asklepios, 120; of Augustus, 116; of dead, 44; of great men, 115; of heroes, 19; of Isis, 128; of Julius Cæsar, 115; of love, 59; of man, 257; of Osiris, 128; of Plato, 109; of Ptolemies, 112; of Romulus, 61, 115; of rulers, 19; of Seleucids, 112; of Vespasian, 19

Deities, as physicians, 239; images of, 178; of Gentiles, 12

Deity, in prophets, 89 ff.; secret name of, 164; union with, 261; visibility of, 57

Delphi, 62, 90, 109, 123

Demeter, 112, 118, 122, 154, 226, 257, 273; healer, 239

Demetrius, hymn to, 112; son of Poseidon, 136

Democritus, 78, 97

Demon, of Socrates, 98

Demons, activity of, 5; cup of, 32; enemies of soul, 247; evil, 247; good, 246; inspiration by, 92; intermediaries, 98; Jewish belief

in, 11; of Gentiles, 12, 96; origin of, 247; protection from, 255; sacrifices to, 182

Demosthenes, 160

Destiny, goddess of, 20

Dio Cassius, 61, 74

Dio Chrysostom, 94, 108, 121

Diocletian, persecution by, 214 f.

Diodorus, 118, 127, 134

Diogenes, of Oenoanda, 21

Diogenes, the Cynic, 182

Dion, 50

Dionysius of Halicarnassus, 188 f.

Dionysus, 90, 116, 121, 143, 257 f.; birth of, 174; civilizing work of, 118; divine parentage of, 134; frenzied rites of, 254; healer, 239; orgies of, 176; resurrection of, 123; tomb of, 123; victory over death, 122

Dives, 103

Divination, 70

Divine parentage, of Alexander the Great, 135; of Apollonius; of Asklepios, 135; of Augustus, 136 f.; of Castor, 134; of Dionysus, 134; of Hercules, 133; of heroes, 133; of Jesus, 144; of Nero, 137; of philosophers, 137 ff.; of Pollux, 134; of Pompey, 136; of Pythagoras, 138; of Scipio Africanus, 136; of Theagenes, 135; of Tyana, 138; Roman view of, 136 ff.

Divine sanctions, among Jews, 5

Dodona, 87, 90

Domitian, assassination of, 74

Dreams, 102

Dualism, of Plato, 99

Ecstacy, Christian, 96

Education, Christian, 311, 321 ff.; Gentile, 306; Greek, 315; Jewish, 314 ff.

Egypt, deliverance of Hebrews from, 8

Elijah, 9, 89, 133, 139, 299; apparition of, 39

Elisha, 9, 89